IMAGES
of America

EAST HANOVER

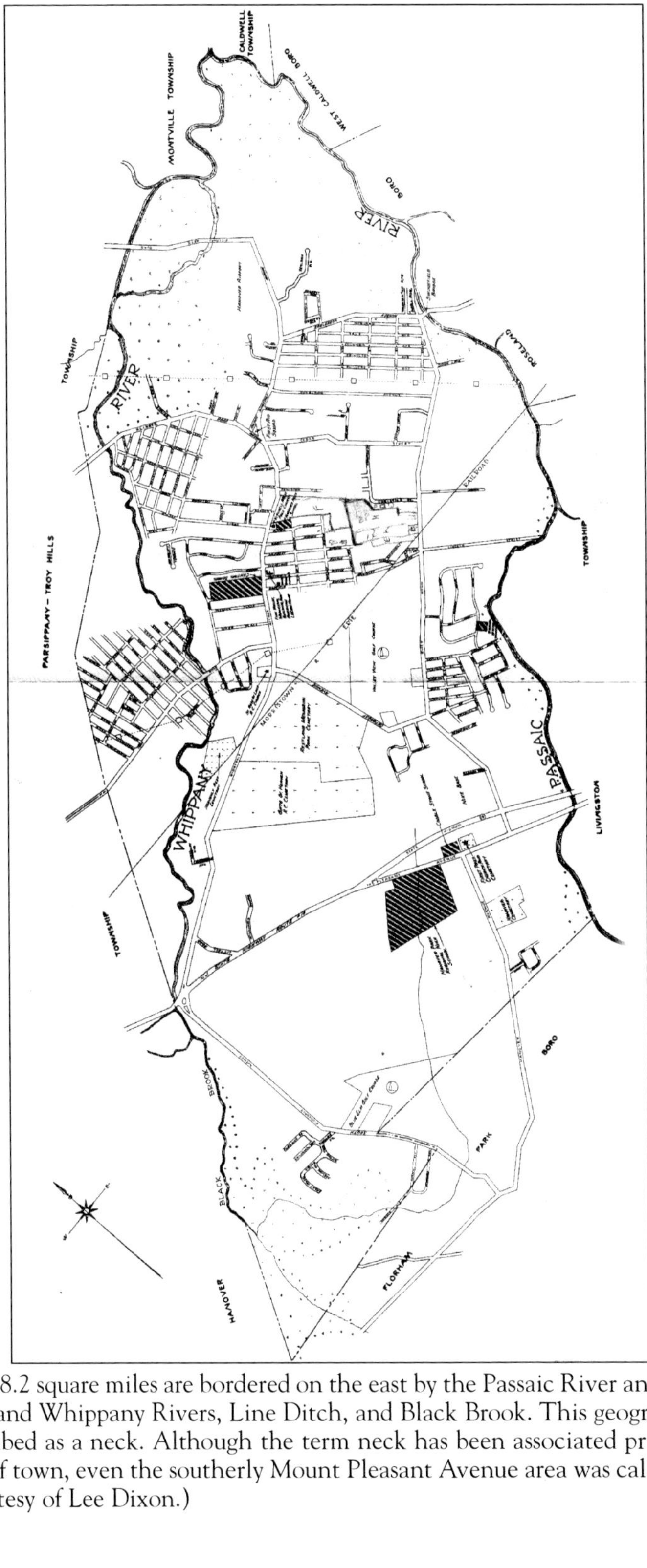

East Hanover's 8.2 square miles are bordered on the east by the Passaic River and on the west by the Rockaway and Whippany Rivers, Line Ditch, and Black Brook. This geographic formation has been described as a neck. Although the term neck has been associated primarily with the northern half of town, even the southerly Mount Pleasant Avenue area was called neck as early as 1754. (Courtesy of Lee Dixon.)

IMAGES
of America

EAST HANOVER

Steve Swanbeck

ARCADIA
PUBLISHING

ISBN 978-0-7385-0965-5

Published by Arcadia Publishing
Charleston, South Carolina

Printed in the United States of America

Library of Congress Catalog Card Number: 2001094294

For all general information contact Arcadia Publishing at:
Telephone 843-853-2070
Fax 843-853-0044
E-mail sales@arcadiapublishing.com
For customer service and orders:
Toll-Free 1-888-313-2665

Visit us on the Internet at www.arcadiapublishing.com

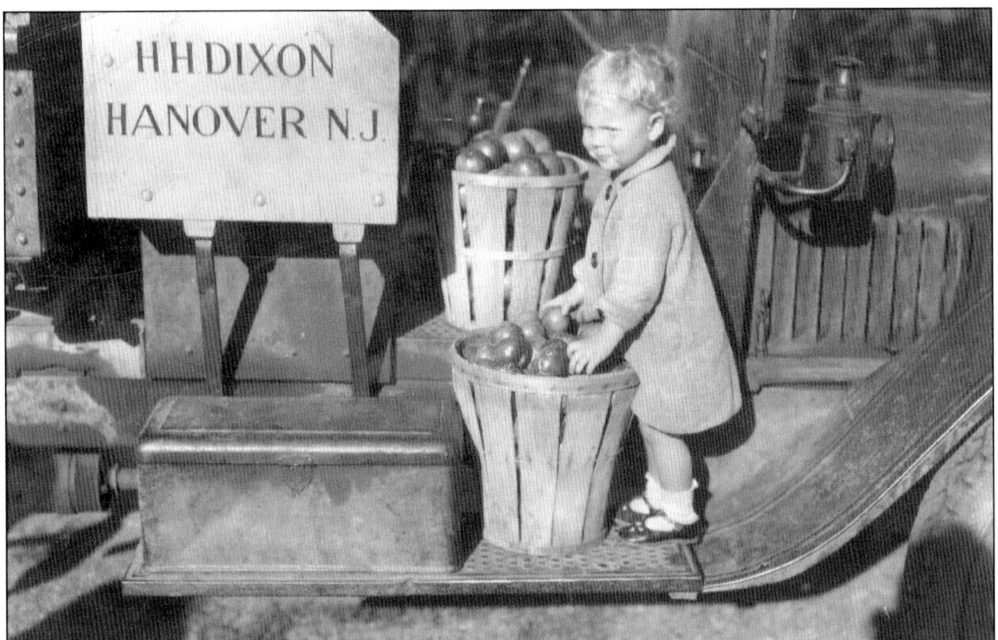

Lee Dixon helps his father load up the truck before it heads off to the wholesale produce market in Newark in 1934. The Dixons owned a 42-acre farm on River Road. Although the township was incorporated as East Hanover in 1928, it was generally referred to as Hanover long thereafter. (Courtesy of Lee Dixon.)

Contents

Acknowledgments 6

Introduction 7

1. Early European Settlement 9
2. Agricultural Heritage 21
3. East Hanover Inc. 43
4. Protecting the Township 71
5. Going to School 85
6. Sports and Leisure 101
7. Around Town 115

ACKNOWLEDGMENTS

It took a village to make this book possible. Some generous people searched their attics, cellars, closets, and albums to find the photographs and documents that provide these memorable snapshots of East Hanover's history.

I would like to extend my sincere appreciation to Betty Albert, Gus Auermuller, Don Bender, George and Sylvia Busold, Betty Cardarella, Fred Costanzo, Don Courter, Lee Dixon, East Hanover Department of Public Services, East Hanover Fire Department, East Hanover First Aid Squad, East Hanover Historical Society, East Hanover Library, East Hanover Town Hall, John Esposito, First Presbyterian Church of Hanover, Barbara Flowers, Catherine Froling, Marge Glutting, Margaret Griffith, Clyde and Bunny Grossmann, Ray Grossmann, Ken Hadley, Hannover Fairs USA, Hanover Cemetery Association, Hanover Park High School, Weetona Hobby, Helen and James Iradi, Tom Iradi, Herb and Jeanette Johnston, Kitchell Memorial Presbyterian Church, Cassandra and Donna Kupper, Scott Lutz, Morris County Library, Novartis, Anthony and Anne Pellecchia, Ralph and Rita Politi, John Rello, Bob Riley, Mrs. Roche, Evelyn and Jim Ross, Liveria and Norwood Ross, Everett Rowley Jr., St. Rose of Lima Church and Academy, Bill Schaeffer, George and Pamela Schaeffer, Bill Shrader, Shirley Shrader, Gregory and Pamela Smith, Dorothy Swet, Pete Tamburro, Christine and Carl Vidal, Orrin Whaites, Edna and Henry Zaleski, Vivian Zakarian. I am also grateful to those who contributed in many different ways to help produce this book. Finally, thanks, Lynne, for keeping an eye on Alison and Amie while I was off hunting for photographs.

Two additional sources of reading for anyone who enjoys East Hanover history are *Gateway to Morris*, by Peter J. Tamburro Jr., and *The Story of Hanover, New Jersey*, by Edna A. Dixon and Edward Dixon. They were helpful references for this book. Check with the East Hanover Library.

INTRODUCTION

Mark Twain would have felt right at home in East Hanover. On hot summer afternoons in the 1800s, children peeled off their clothes and swam in the cool, meandering waters of the Passaic River. A good day fishing in the Passaic yielded a string of carp or catfish. Just about everybody went barefoot. There were two neighborhood schoolhouses—one on Ridgedale Avenue near Cedar Street, the other on Mount Pleasant Avenue across from the church. Some students studied hard and received excellent marks; others played hooky on occasion.

Going much further back in time, East Hanover's first residents were the Lenni Lenape Indians. They lived here for thousands of years before European settlers arrived. Two rivers and fertile soil provided sustenance. High ground on what is now land owned by Novartis offered strategic protection for one Native American settlement. Artifacts have been unearthed throughout the township.

The Lenni Lenape sold their property in the early 1700s. The first European settlers came to this rural area from places like Newark and Elizabeth to farm the land. There were 200 to 400 residents by the time of the Revolutionary War. Patriots guarded Cook's Bridge on Mount Pleasant Avenue from the threat of nearby British soldiers. The First Presbyterian Church of Hanover served as a medical facility during the war.

In addition to the farmers, the blacksmith, shoemaker, weaver, and tailor all plied their trades. Wheat was taken to the gristmill in Whippany or Montville to be ground into flour. It was transported along roads like Mutton Lane (now River Road) or Dumpling Lane (now Troy Road). On the way home, a thirsty farmer could stop for a quick drink at a local tavern. Shopping was a full-day event that included hooking up the horse and wagon and setting off for the market in Newark.

Church was an important part of spiritual and social life. The First Presbyterian Church of Hanover is the oldest place of worship in Morris County. It started in Whippany in 1718 and moved to Mount Pleasant Avenue in 1755. Eventually, there was a need for a church meeting place in the northern part of town. The Bethel Society of Hanover became an offshoot of the First Presbyterian Church in 1898. It is now Kitchell Memorial Presbyterian Church. St. Rose of Lima Church followed more than a half century later.

The township, however, was multifaceted. Even as spirited preachers reminded their congregations of the evils of drink and other temptations, whiskey stills simmered throughout town. During Prohibition, at least one still was raided and destroyed by federal agents.

East Hanover was originally part of greater Hanover Township, which at one point encompassed much of what is today Morris County. As the population increased, it became more difficult to govern the town's widespread residential villages. Eventually, many East Hanoverians were ready for self-governance. During the spring of 1928, more than 1,500 registered voters of Hanover Township went to the polls in a special election to accept or reject a referendum incorporating the Township of East Hanover. The vote was 945 yes, 512 no. East Hanover became a separate municipality on May 9.

As far back as the Revolutionary War, young people from East Hanover packed their bags, kissed their loved ones goodbye, and headed off to war when duty called. Some of them never returned. A number of them are buried in the town's five cemeteries.

From the mid-20th century onward, East Hanover developed from a farming community into a busy suburb. Housing developments grew from cornfields. New schools were built. Businesses came to town. The golf course went away. The population increased from 2,151 in 1950 to more than 11,000 today. Onetime dirt roads are now oftentimes backed up with traffic—progress to some, too much development for others.

This book takes a look at the way things used to be.

One

Early European Settlement

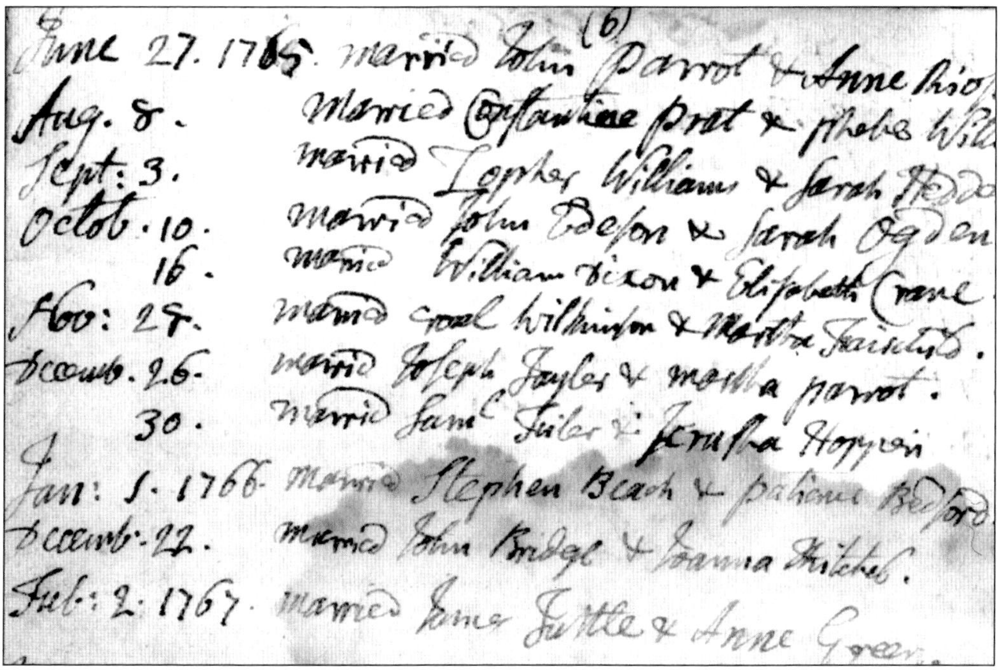

Little did Rev. Jacob Green know that a marriage he performed in 1765 would, generations later, beget one of the world's greatest inventors. This handwritten entry (fourth down) in the reverend's marriage book documents that he performed the marriage of John Edison and Sarah Ogden on October 10 at the First Presbyterian Congregation of Hanover on Mount Pleasant Avenue. They are the great-grandparents of Thomas Alva Edison. (Courtesy of the First Presbyterian Church of Hanover.)

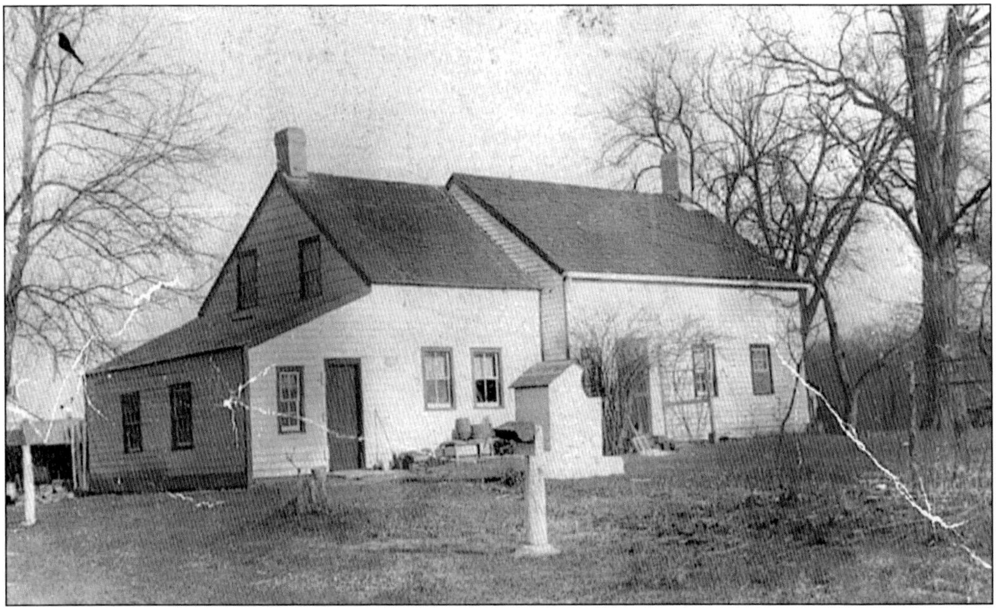

This is believed to be the oldest house in town. It was built by David Douglass in 1740 at the northern end of what is now Ridgedale Avenue. Aaron Kitchell was born four years later and lived around the bend. He became a U.S. congressman and then a U.S. senator in 1807. This early-1900s photograph shows the Douglass house after an addition had been added to the left side of the original structure. (Courtesy of Helen and James Iradi.)

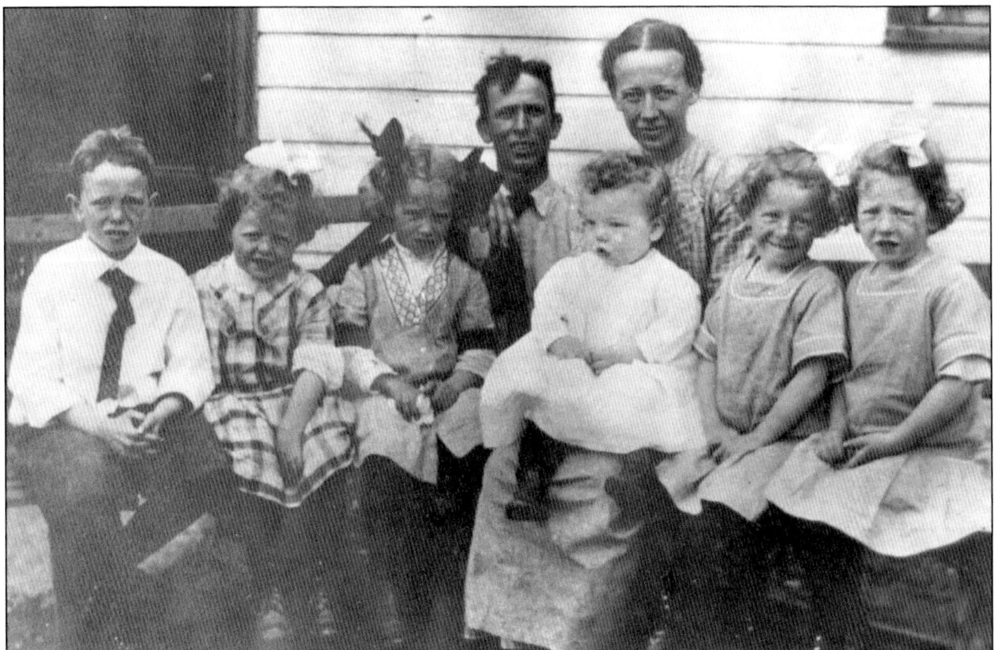

The Little family lived in the Douglass house in the early 1900s. It was a farm then with more than five acres of land. Members of the Little family included, from left to right, Harold, Ruth, Margaret, Charles, Roger (on lap), Frances M., Frances C., and Charlotte. (Courtesy of Helen and James Iradi.)

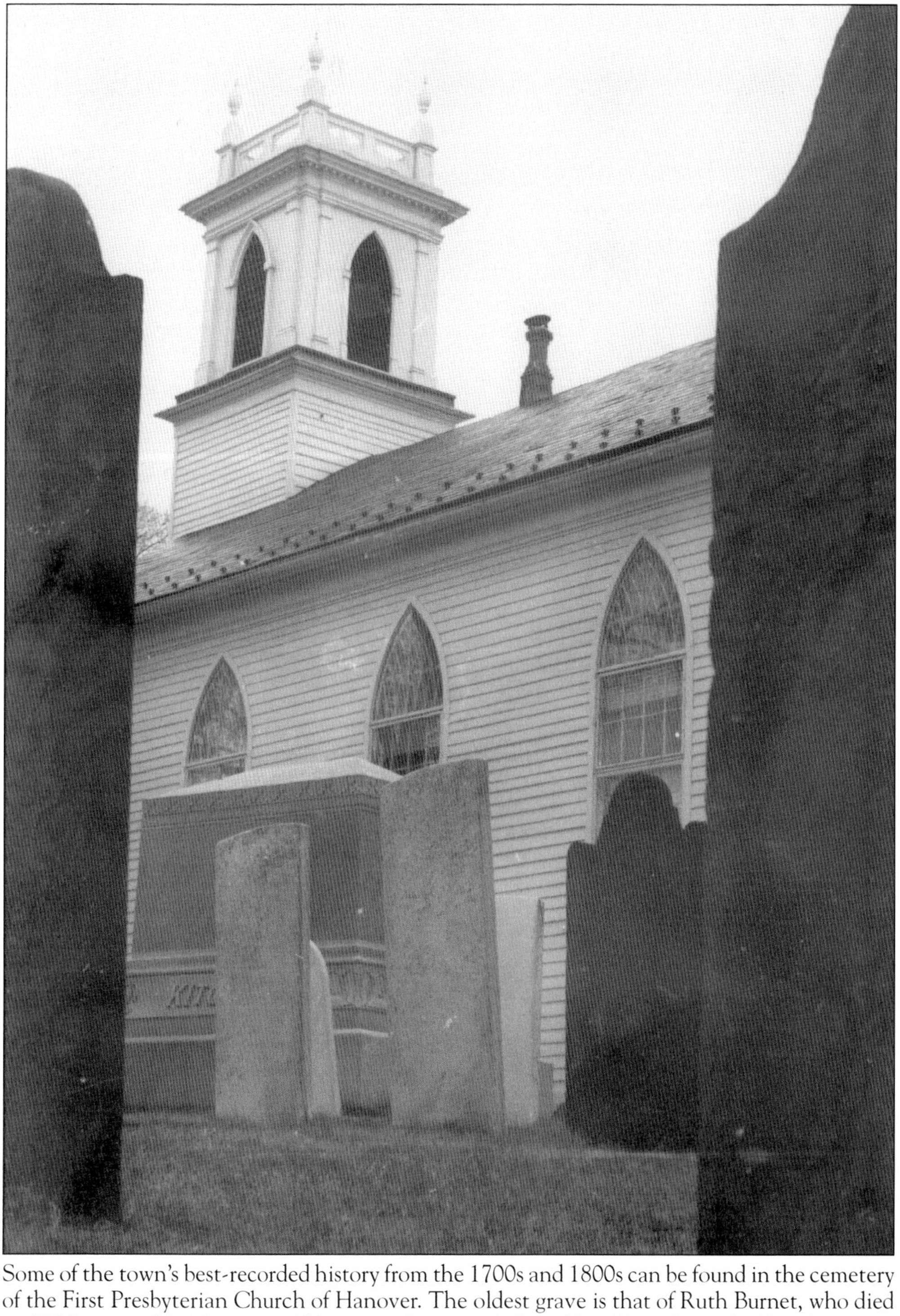

Some of the town's best-recorded history from the 1700s and 1800s can be found in the cemetery of the First Presbyterian Church of Hanover. The oldest grave is that of Ruth Burnet, who died in 1750 at age 38. There are 879 graves there, including 38 soldiers from the Revolutionary War, Sen. Aaron Kitchell, and David Young, author of the *Farmers' Almanac*. (Courtesy of Henry Malmquist Jr. and the First Presbyterian Church of Hanover.)

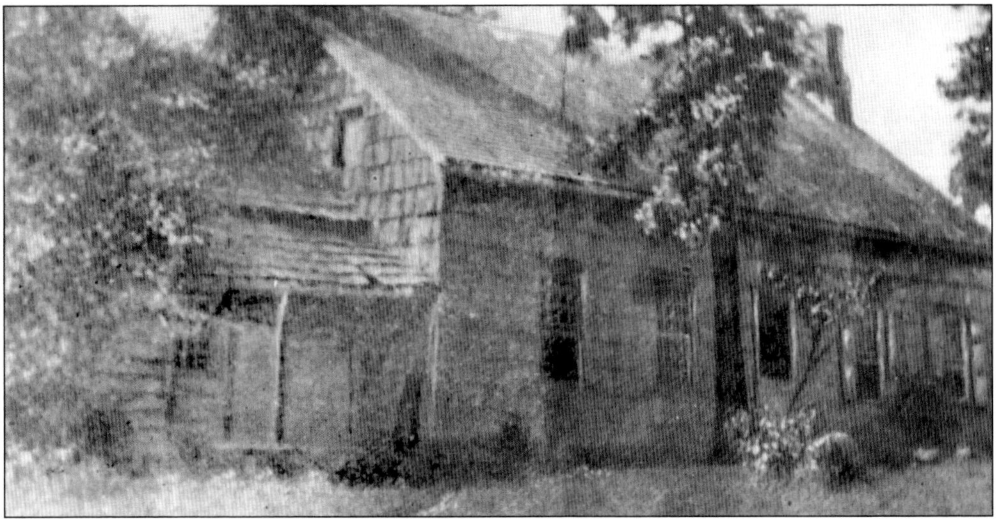

The Old Parsonage on Hanover Road was built in 1757 for Rev. Jacob Green, pastor of the First Presbyterian Congregation of Hanover from 1745 to 1790. He was an extraordinary man who had a significant impact on Colonial history in this area. He was a patriot, political activist, and fervent abolitionist. Despite his Harvard degree, Reverend Green did not earn much as a man of the cloth, so he also worked as a teacher, doctor, miller, distiller, and Princeton University trustee. He started the town's first school in 1774. In 1776, he was named chairman of the committee that wrote New Jersey's constitution. During the winter of 1777, with George Washington's troops encamped in Morris County, he helped save many lives by recommending a controversial inoculation program when a smallpox epidemic broke out. He utilized the church on Mount Pleasant Avenue as a medical facility during the Revolutionary War for both the Continental Army and British soldiers. Reverend Green is buried in the church cemetery. The Old Parsonage on Hanover Road is today a private home. (Courtesy of Everett Rowley Jr.)

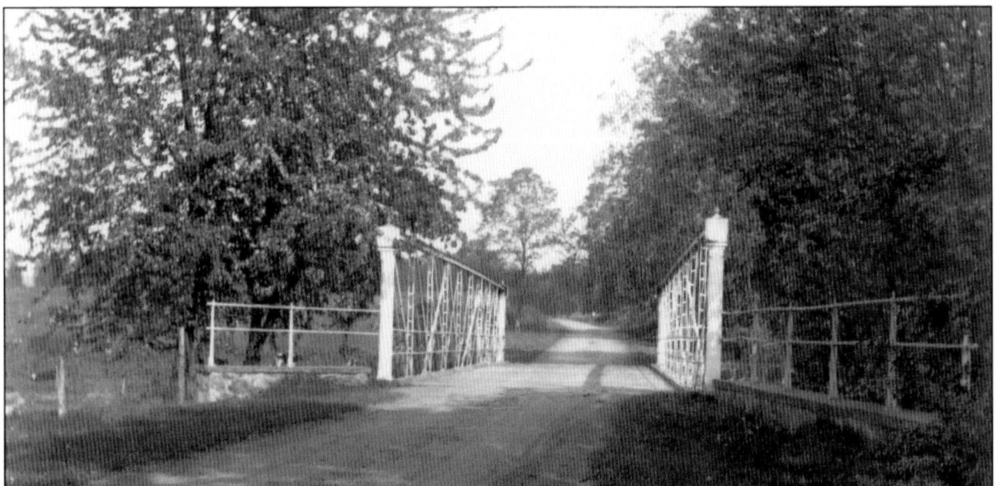

Cook's Bridge over the Passaic River on Mount Pleasant Avenue has seen its share of action. It was guarded by locals during the Revolutionary War against the threat of British soldiers entering Morris County. In the 1800s, it was a toll bridge along the Newark and Mount Pleasant Turnpike. It has been rebuilt on more than one occasion, rerouting traffic and testing travelers' patience during restoration. (Courtesy of the East Hanover Historical Society.)

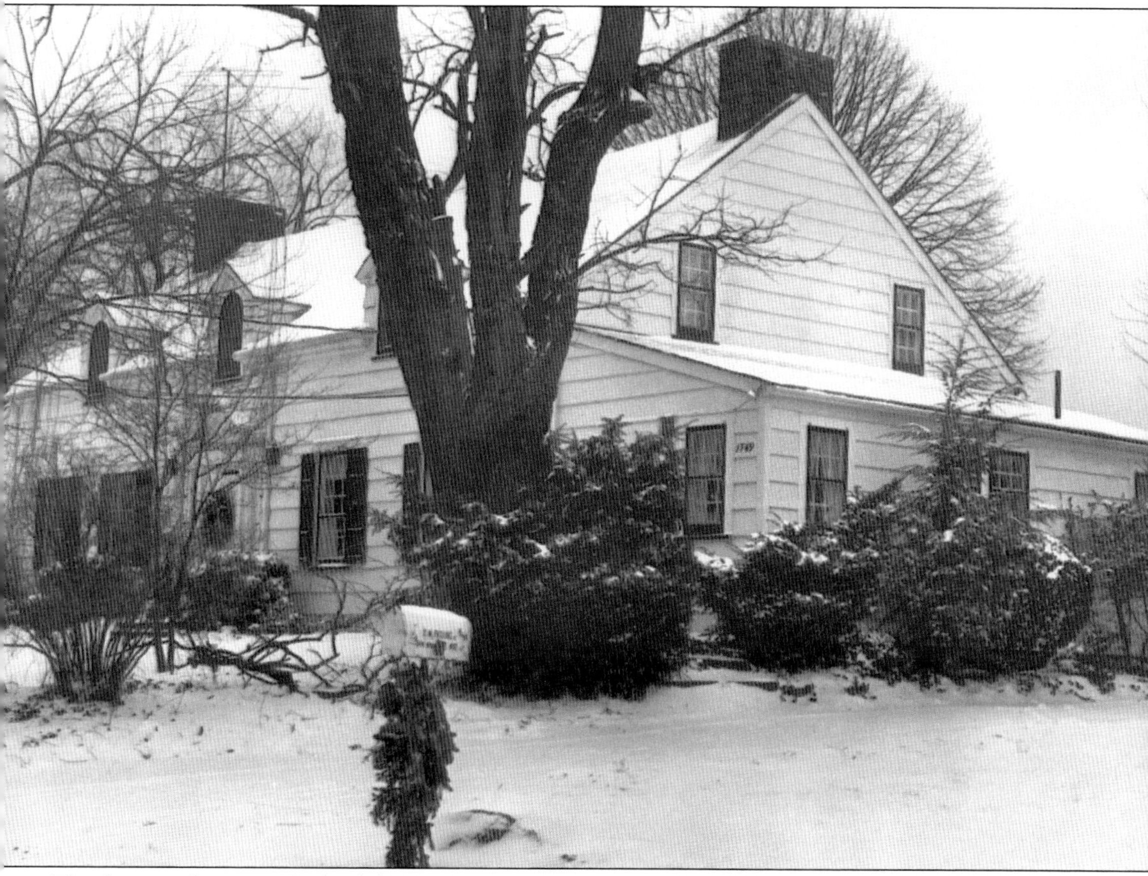

This historic home on Ridgedale Avenue near Eagle Rock Avenue dates from 1749. Adoniram Pruden bought the house and property from Moses Tuttle of Pequannock for 625 pounds. The property stretched from the Whippany to the Passaic Rivers. Now a private residence, the house still has an original brick oven in a fireplace, where bread was baked in Colonial times. There is also a secret hiding place settlers used in case of attack. The Tuttle family had extensive land holdings in the northern part of town. (Courtesy of Catherine Froling.)

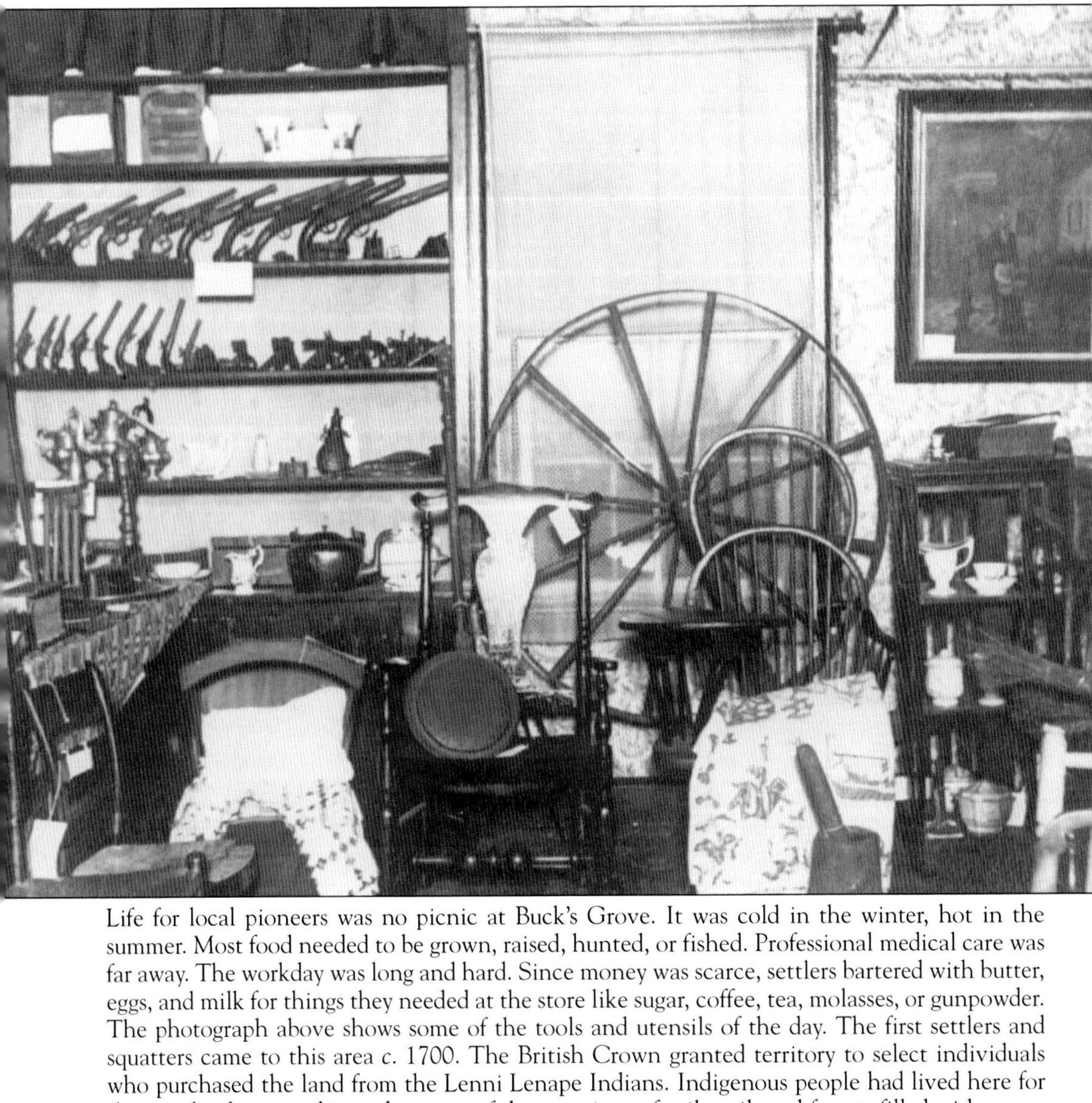

Life for local pioneers was no picnic at Buck's Grove. It was cold in the winter, hot in the summer. Most food needed to be grown, raised, hunted, or fished. Professional medical care was far away. The workday was long and hard. Since money was scarce, settlers bartered with butter, eggs, and milk for things they needed at the store like sugar, coffee, tea, molasses, or gunpowder. The photograph above shows some of the tools and utensils of the day. The first settlers and squatters came to this area *c.* 1700. The British Crown granted territory to select individuals who purchased the land from the Lenni Lenape Indians. Indigenous people had lived here for thousands of years, taking advantage of the two rivers, fertile soil, and forests filled with game. (Courtesy of Everett Rowley Jr.)

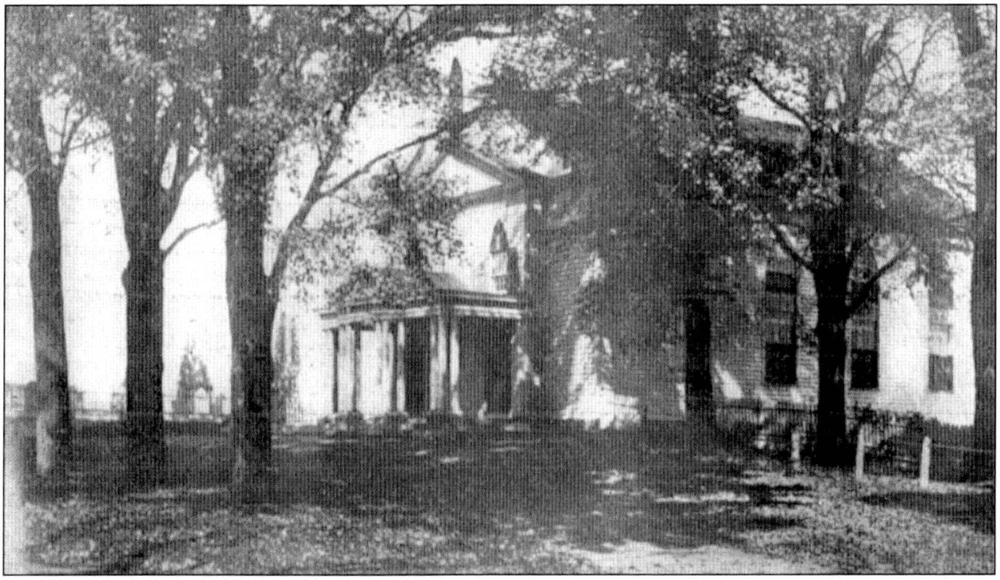

The First Presbyterian Church of Hanover is the oldest religious congregation in Morris County. It was established in Whippany in 1718 and moved to Mount Pleasant Avenue in 1755. The present building was constructed in 1835. This is the original mother church to several congregations, including Kitchell Memorial Presbyterian in East Hanover, Calvary Presbyterian in Florham Park, and Olivet Chapel in Livingston. (Courtesy of the First Presbyterian Church of Hanover.)

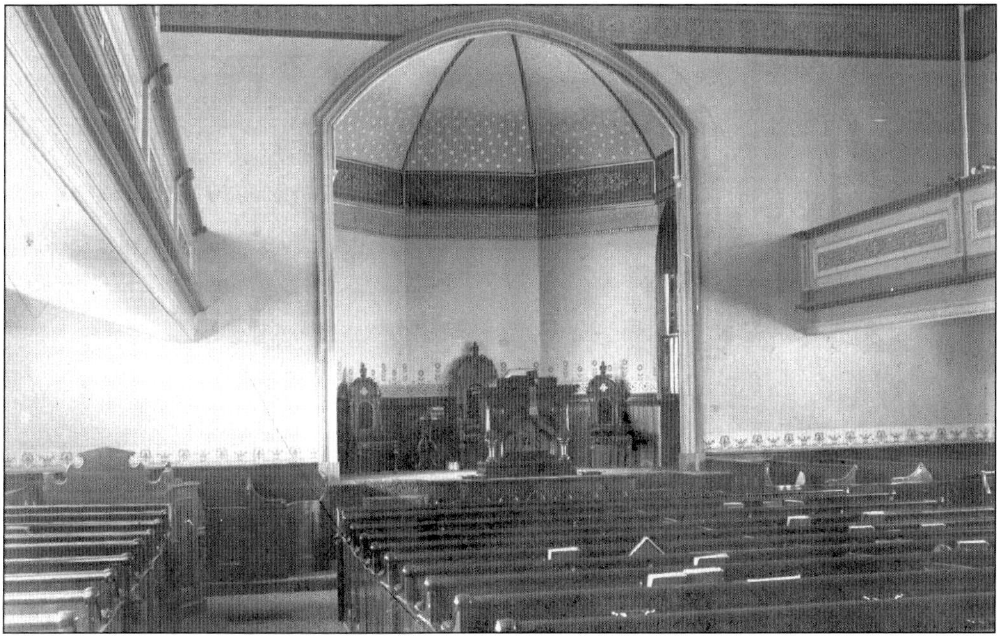

This pre-1912 postcard shows the inside of the First Presbyterian Church of Hanover. The interior of the sanctuary slopes downward from back to front so parishioners can better see the pastor and vice versa. Long ago, seating was in family pews that were rented on an annual basis. Special benches kept feet raised above the cold floor on winter Sunday mornings. (Courtesy of the First Presbyterian Church of Hanover.)

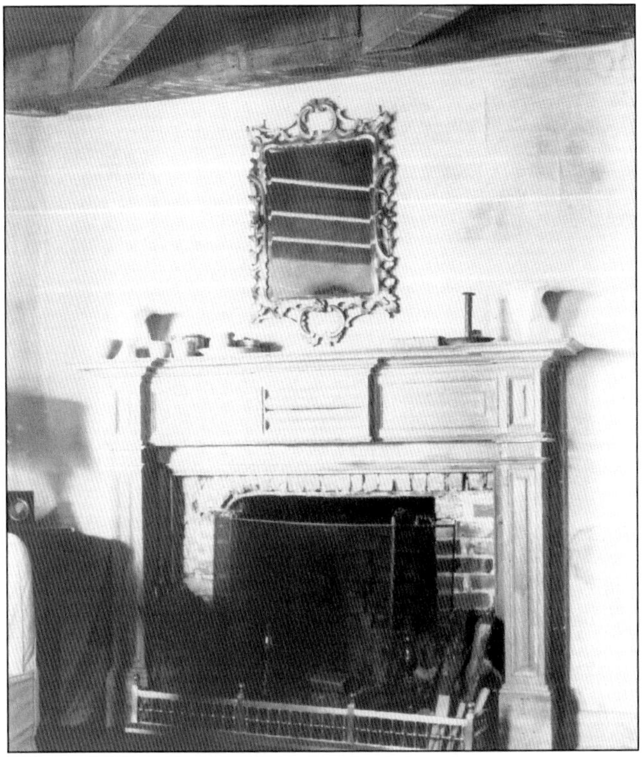

Fireplaces were used for heating and cooking until they were eventually replaced by wood- or coal-burning stoves. This fireplace, in the parlor of the Halfway House, dates from the 1700s and was used for heating into the 1900s. (Courtesy of the East Hanover Historical Society.)

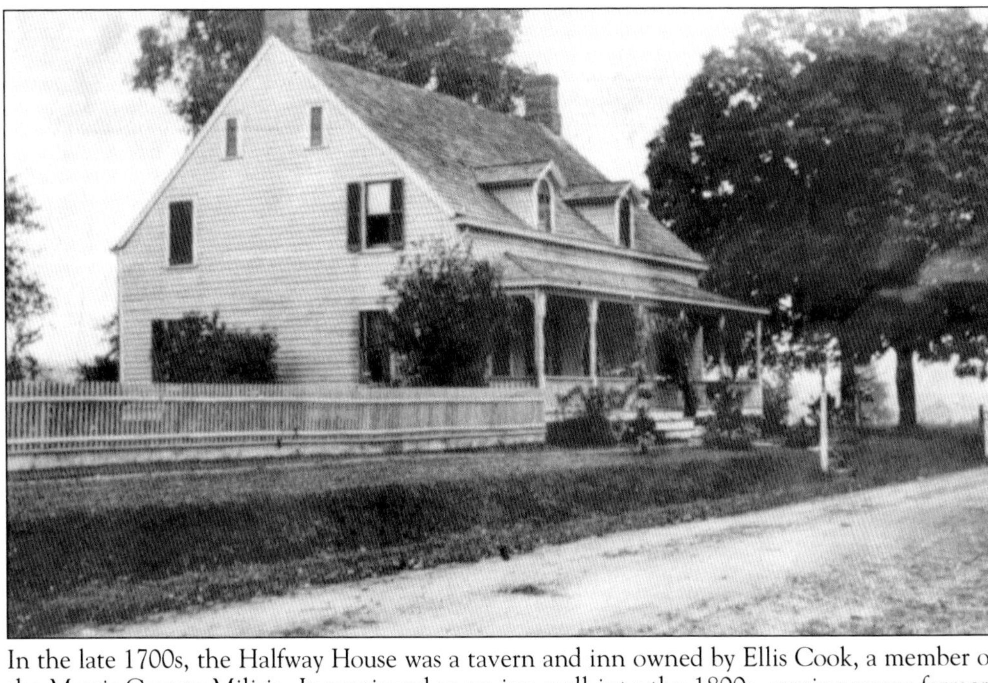

In the late 1700s, the Halfway House was a tavern and inn owned by Ellis Cook, a member of the Morris County Militia. It continued as an inn well into the 1800s, serving weary farmers who carted their produce from northwestern New Jersey to markets in Newark. It is located about halfway along the journey. Today, the Halfway House is home to the East Hanover Historical Society. (Courtesy of Pete Tamburro.)

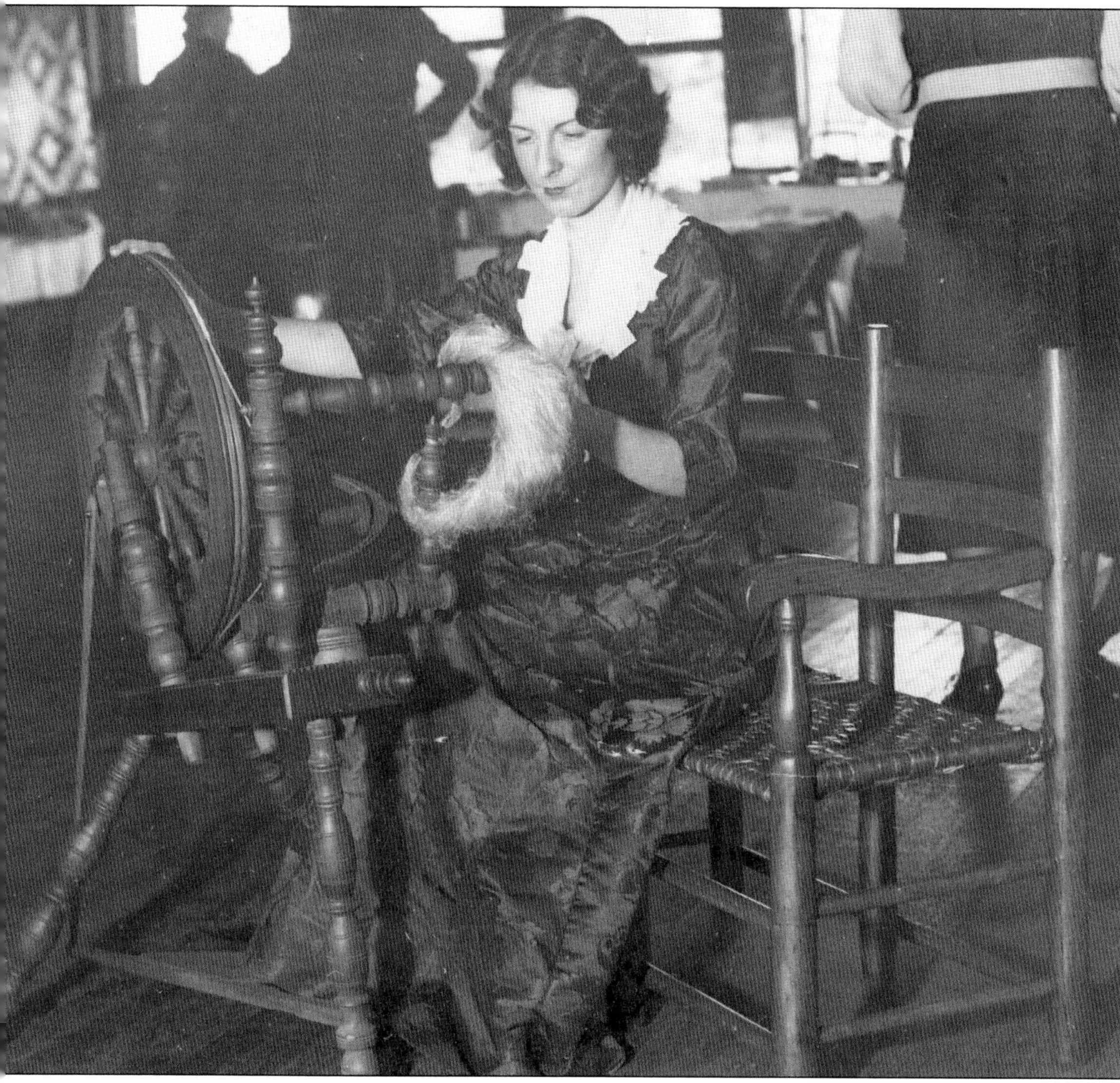

Hazel Bright demonstrates spinning during a celebration at the First Presbyterian Church in 1935. Colonial housewives spun wool and cloth for clothing and household linens in pioneer days. Some spinsters earned a few shillings creating garments for their neighbors. Great pride was taken by the creators of handmade apparel. Clothing that was useable was handed down to children or siblings. When it was worn out, the material went to make rag rugs. Shoes were so valuable that most people went barefoot in the summer. Often, churchgoers carried their shoes on Sunday mornings and put them on when they arrived at the sanctuary. Women also sewed clothing by hand, made soap and candles, churned cream to make butter, washed and ironed the clothes, and did most of the cooking. (Courtesy of the East Hanover Historical Society.)

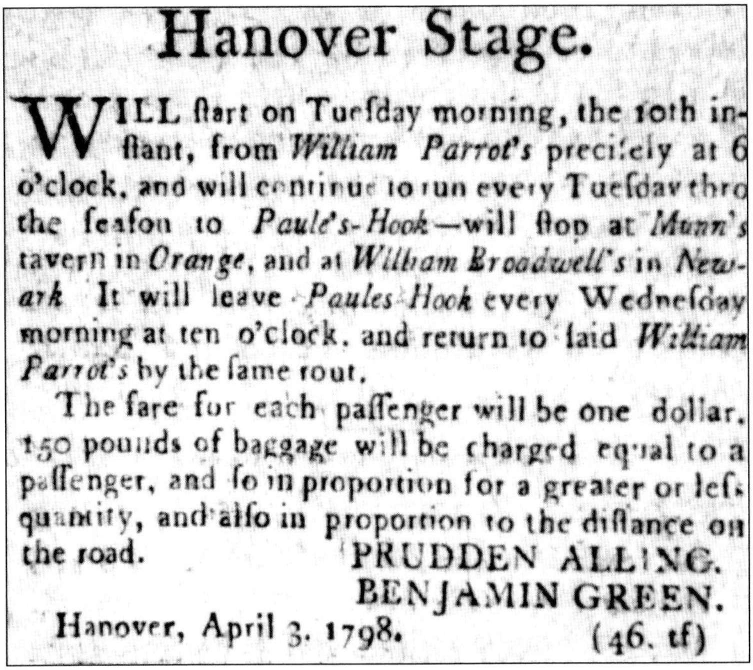

Hanover Stage.

WILL ſtart on Tueſday morning, the 10th inſtant, from *William Parrot's* preciſely at 6 o'clock, and will continue to run every Tueſday thro the ſeaſon to *Paule's-Hook*—will ſtop at *Munn's* tavern in *Orange*, and at *William Broadwell's* in *Newark*. It will leave *Paules Hook* every Wedneſday morning at ten o'clock, and return to ſaid *William Parrot's* by the ſame rout.

The fare for each paſſenger will be one dollar. 150 pounds of baggage will be charged equal to a paſſenger, and ſo in proportion for a greater or leſs quantity, and alſo in proportion to the diſtance on the road.

PRUDDEN ALLING.
BENJAMIN GREEN.

Hanover, April 3. 1798. (46. tf)

Stagecoach travel began in the late 1700s when roads were built that could accommodate wheels. Before then, people got around by horseback or foot. This advertisement, dated April 3, 1798, announces that the Hanover Stage is opening for the season. In all likelihood, it did not run in the winter; the roads were not that good. (Courtesy of Pete Tamburro and Alfredo Fanelli.)

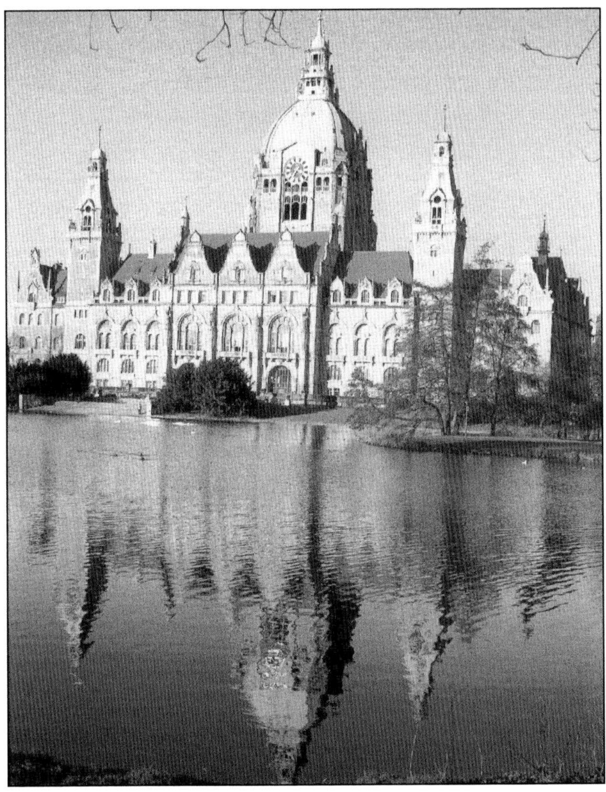

Although this building is not in East Hanover, there is an important connection between it and the township. This is city hall in Hannover, Germany. There are 64 Hanovers in the United States, including East Hanover. All can trace the origin of their names to this northern German city, which dates back to A.D. 950. (Courtesy of Hannover Fairs USA.)

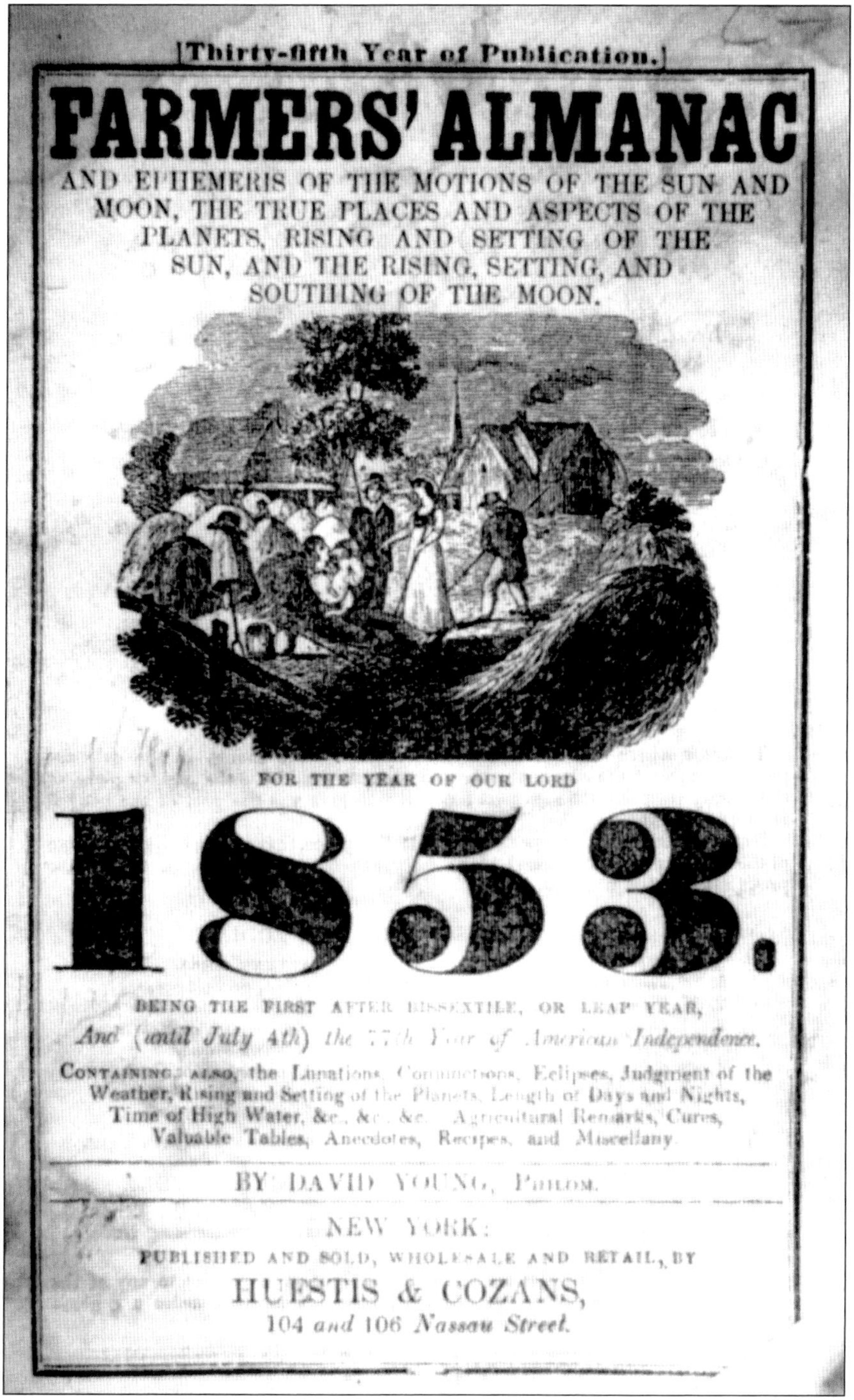

[Thirty-fifth Year of Publication.]

FARMERS' ALMANAC

AND EPHEMERIS OF THE MOTIONS OF THE SUN AND MOON, THE TRUE PLACES AND ASPECTS OF THE PLANETS, RISING AND SETTING OF THE SUN, AND THE RISING, SETTING, AND SOUTHING OF THE MOON.

FOR THE YEAR OF OUR LORD

1853.

BEING THE FIRST AFTER BISSEXTILE, OR LEAP YEAR,

And (until July 4th) the 77th Year of American Independence.

CONTAINING ALSO, the Lunations, Conjunctions, Eclipses, Judgment of the Weather, Rising and Setting of the Planets, Length of Days and Nights, Time of High Water, &c., &c., &c. Agricultural Remarks, Cures, Valuable Tables, Anecdotes, Recipes, and Miscellany.

BY DAVID YOUNG, PHILOM.

NEW YORK:

PUBLISHED AND SOLD, WHOLESALE AND RETAIL, BY

HUESTIS & COZANS,

104 *and* 106 *Nassau Street.*

David Young was a local man of keen intellect. Born on January 27, 1781, he was recognized in his youth as somewhat of a genius. As an adult, he became a noted astronomer, writer, and mathematician. Young was most famous for writing and editing the *Farmers' Almanac*. This 1853 edition was published posthumously. He died on February 13, 1852, and is buried in the First Presbyterian Church cemetery. (Courtesy of Pete Tamburro and Alfredo Fanelli.)

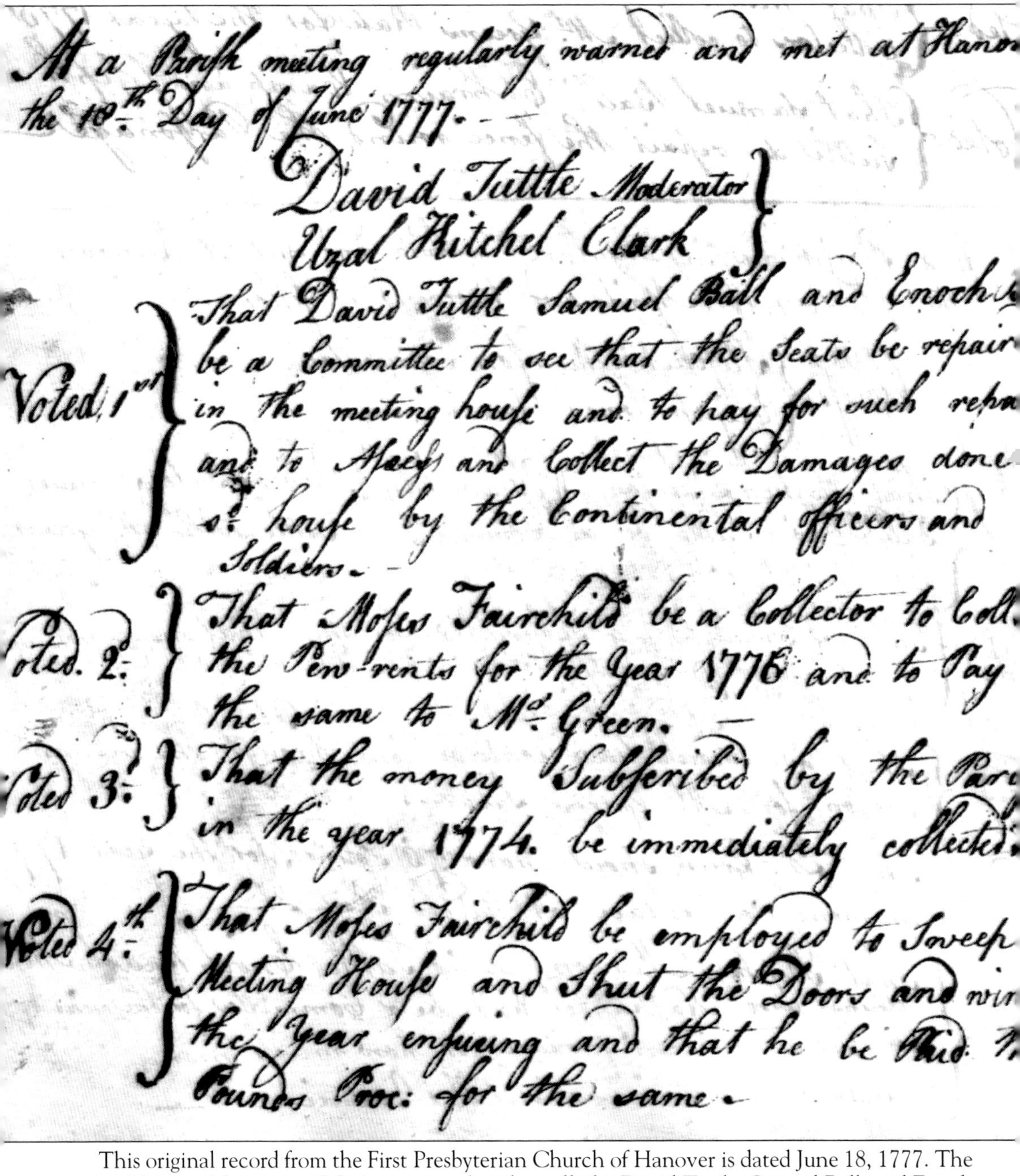
At a Parish meeting regularly warned and met at Hanov
the 18th Day of June 1777 — —

David Tuttle Moderator
Uzal Kitchel Clark

Voted 1st That David Tuttle Samuel Ball and Enoch
be a Committee to see that the Seats be repair
in the meeting house and to pay for such repa
and to Assess and Collect the Damages done
sd house by the Continental officers and
Soldiers —

Voted 2d That Moses Fairchild be a Collector to Coll
the Pew-rents for the Year 1776 and to Pay
the same to Mr Green. —

Voted 3d That the money Subscribed by the Pari
in the year 1774. be immediately collected.

Voted 4th That Moses Fairchild be employed to Sweep
Meeting House and Shut the Doors and win
the Year ensuing and that he be Paid
Pounds Proc: for the same —

This original record from the First Presbyterian Church of Hanover is dated June 18, 1777. The parishioners' first vote of their meeting that day calls for David Tuttle, Samuel Ball, and Enoch Beach to have seats at the church repaired and to then send the bill to the Continental Army. It seems some patriots caused enough damage for the church elders to take action. (Courtesy of the First Presbyterian Church of Hanover.)

Two

Agricultural Heritage

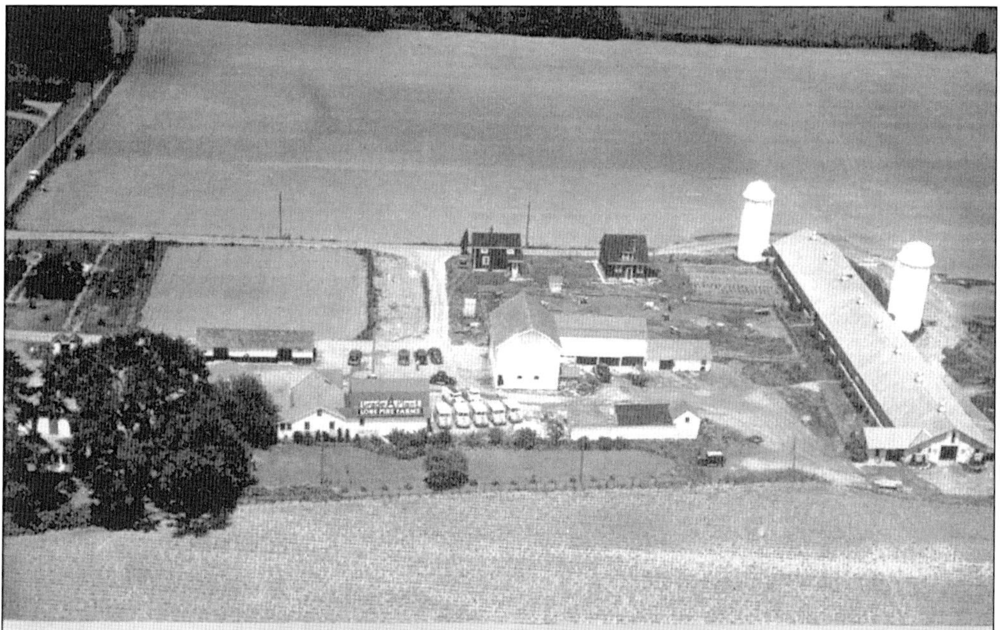

This postcard of Lone Pine Farm shows the 50-acre dairy in its heyday. It was started in 1905 by Raymond and Emma Durham, who later passed it on to their children. The farm eventually ceased operations in 1985. At one time, as many as 200 cows grazed in the fields along Route 10 and River Road. Customers could buy milk, eggs, and ice cream in a store at the farm site. (Courtesy of John Esposito.)

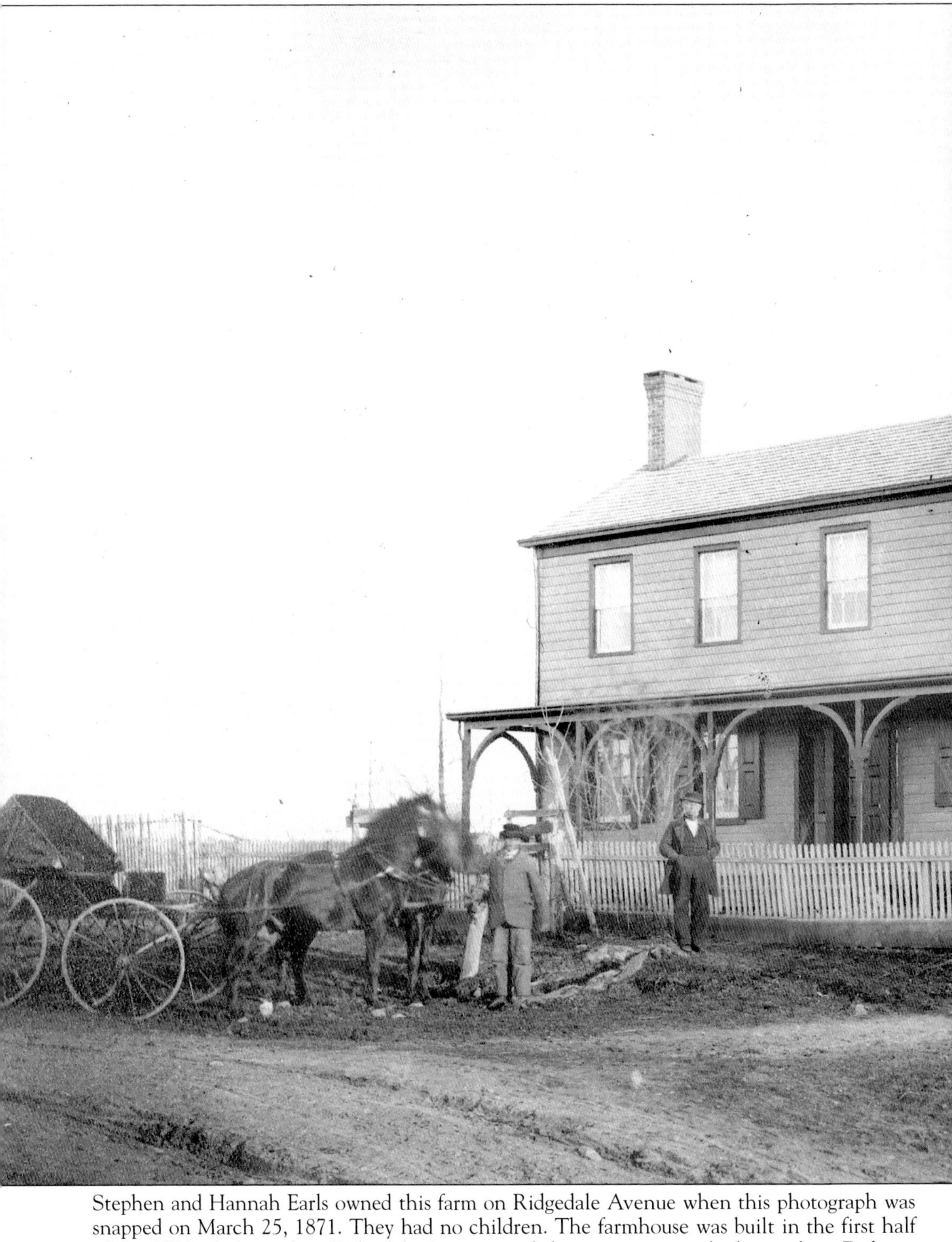

Stephen and Hannah Earls owned this farm on Ridgedale Avenue when this photograph was snapped on March 25, 1871. They had no children. The farmhouse was built in the first half of the 1800s. It fronted on Ridgedale Avenue, and the property stretched east along Deforest Avenue into what is now Restland Memorial Park. A lumberyard opened behind the house in

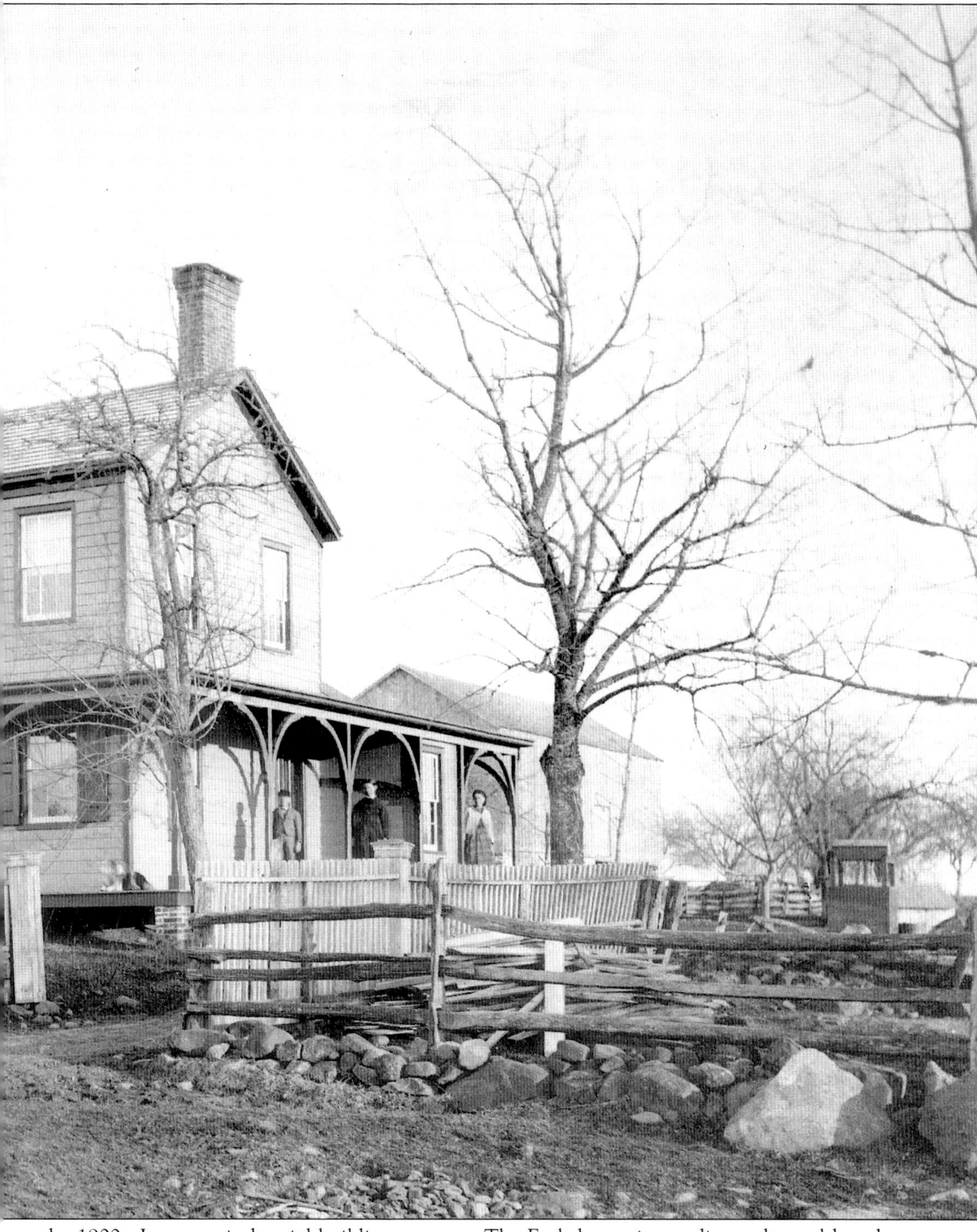

the 1900s. Later, an industrial building went up. The Earls house is standing today—although a number of changes have been made—several doors south of the post office. (Courtesy of the East Hanover Historical Society.)

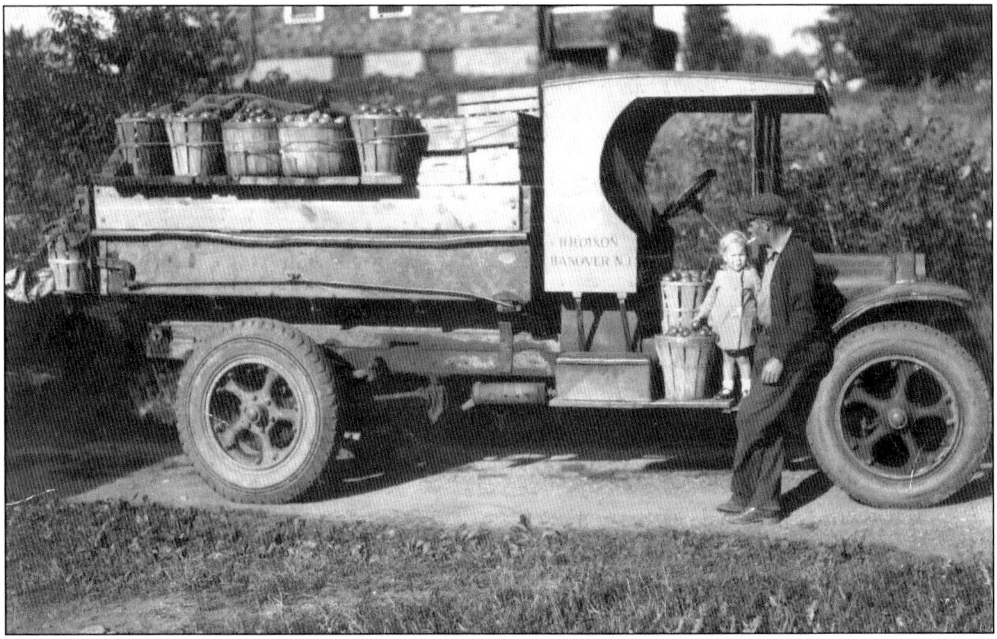

Horace Dixon and his son Lee take a break after packing up the truck on their River Road farm in 1934. Several times a week during the season, Horace would truck his produce to the Newark wholesale market, where he rented space and sold produce from the tailboard to hotels, restaurants, retailers, commissioned merchants, steamship suppliers, and others. (Courtesy of Lee Dixon.)

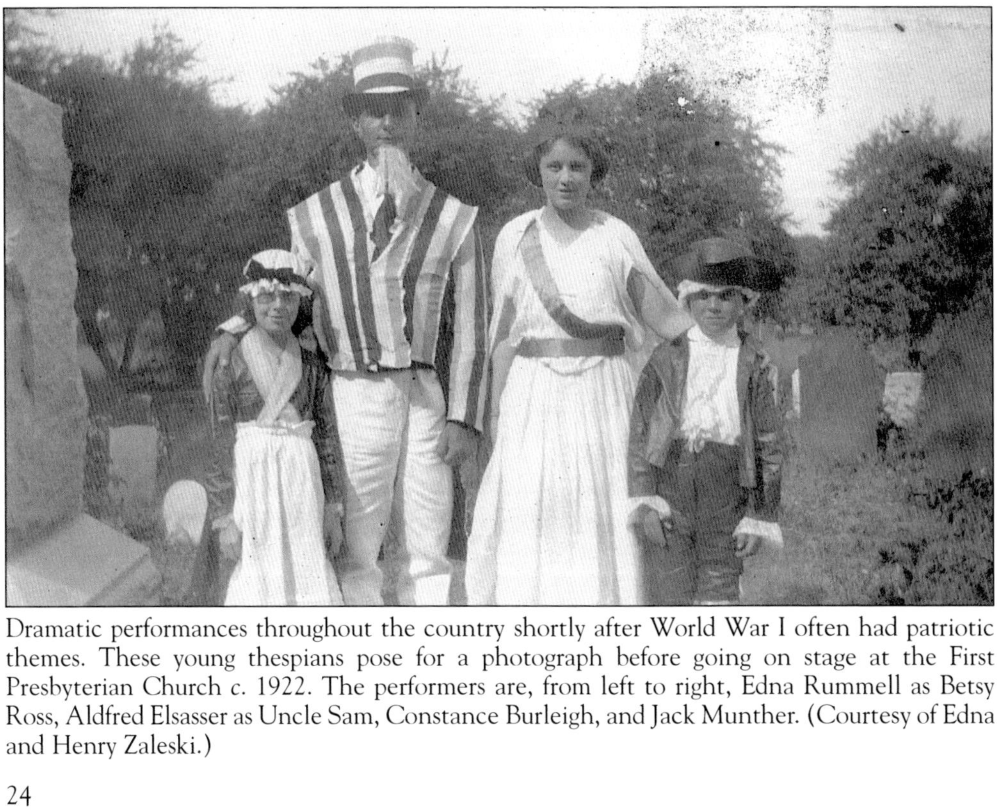

Dramatic performances throughout the country shortly after World War I often had patriotic themes. These young thespians pose for a photograph before going on stage at the First Presbyterian Church c. 1922. The performers are, from left to right, Edna Rummell as Betsy Ross, Aldfred Elsasser as Uncle Sam, Constance Burleigh, and Jack Munther. (Courtesy of Edna and Henry Zaleski.)

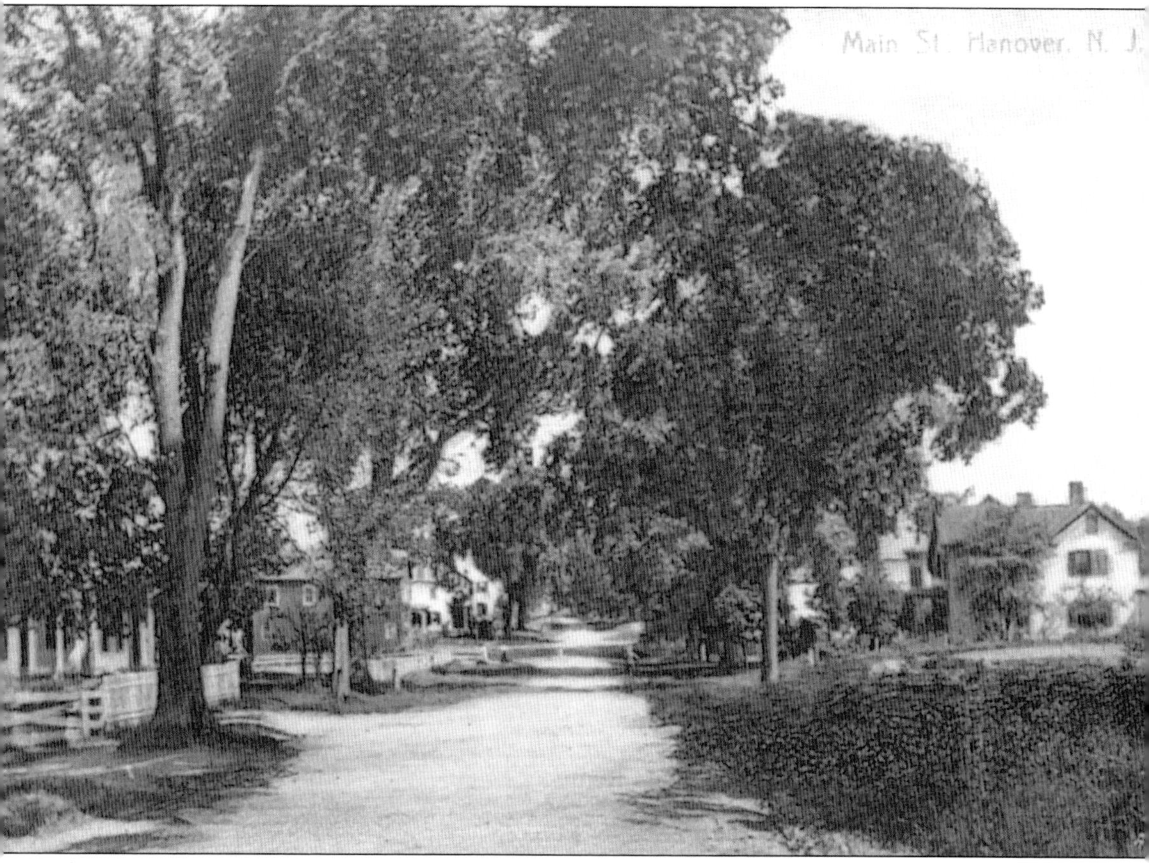

This postcard, dated September 8, 1908, was sent from what is now East Hanover to Jersey City. "You ought to be up here. We are enjoying ourselves greatly," the writer told her sister. At around that time, people came here then to escape the hustle and bustle of urban life. The scene is Mount Pleasant Avenue, which at the time was also referred to as Main Street, in the village known as Hanover from the 1700s through much of the 1900s. There were businesses, a church, general store, post office, and residences lining Main Street—a real village setting. The northern part of town was known as Hanover Neck. There were homes and several stores throughout the neck, but not a central village like this in the 1700s and 1800s. (Courtesy of the Morris County Library.)

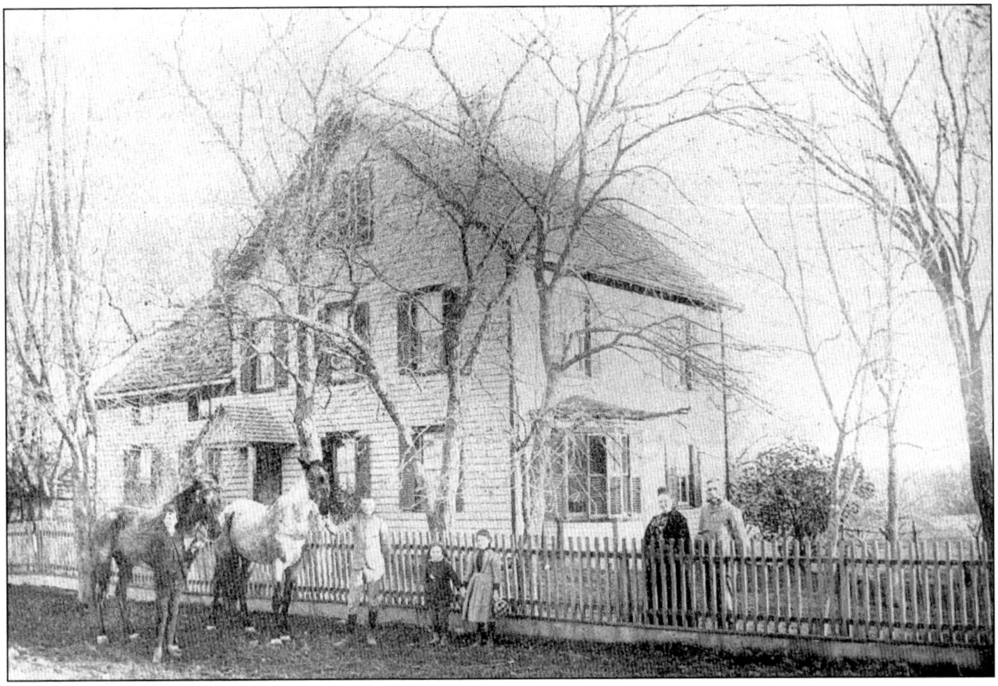

The Whaites family home is shown in the late 1800s. It was located near where the Ford dealer is today on Route 10. Shown, from left to right, are Percy, Ernest, Orrin, and Aida Whaites; Sara Courter; and Frank Whaites. Orrin became the local postmaster in 1910. He is also the original source of some of the old photographs in this book. (Courtesy of the East Hanover Historical Society.)

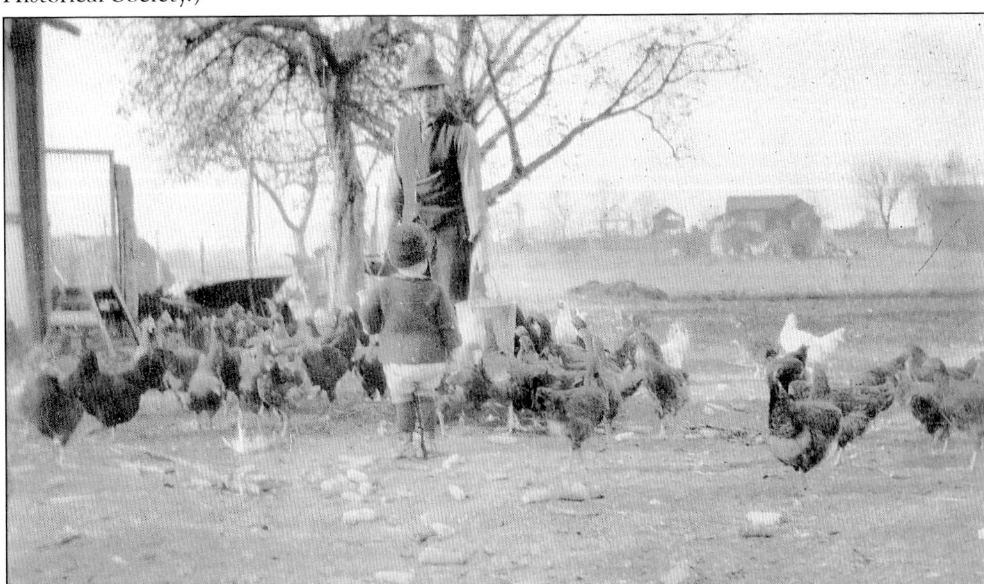

It was common for many residents to raise some of their own food in 1927. In addition to chickens, some people had a few cows, pigs, horses, and sheep. Some homes also had fruit trees; the fruit was eaten as is or used to make cider, vinegar, and sometimes whiskey known as Jersey Lightning. (Courtesy of Herb Johnston.)

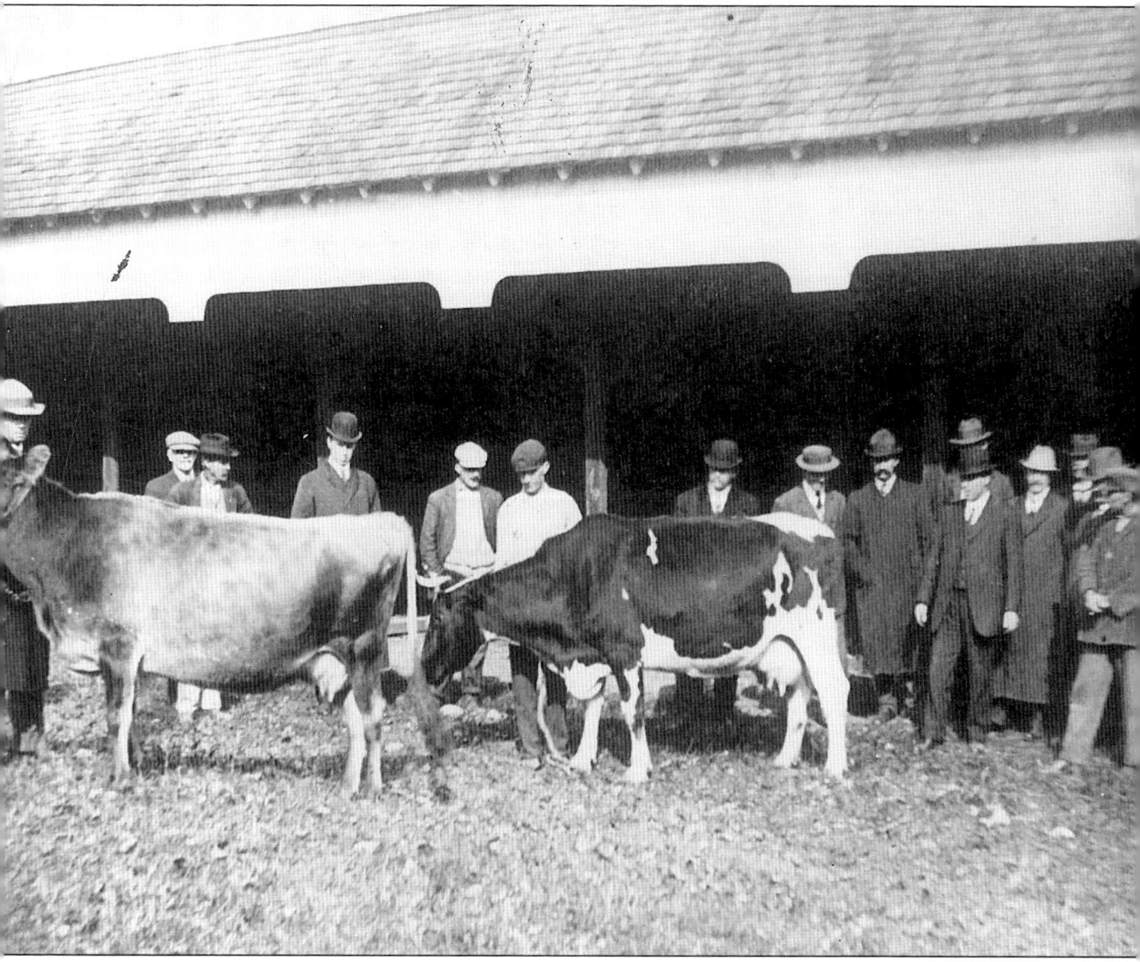

A local chapter of a grange society started in the late 1800s and held its meetings above the blacksmith shop at the corner of Mount Pleasant Avenue and River Road. This photograph was taken nearby—across the street from the First Presbyterian Church, where the annual fair is held today. It is likely a granger get-together, perhaps an auction. Every year, grangers and thousands of guests enjoyed a picnic at Tuttle's Grove along the Passaic River next to the Swinefield Bridge. It was a memorable event, with lots to eat and drink, games, boat rides, and plenty of things to talk about. (Courtesy of Everett Rowley Jr.)

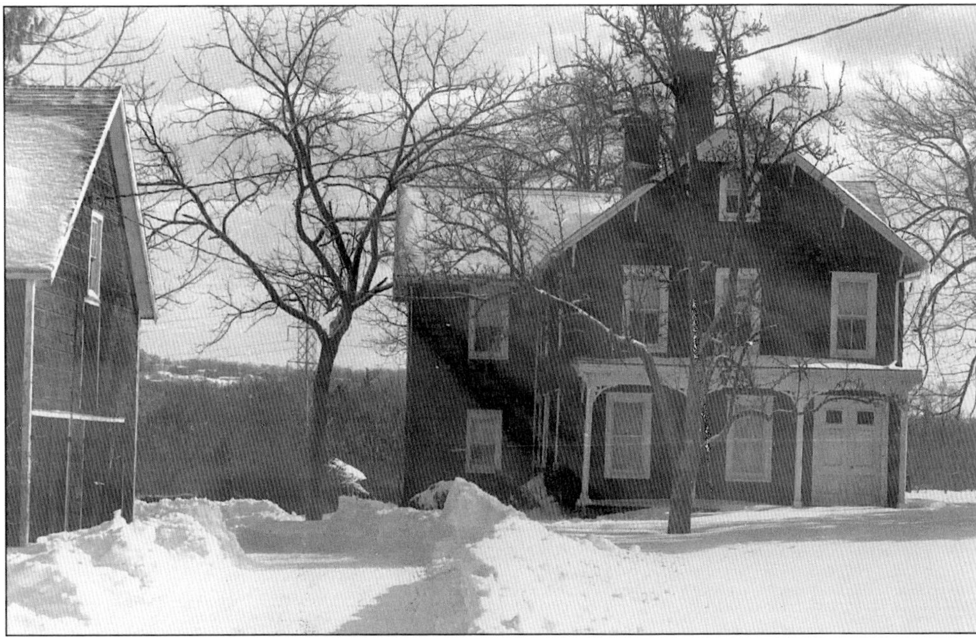

This Gothic Revival farmhouse was built in the mid-1800s by George Petry, who came from Totowa and purchased the property from James Lewis. The Petry farm, on River Road across from Cedar Street, was an active dairy farm run by the family into the latter half of the 20th century. (Courtesy of Gus Auermuller.)

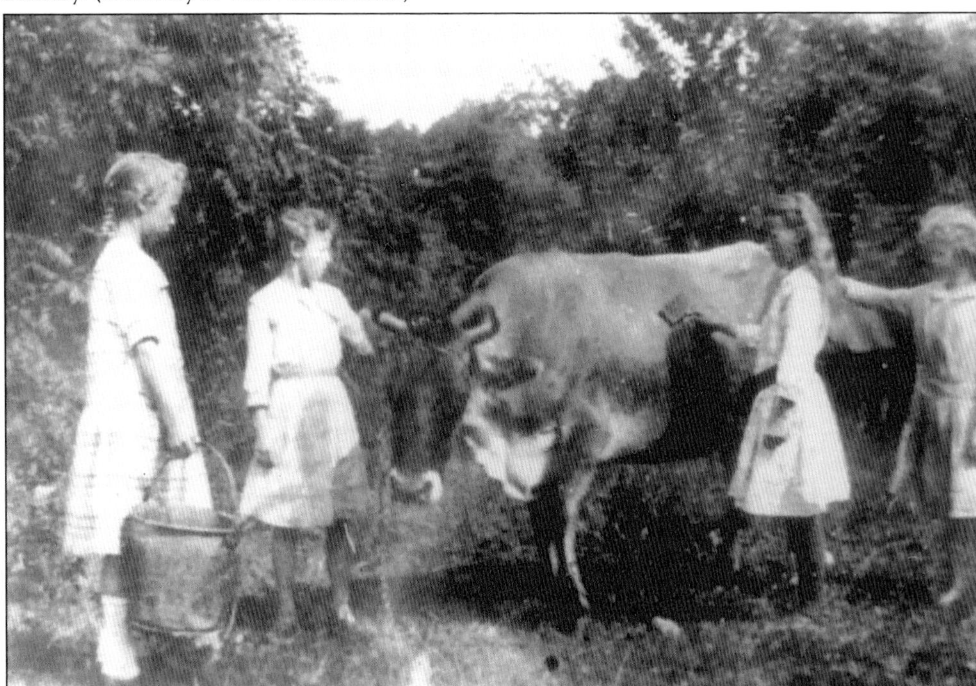

Milking the cows was one of the many chores children had to do if they lived on a farm. Shown here getting ready to go to work in the early 1900s are, from left to right, Margaret, Charlotte, Frances, and Ruth Little at their farm on Ridgedale Avenue. (Courtesy of Helen and James Iradi.)

The Morristown & Erie Railroad originated with the Whippany River Railroad that began in 1895. Over the years, it changed ownership, was rebuilt, expanded, and eventually connected Morristown and Essex Fells, carrying both passengers and freight. Had a passenger used this October 1923 ticket, he or she could have made the 11-mile trip between Morristown and Essex Fells in 37 minutes. (Courtesy of John Esposito.)

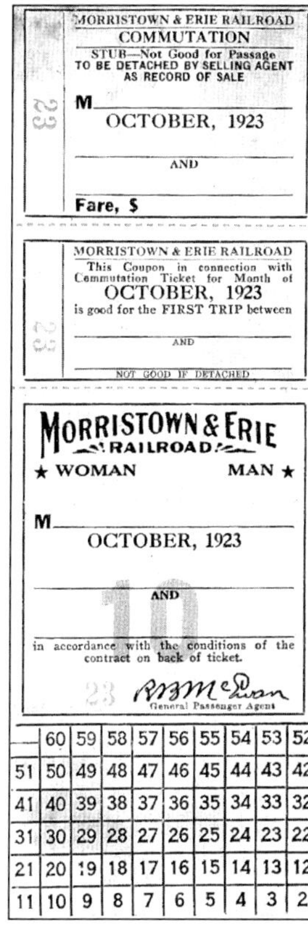

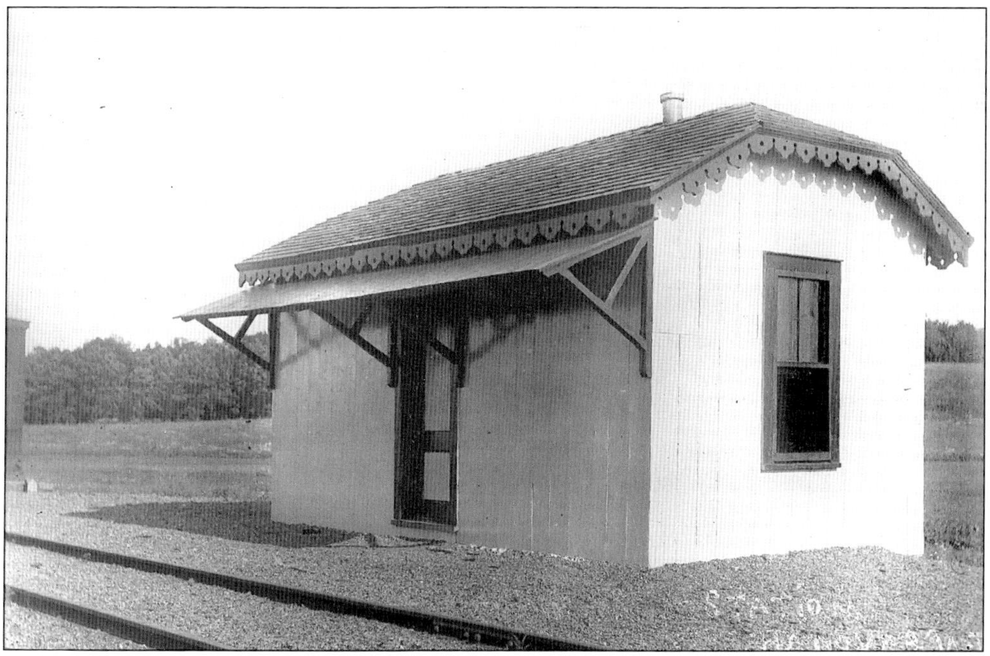

One of the Morristown & Erie Railroad stops was the Hanover Station on Deforest Avenue. This is what the station looked like in the 1920s. When passenger service was discontinued, the depot became the site of a fuel dealer. (Courtesy of the East Hanover Historical Society.)

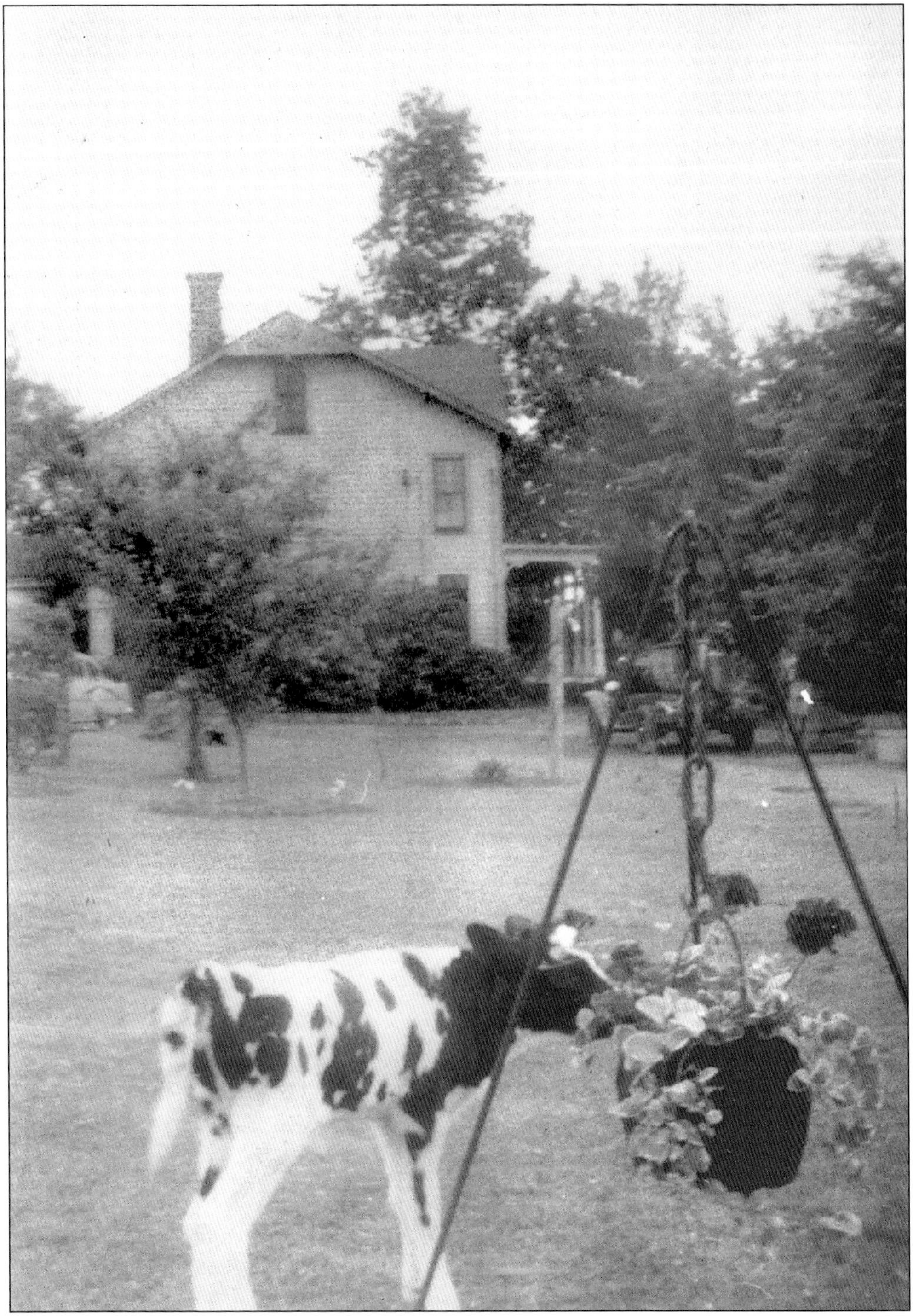

Honeybee investigates a potted plant at the McNaughton farm on South Ridgedale Avenue in the early 1950s. The camera is looking south on Ridgedale. Today the big farmhouse would be sitting in the middle of Tiffany Drive. (Courtesy of George and Sylvia Busold.)

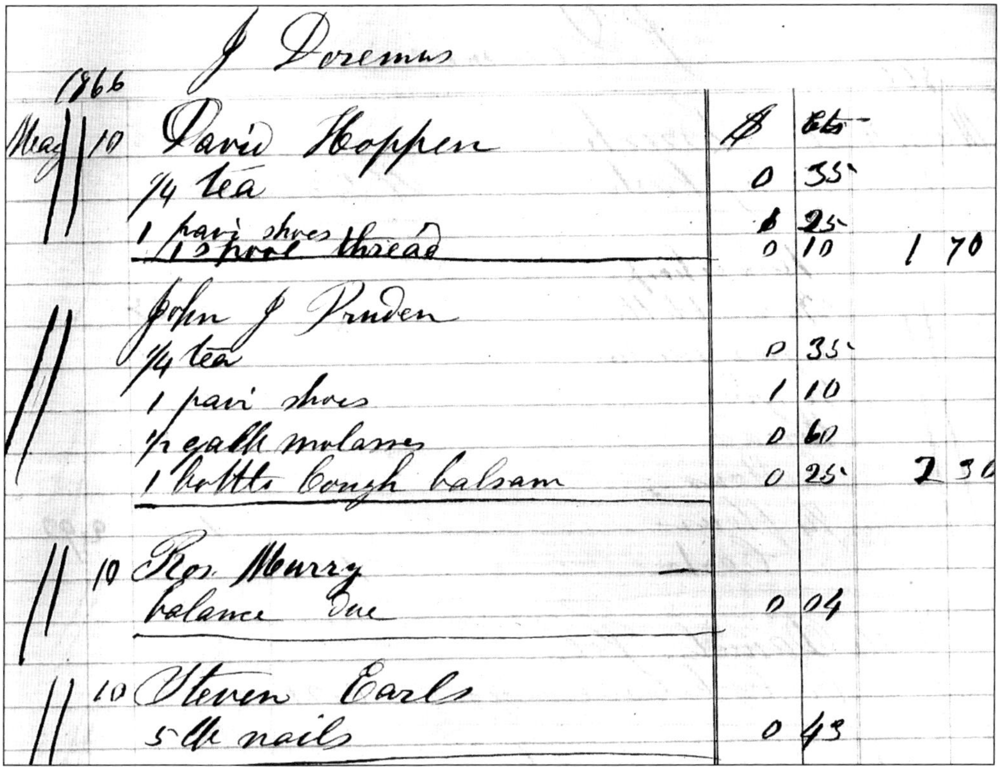

J Doremus

1866			$	Cts	
May	10	David Hoppen			
		1/4 tea	0	35	
		1 pair shoes	1	25	
		1 spool thread	0	10	1 70
		John J Pruden			
		1/4 tea	0	35	
		1 pair shoes	1	10	
		1/2 gall molasses	0	60	
		1 bottle Cough balsam	0	25	2 30
	10	Rev. Murry			
		balance due	0	04	
	10	Steven Earls			
		5 lb nails	0	43	

This is a page from the original 1866 accounts ledger for the general store owned by Jeremiah Doremus (see below). One of the entries on May 10 is for Steven Earls, who bought five pounds of nails for 43¢. He undoubtedly went home to use them on his farm, which can be seen on pages 22 and 23. (Courtesy of Herb Johnston.)

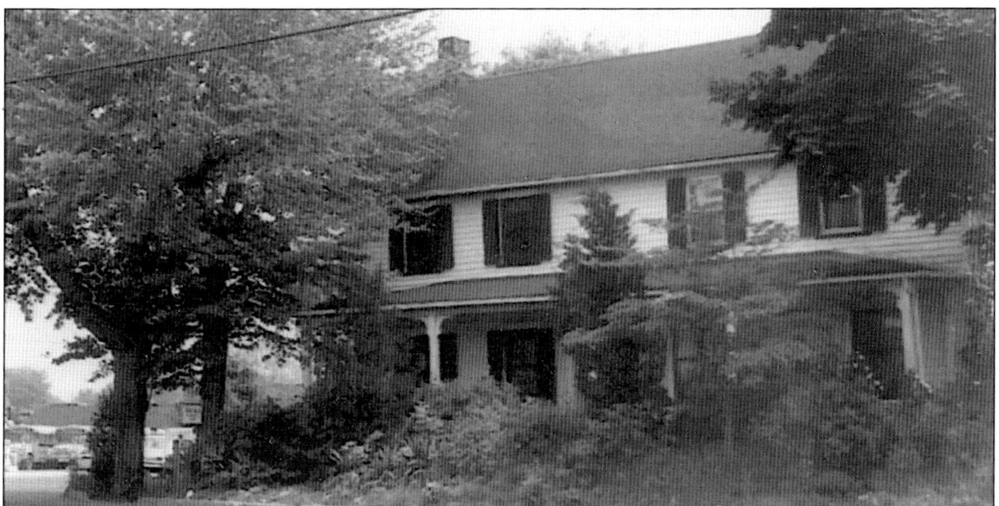

The town's first post office opened here on December 12, 1818, in the general store at the corner of Ridgedale and Eagle Rock Avenues. The first postmaster was Joshua Perry. Store owners in early years included Jeremiah Doremus, John Polhemus, and Frank Hopping. Young men often hung around the store and shot the breeze. (Courtesy of Catherine Froling.)

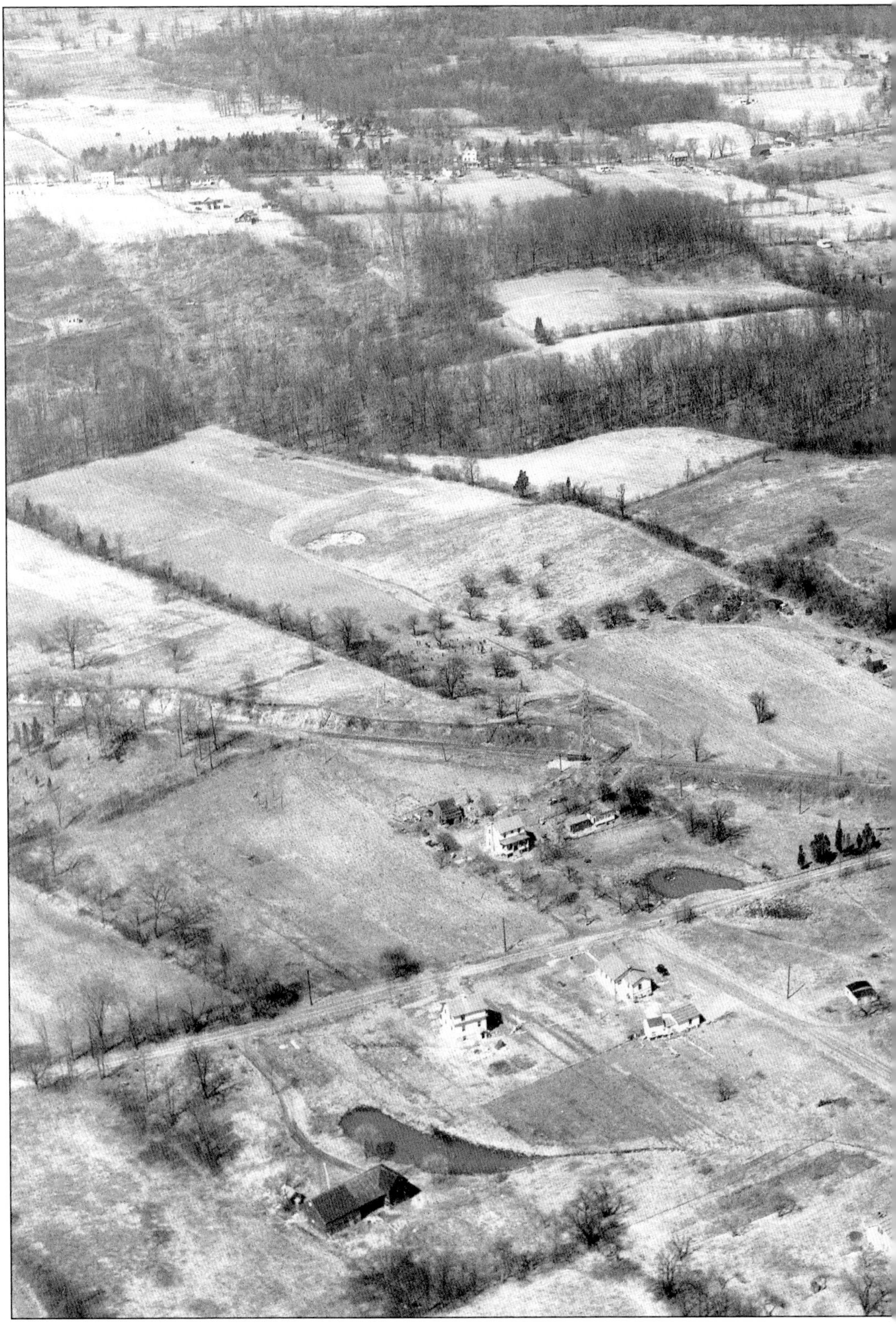

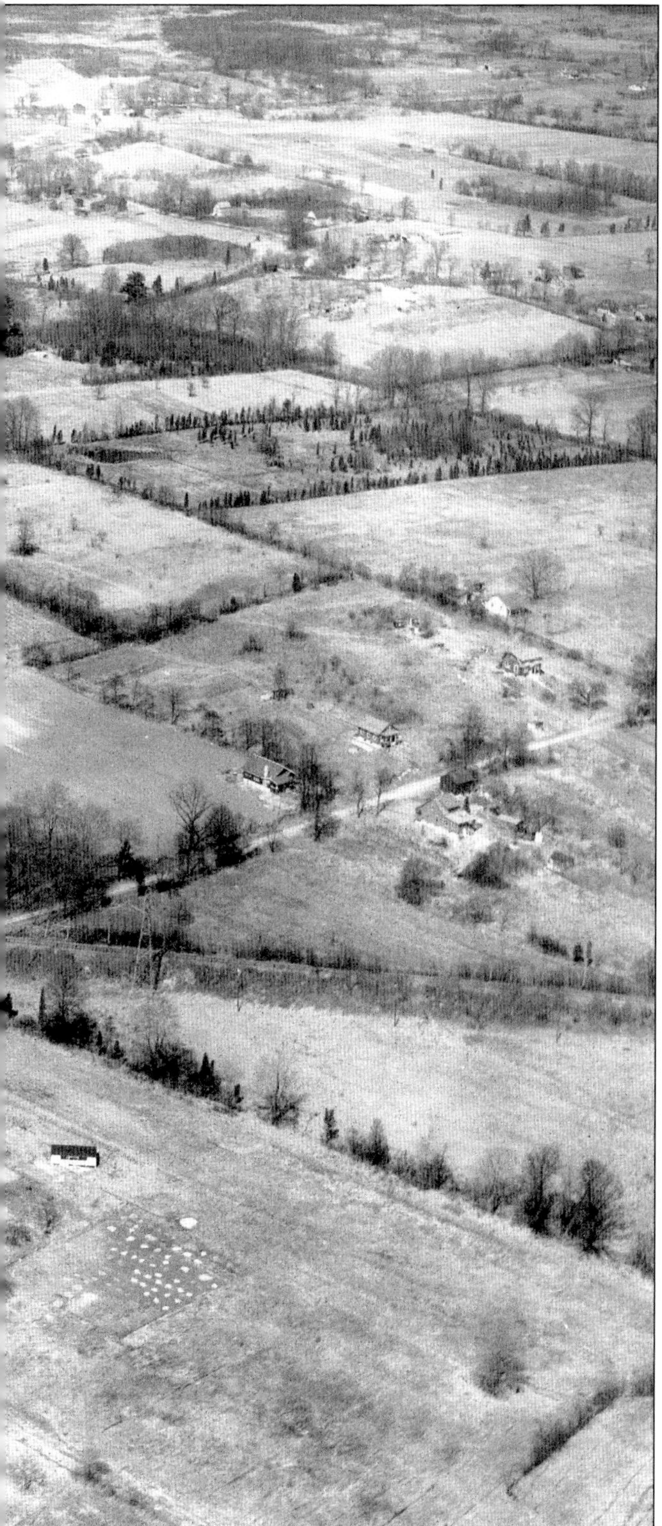

This aerial photograph of the Dixon farm on River Road was taken on March 24, 1929, by Eric Dixon of East Hanover. He had taken off from the first airport in town, which was located near to what is now the bowling alley on Route 10. Eric was an aerial photographer for the military in World Wars I and II. He was a relative of Horace Dixon, the owner of this farm. In addition to agriculture on the 42-acre spread, the Dixons also had a sand and gravel business. The first borrow pits can be seen as small spots in the mid-to-upper right and mid-to-upper left of the photograph. Ancient sea fossils have been found at the sandpits. (Courtesy of Lee Dixon.)

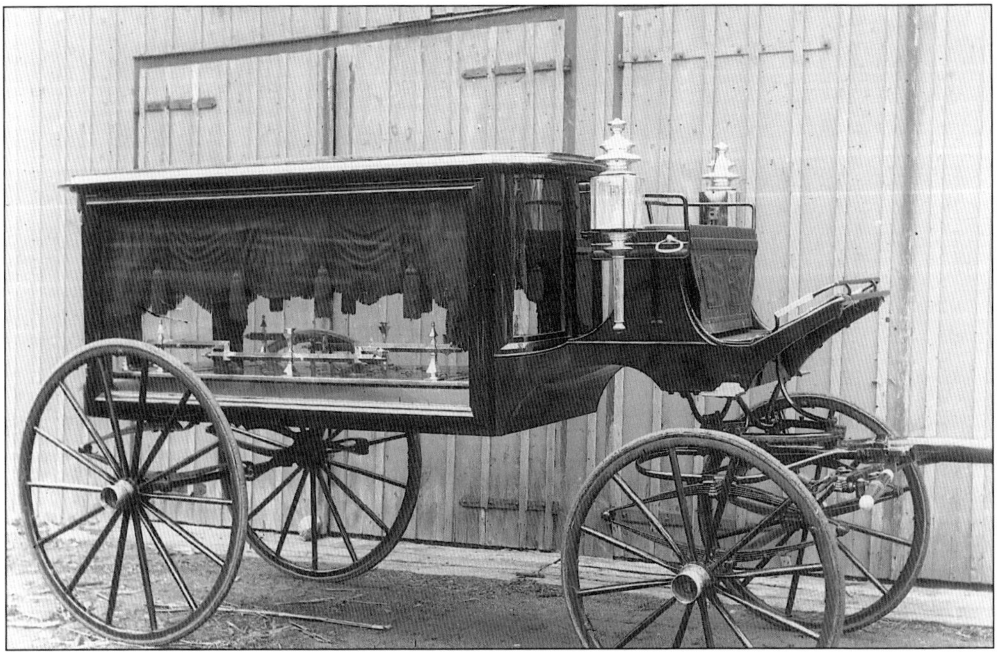

Funeral carriages like this one were used in the 1800s for burials in the town's two cemeteries. The first interment at the Hanover Cemetery (below) on Hanover Road was the wife of Joseph Hedges. She died in August 1849. (Courtesy of the East Hanover Historical Society.)

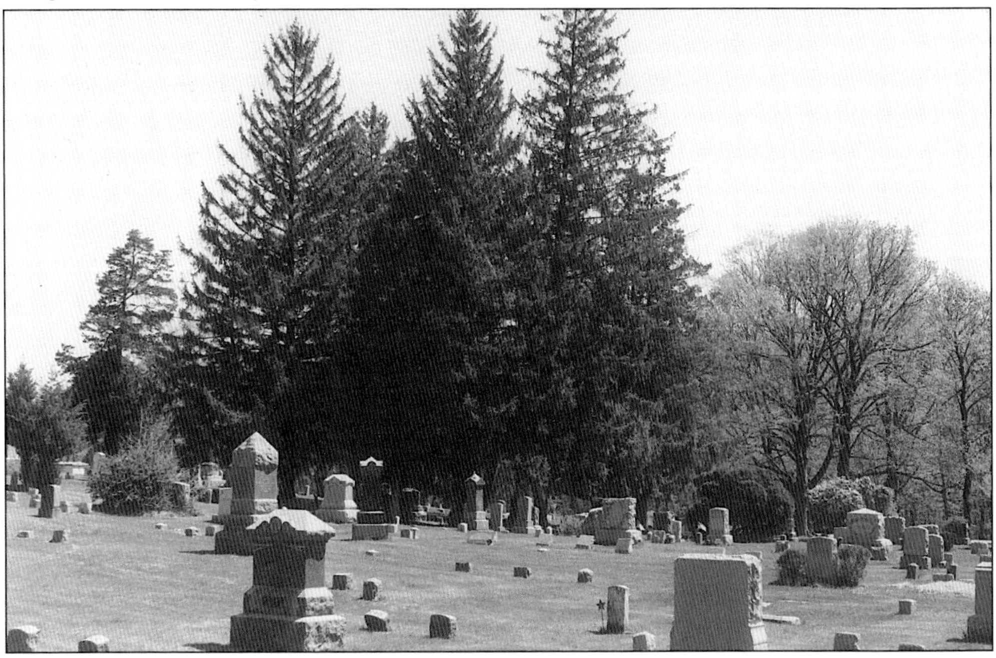

Although the Hanover Cemetery is an independent, nonprofit entity and not affiliated with the church, it was incorporated in 1849 because the cemetery at the First Presbyterian Church was nearly filled. A group of people from the church who wanted a burial place for their families secured land in the neighborhood and formed the Hanover Cemetery Association. (Courtesy of the Hanover Cemetery Association.)

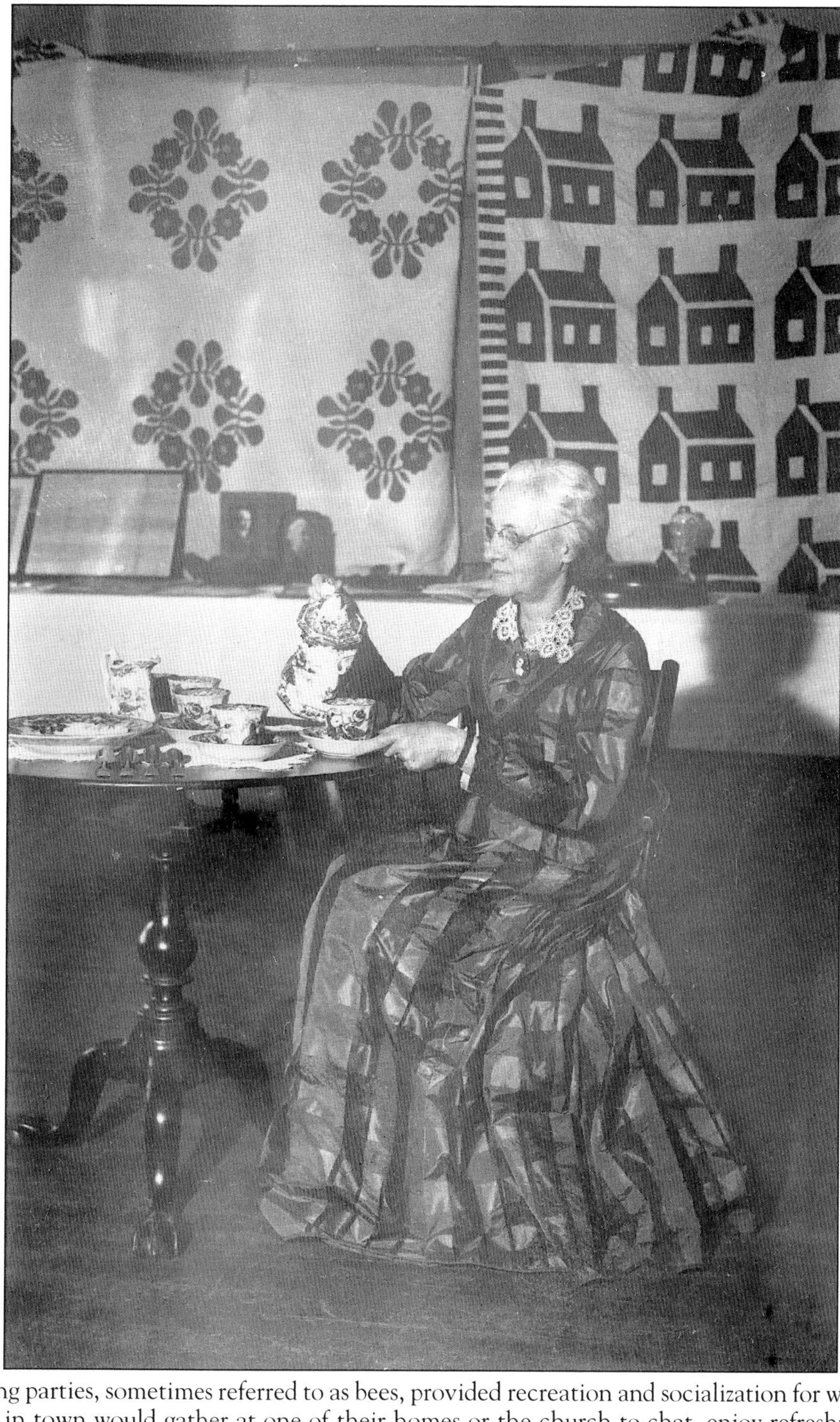

Quilting parties, sometimes referred to as bees, provided recreation and socialization for women. Ladies in town would gather at one of their homes or the church to chat, enjoy refreshments, and create beautiful bed covers by hand. In this photograph, Mrs. Woodward takes a break from demonstrating the craft at a church celebration in 1935. Corn-husking parties were another way to unwind for both women and men. (Courtesy of Everett Rowley Jr.)

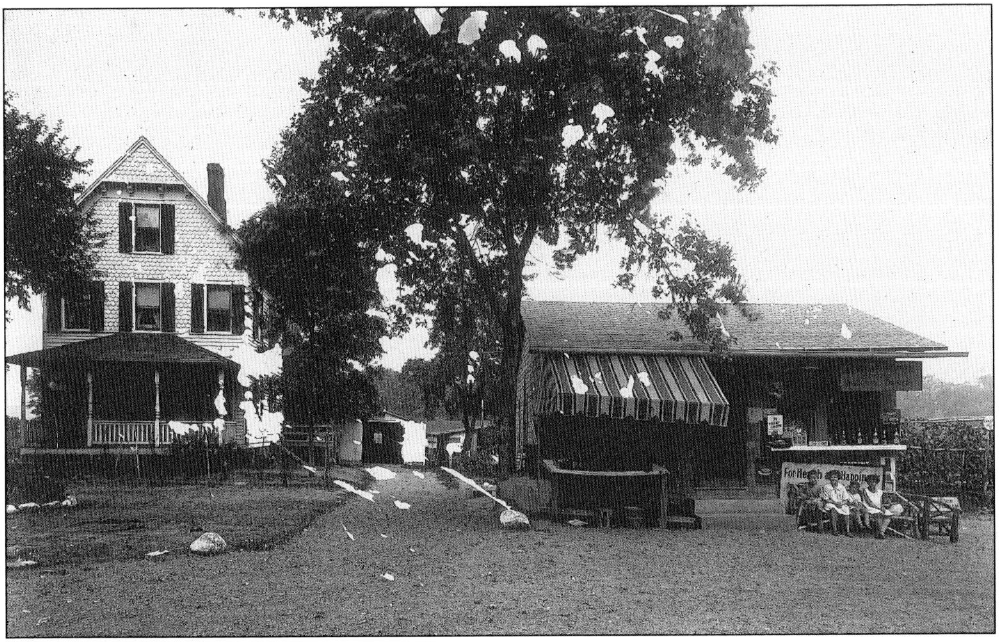

The Pellecchia family's produce stand on Mount Pleasant Avenue sold vegetables, fruits, ice cream, candy, and smoking supplies. Most of the produce was grown on their three-acre farm. This *c.* 1928 photograph shows the stand and family farmhouse. The Pellecchias also opened the Hanover Bridge Beer Garden here. (Courtesy of Anthony and Anne Pellecchia.)

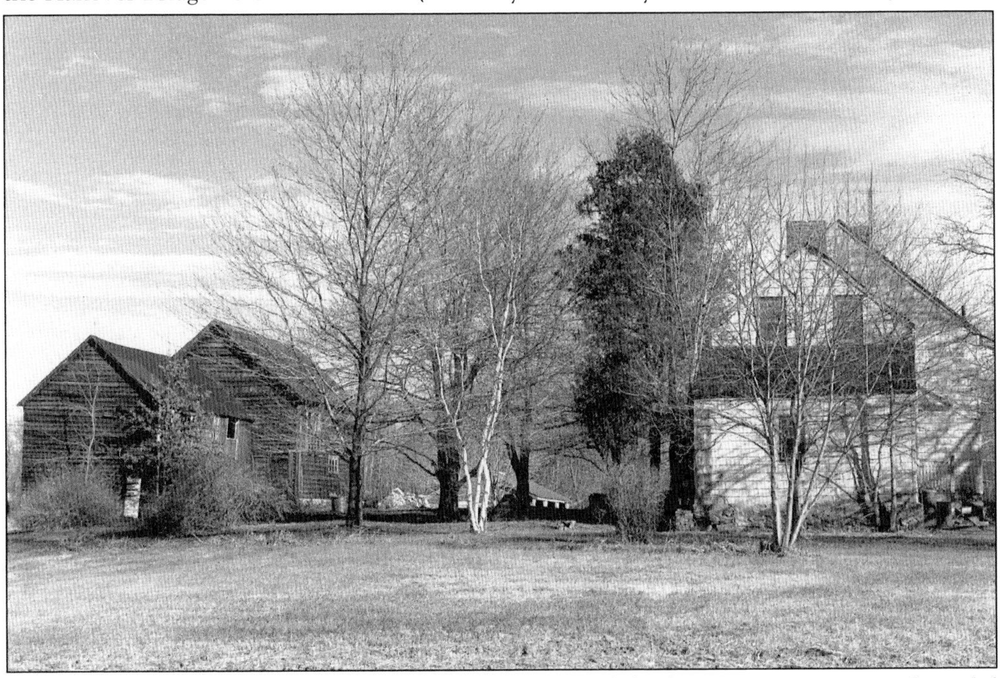

The Sharkey Brothers Farm on Troy Road grew some of the best Jersey corn around, as did some of the other farms in town. It was owned by Roy and Ray Sharkey. On this clear winter afternoon, the barns can be seen on the left and the farmhouse on the right. (Courtesy of Gus Auermuller.)

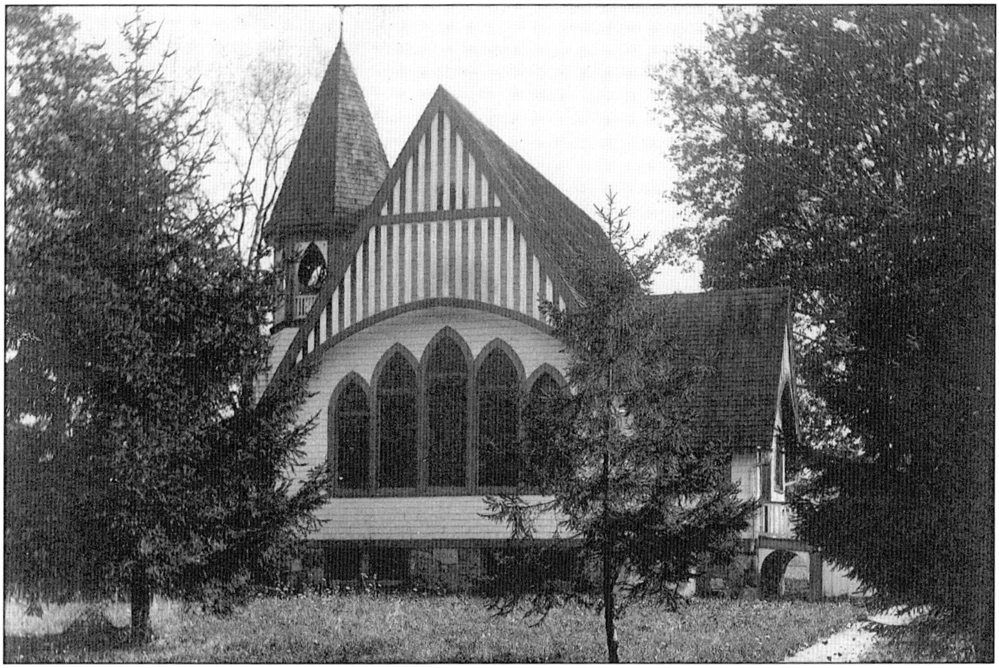

When this photograph was taken in 1918, Kitchell Memorial Presbyterian Church was the Bethel Society of Hanover, one of three outlying chapels of the mother church, the First Presbyterian Church of Hanover. The society dates back to 1893. The first service was held in this building on April 3, 1898, which at the time was a one-room structure with a dirt cellar and bell tower that cost $106. (Courtesy of the First Presbyterian Church of Hanover.)

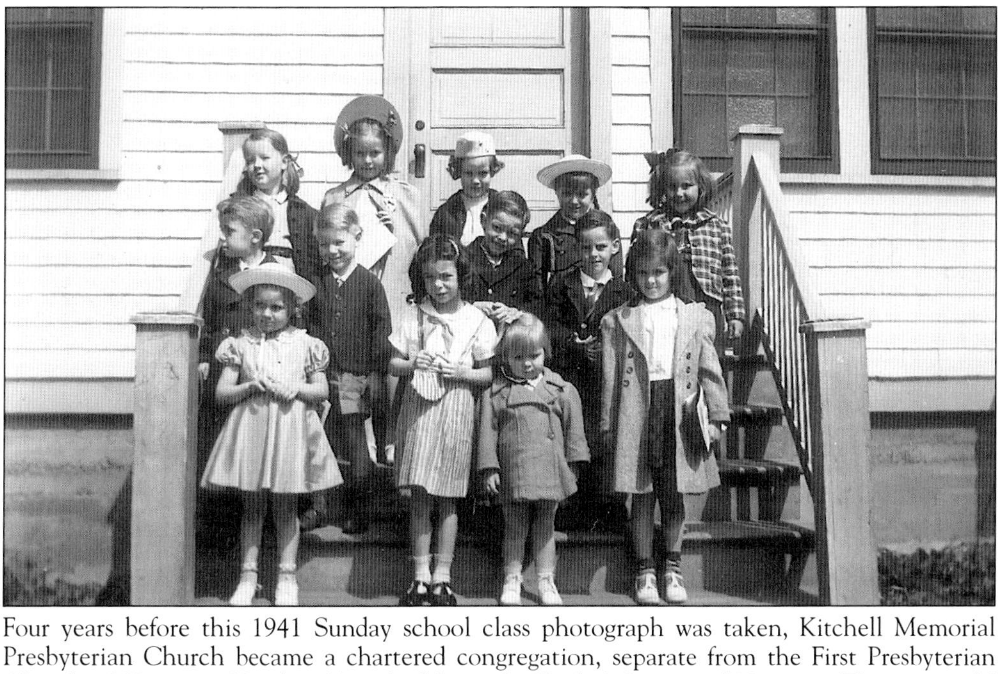

Four years before this 1941 Sunday school class photograph was taken, Kitchell Memorial Presbyterian Church became a chartered congregation, separate from the First Presbyterian Church of Hanover. Until 1937, it had been the Bethel Society of Hanover. There were 36 registered members in 1937. (Courtesy of Evelyn and Jim Ross.)

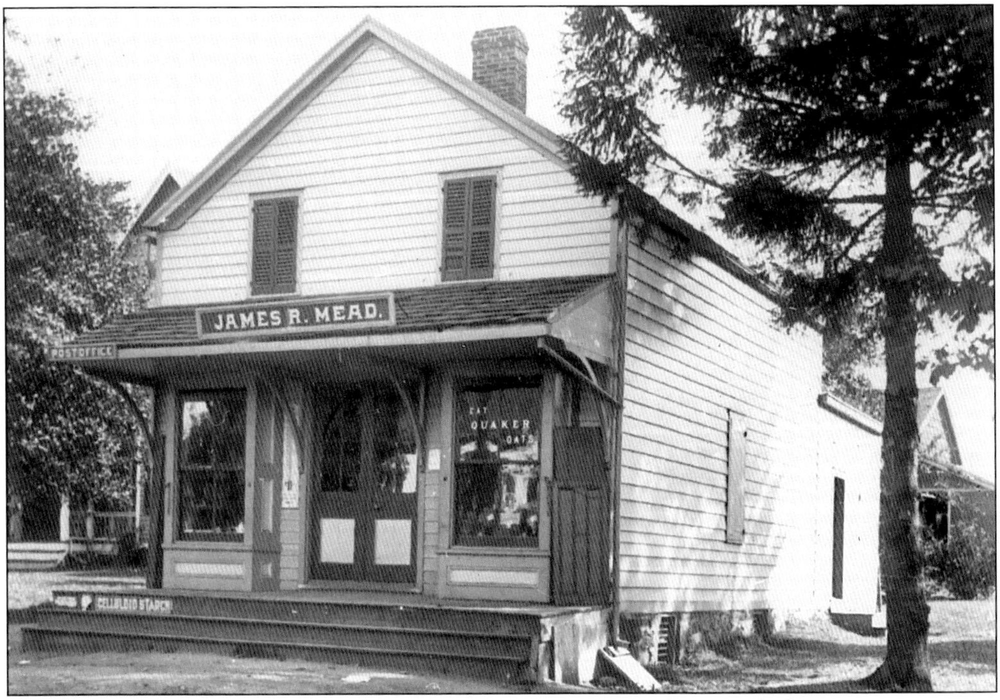

This was the general store and post office that serviced the southern end of town. It was a store as far back as the early 1800s and became the town's second post office c. 1900. The post office sign can be seen on the left corner of the portico. The building stands today on Mount Pleasant Avenue across from River Road. (Courtesy of Gus Auermuller.)

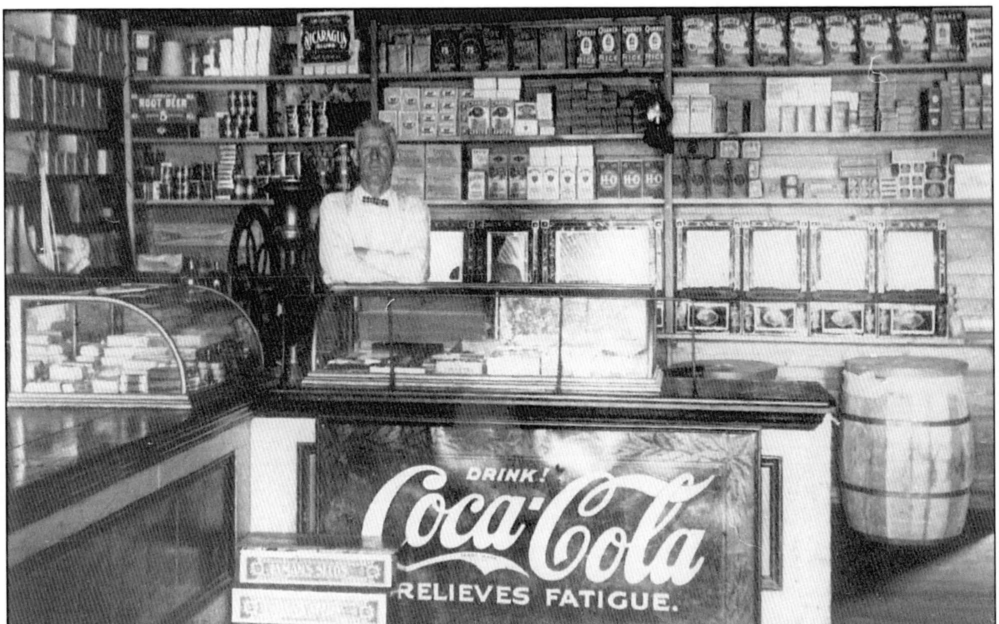

Mead's looked like the quintessential country store around the beginning of the 20th century. The proprietor in the photograph is believed to be James Mead, who was also the postmaster. Coca-Cola was a big advertiser even then. (Courtesy of Gus Auermuller.)

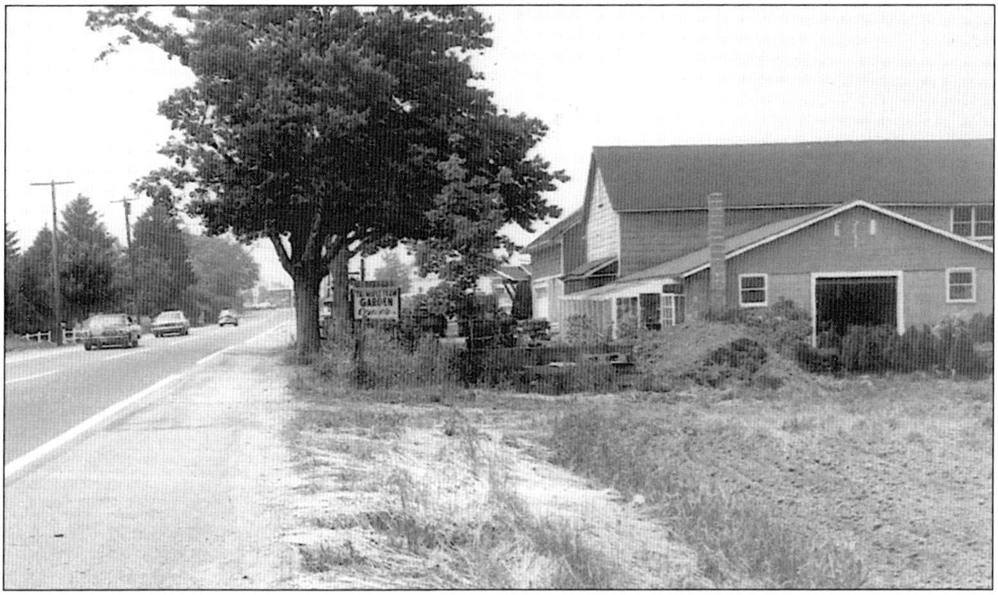

The Ferraiuolo farm on Eagle Rock Avenue was most likely the oldest operating farm in town. It dated back to the 1700s, when it began with the Tuttle family. Anthony Ferraiuolo purchased the farm from the Tuttles in the early 1900s. He passed it along to his children, who kept the farm stand going until a few years ago. Produce was grown here and sold at the stand, and dairy cows grazed on the property until 1963. (Courtesy of Catherine Froling.)

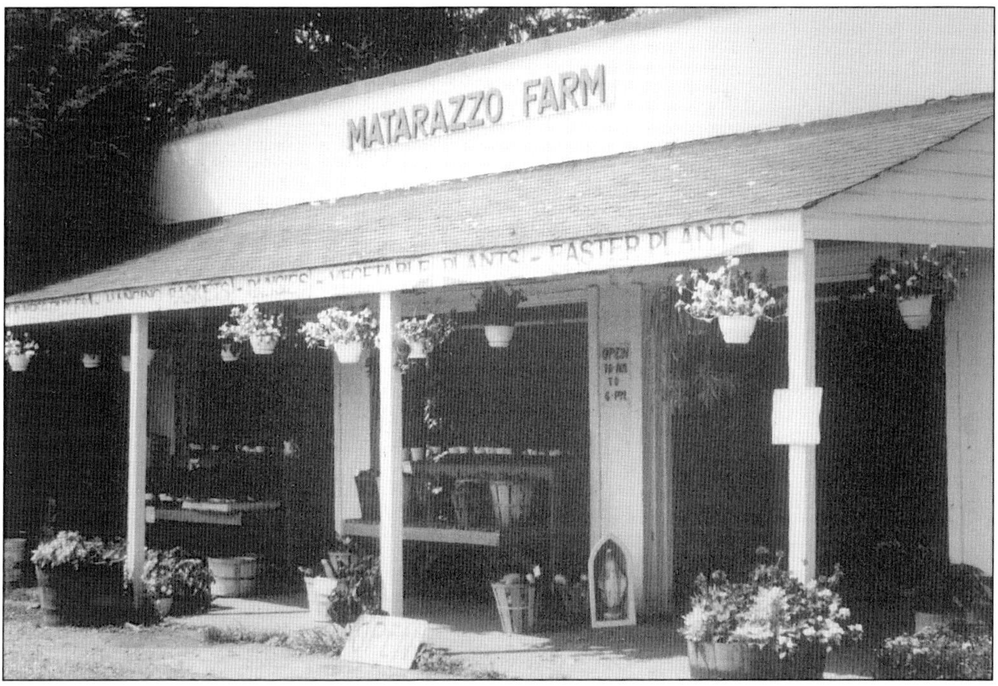

The Matarazzo Farm opened on River Road in 1940. Started by Andrew and Sabina Matarazzo, it originally included 66 acres of land. Fresh vegetables, flowers, plants, and fruits were sold at this roadside stand. The Matarazzo family also trucked some of their produce to the Newark markets. (Courtesy of the East Hanover Historical Society.)

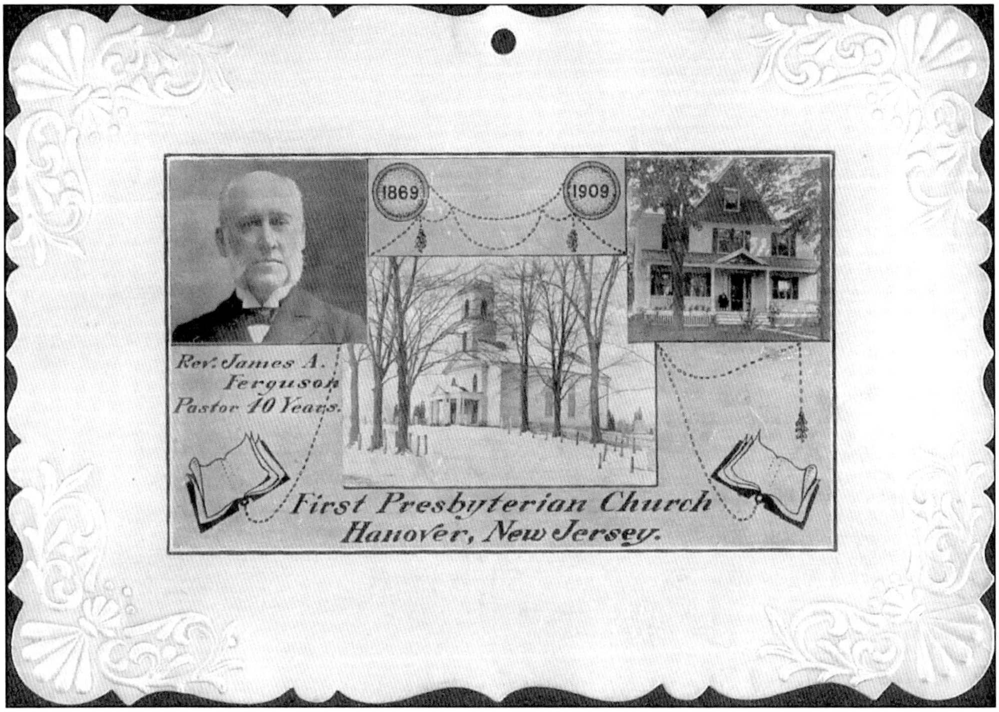

Rev. James A. Ferguson, pastor of the First Presbyterian Church from 1869 to 1909, was honored with this commemorative plaque. This is what he suggested about church attendance in an 1886 manual: "It is easy to stay at home, as many know, if the day is cold or the weather threatening, or the body weary, or the rising late, or if the house is full of company. But the true disciple will not allow small reasons to hinder his performance of duty." (Courtesy of Don Courter.)

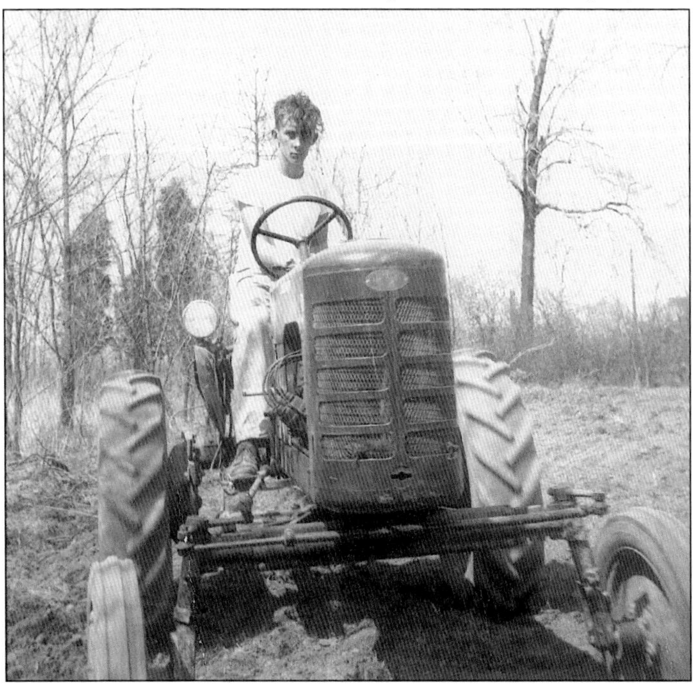

George Busold takes the tractor out at the Stickles farm on South Ridgedale Avenue in the 1950s. Today, George is responsible for much more sophisticated equipment; he is the fire chief of East Hanover. (Courtesy of George and Sylvia Busold.)

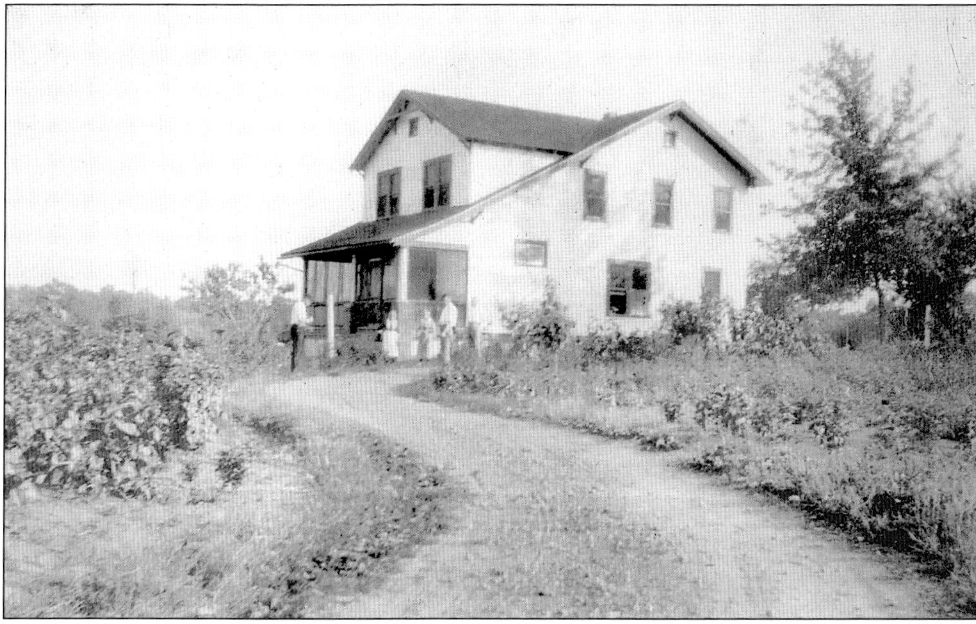

Taxes on the Johnston place on Eagle Rock Avenue came to $92.44 in 1922 for this two-story home on three and one-half acres. The tax bill shows that present-day East Hanover was then part of Hanover Township. This house still stands today next to the public tennis courts. (Above and below courtesy of Herb Johnston.)

Usher's Form 200

First Half of Tax Due
APRIL 1, 1922
Delinquent After
June 1st

Second Half of Tax Due
DEC. 1, 1922
Delinquent After
December 1st

Unpaid taxes on land with interest, etc. become a lien on and after December 1st. (Chap. 237, Laws of 1918).

When any municipal lien on real property remains unpaid on July 1st in the year following the date when it became in arrears (December 1st) the Collector shall enforce the lien by sale of the property. (Laws of 1918. Chapter 237, sec. 16).

COLLECTOR'S TAX NOTICE

1922

Township of Hanover

County of Morris, N. J.

E. HALSEY BALL, Collector Boonton, N. J.

Interest at rate of 9% will be charged on delinquent taxes.

MRS. Bertha Johnson
475 Bergen Ave
Jersey City NJ

Page No. 220 Lot No. 57 lots
Line No. ______ Block No. ______

For the Annual Tax. Assessed for State, County and Local Purposes

TAX RATE 1922
$4.43 Per $100

State Road	.10
State School	.244267
Soldiers' Bonus	.017494
Bridge and Tunnel	.026027
County	1.205960
Special School	2.483370
Local Tax	.312190
District Court	.015542
County Library	.020000
Total	$4.424850

Poll taxes are payable in full not later than June 1st (Chap. 224, Laws of 1920).

Where any personal * * * taxes remain in arrears after December 1st it shall be the duty of the Collector to enforce the same by distress and sale of the goods or chattels or by arrest. (Excerpt from Laws of 1918, Chapter 236, sec. 606.)

Notice of Arrears, Year ______

VALUATIONS

DESCRIPTION and LOCATION	LAND	BUILDINGS	PERSONAL	Total Value of Real and Personal	Deductions or Exemptions	NET Valuations
Beaufort	$ 510	$ 1390	$	$	$	$ 1900

TAXES

	TOTAL AMOUNT OF TAX Dollars	Cts.	1st Half of Tax Dollars	Cts.	2d Half of Tax Dollars	Cts.
	84	17				
Poll Tax						
Discount		47				
Interest	3	80				
TOTAL	92	44				

Received Payment ______ 192__
1st Half
______ Collector of Taxes

Received Payment ______ 192__
2nd Half
______ Collector of Taxes

APPEALS: All appeals must be filed with the Morris County Board of Taxation, Court House, Morristown, N. J., on or before June 15, 1922. Necessary blanks can be secured from the local assessor or by writing the Secretary of the Board at Morristown. Two appeal blanks must be filled out. One copy served on the Clerk of the municipality where the assessment has been levied and the other filed with the Secretary of the Board. No appeal can be filed by law after June 15, 1922, and the Board cannot accept any appeal for filing after that date. This provision of law must be strictly enforced and cannot be waived.

Office Hours of Collector: At his home, Troy Hills, May 24 to June 15, and November 23 to December 15, 1922, from 8 a. m. to 3 p. m., excepting Saturday afternoons, Sundays and Holidays. In addition the Collector will sit for the purpose of receiving taxes at Polhemus Store, Whippany, May 23 and November 20 and at Merchant's Store, Morris Plains, May 25 and November 22 from 9.30 a. m. to 2.30 p. m.

When convenient taxpayers are requested to pay taxes by check or money order.

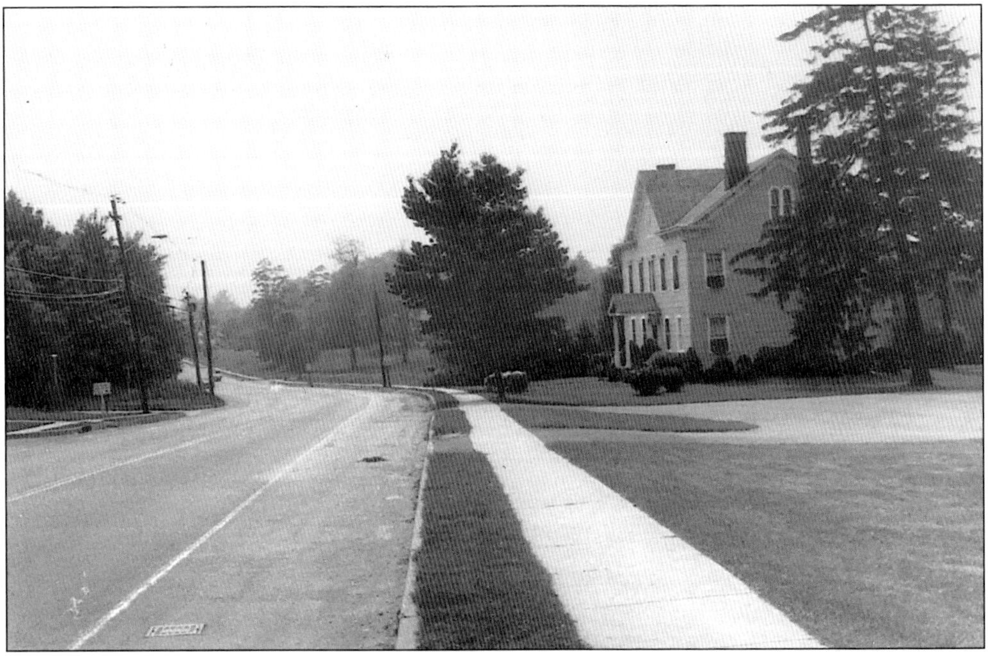

The Goldblatt farmhouse fronted on Ridgedale Avenue near where Berkeley Plaza is today. At one time, this was a large farm that spanned both sides of Ridgedale. The Goldblatt family purchased the farm in the 1920s. Previously it had been owned by the Kitchells, early settlers in town. Bernard Goldblatt was mayor in 1953 and 1954. (Courtesy of Catherine Froling.)

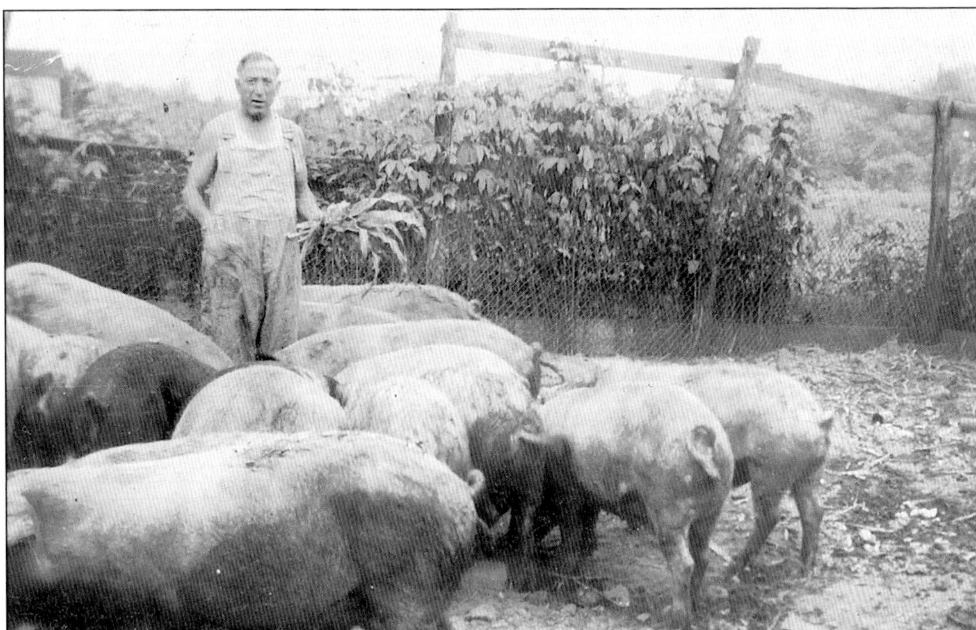

Pigs grazed on farms throughout town for more than 200 years. The Swinefield Bridge over the Passaic River indicates that there must have been quite a few of them at one time. These porkers were raised by Salvadore Iradi Sr. on Homestead Avenue in 1945. (Courtesy of Betty Cardarella.)

Three

EAST HANOVER INC.

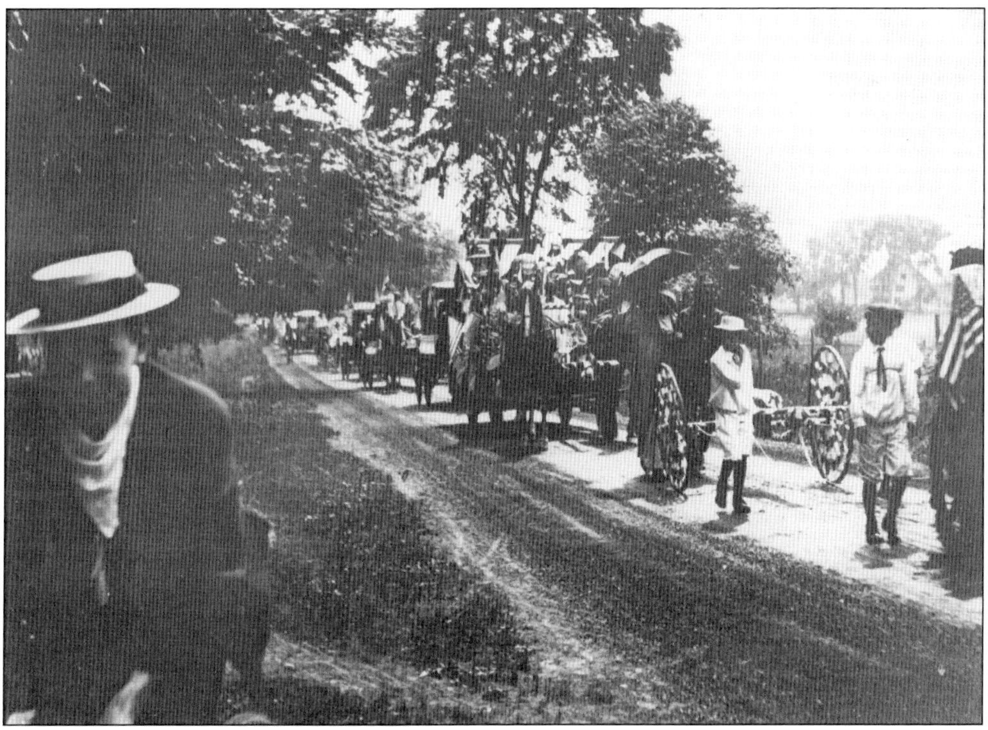

About the time this early-1900s photograph was taken of a local parade, some residents of the eastern section of Hanover Township were becoming politically restless. They believed their interests would be better represented by a more localized government. The march toward East Hanover's separation from Hanover Township had begun. (Courtesy of Everett Rowley Jr.)

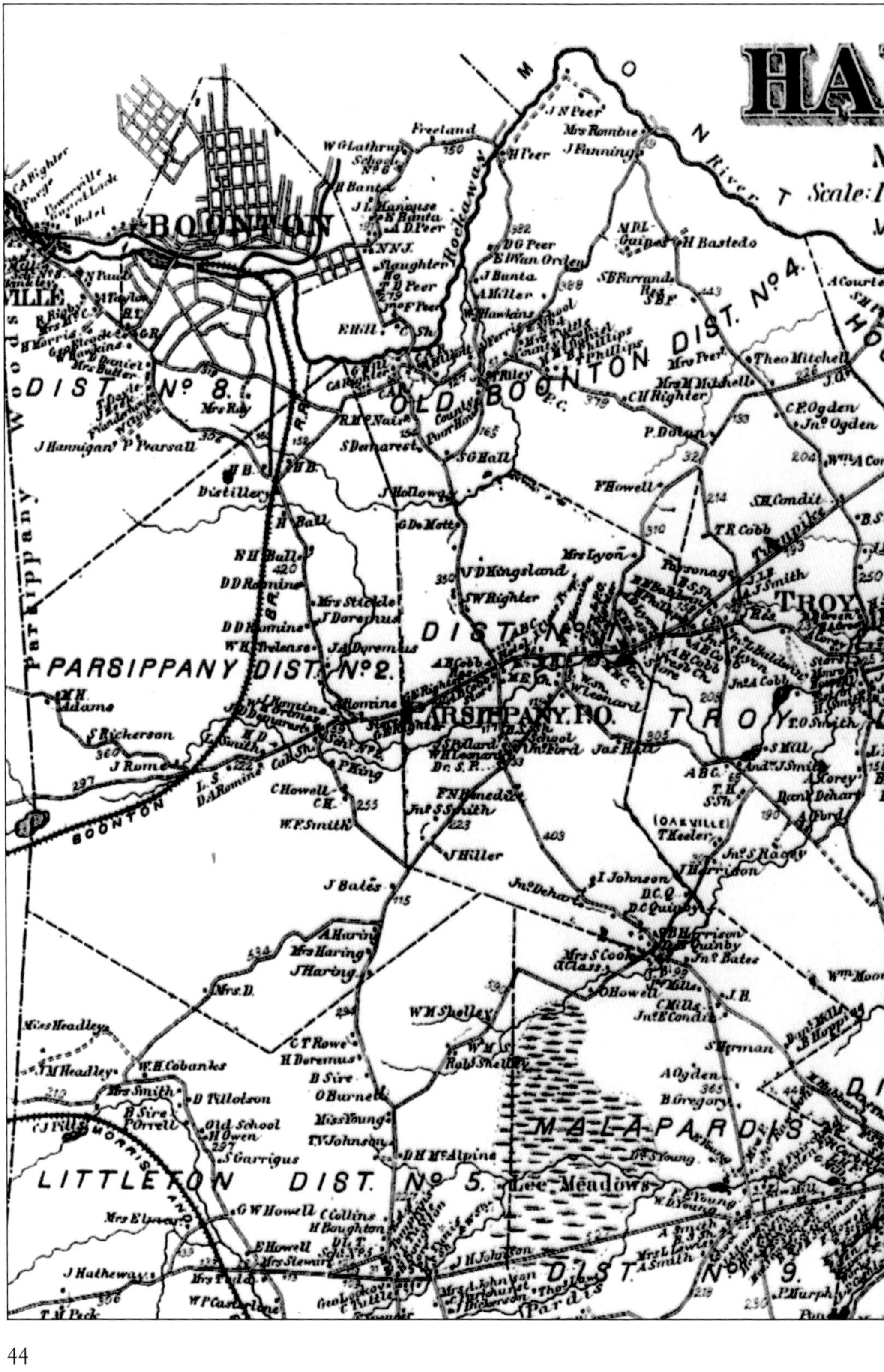
BOONTON
OLD BOONTON DIST. No 4.
DIST No 8.
PARSIPPANY DIST. No 2.
PARSIPPANY P.O.
DIST. No 1
TROY
LITTLETON DIST. No 5.
MALAPARDIS
Lee Meadows
DIST. No 9.
Rockaway
Parsippany
Woods
Distillery
BOONTON
Turnpike
M O N T
River

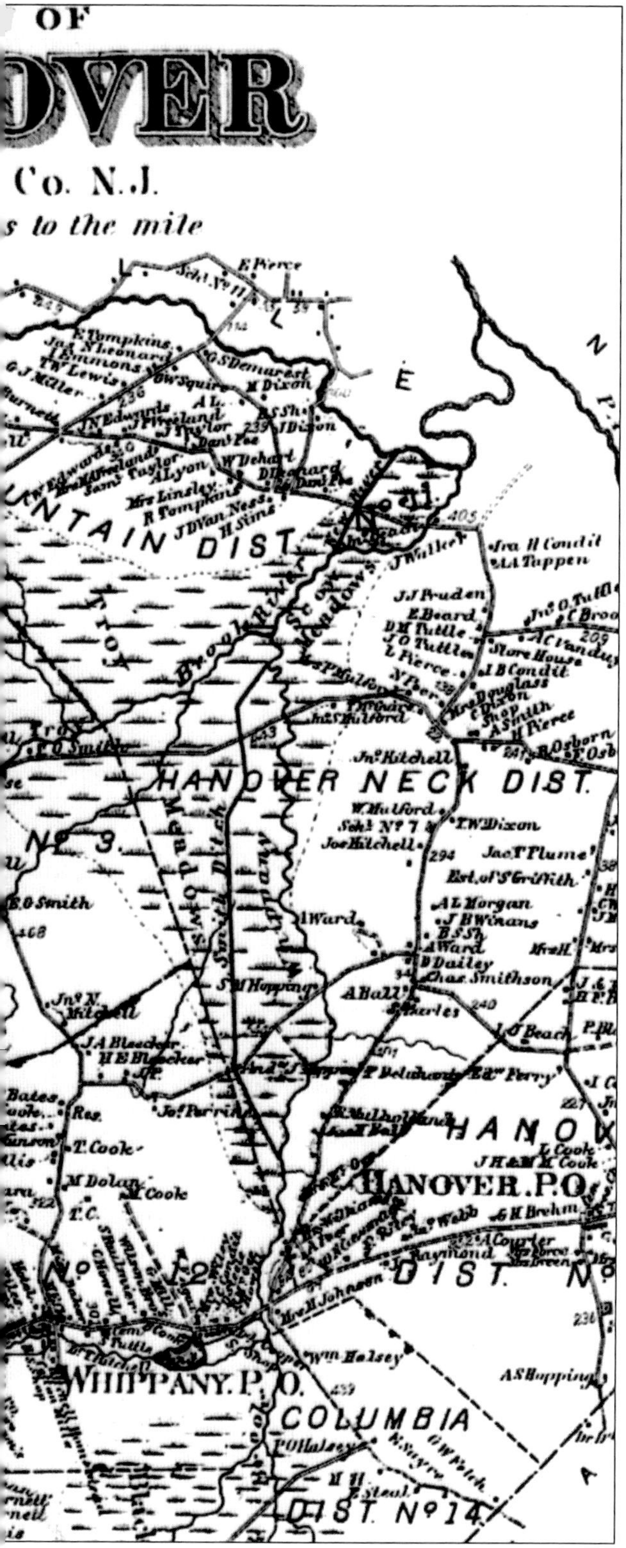

East Hanover was originally part of greater Hanover Township, which at one point encompassed much of what is today Morris County. This 1868 *Atlas of Morris County* by F.W. Beers shows Hanover's size and scope. As populations increased, governing and administering the widespread residential villages became more and more difficult. Eventually, some villages started splitting off and forming their own boroughs and townships. By 1928, many people in East Hanover were ready for self-governance. In a special election, more than 1,500 registered voters of Hanover Township went to the polls to vote on whether or not East Hanover should be incorporated. The vote was 945 yes to 512 no. East Hanover became its own township on May 9. Parsippany did as well. (Courtesy of the Morris County Library.)

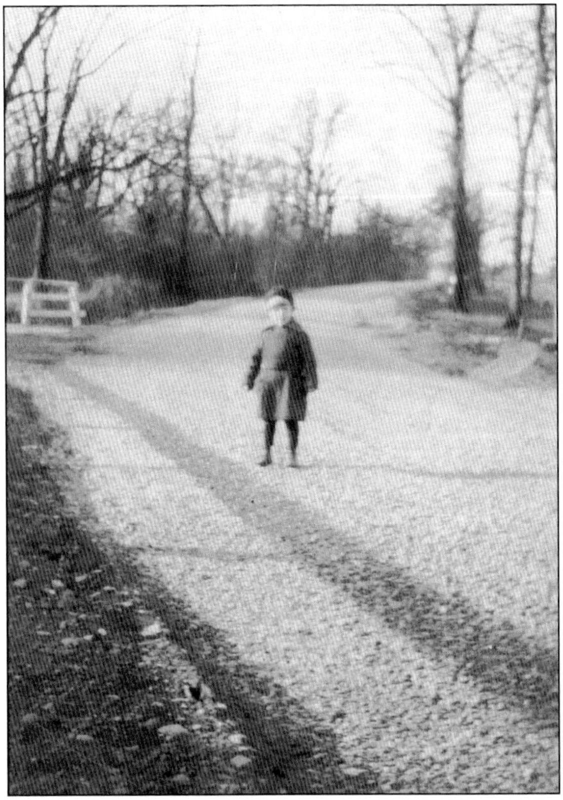

Herbie Johnston stands alone in the Middle of Eagle Rock Avenue in 1929 when it was still a dirt road. Very shortly thereafter, workers began paving the road as Herbie and grandpa look on. A few hundred years earlier, Eagle Rock Avenue had been a Native American trail. A 1930 map of the township shows Eagle Rock Avenue called Swinefield Road. The bridge over the Passaic River is still called Swinefield Bridge. (Courtesy of Herb Johnston.)

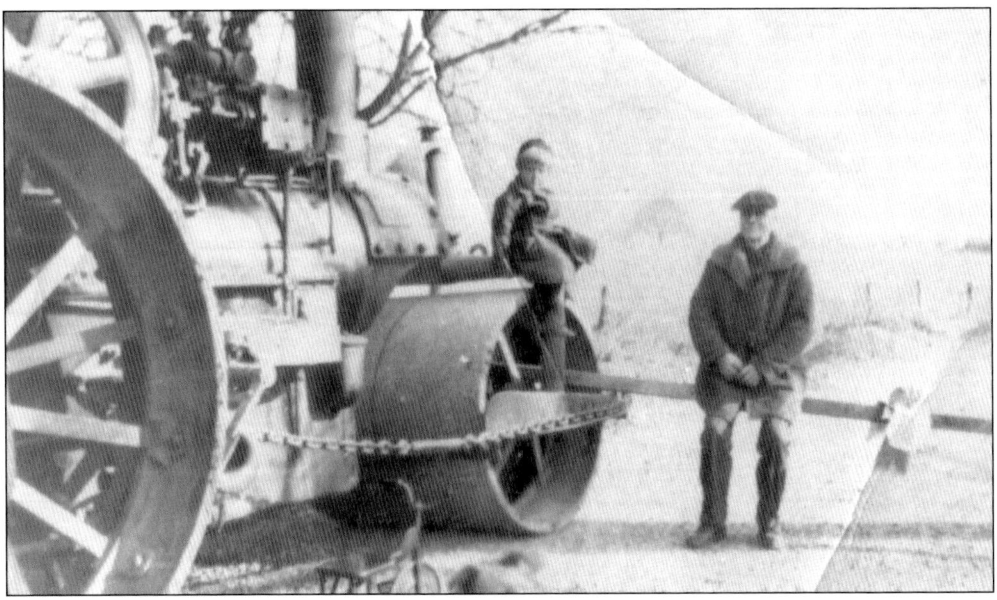

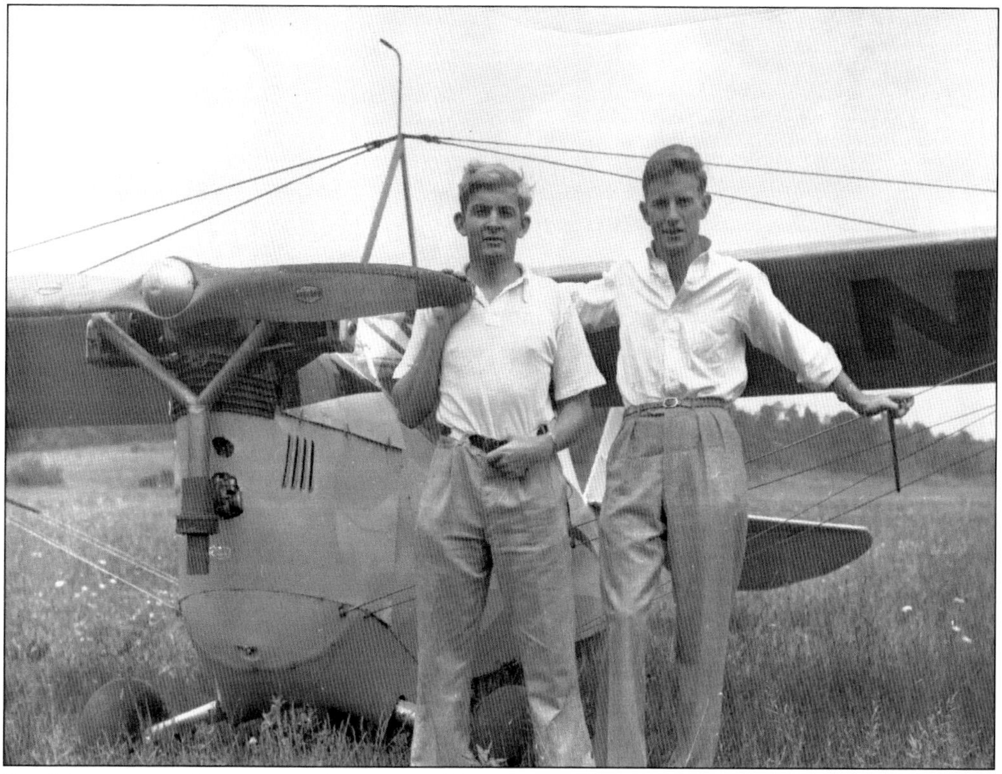

East Hanover was home to early aviation. These young flyers, Everett Rowley Jr. (left) and Bill Ruthfen, stand at the first airport in town, approximately where the bowling alley is today on Route 10. This airfield opened on April 28, 1928, and was described as one of the best fields in New Jersey. The runway was grass, and there was no hanger. It remained active into the 1930s. (Courtesy of the East Hanover Historical Society.)

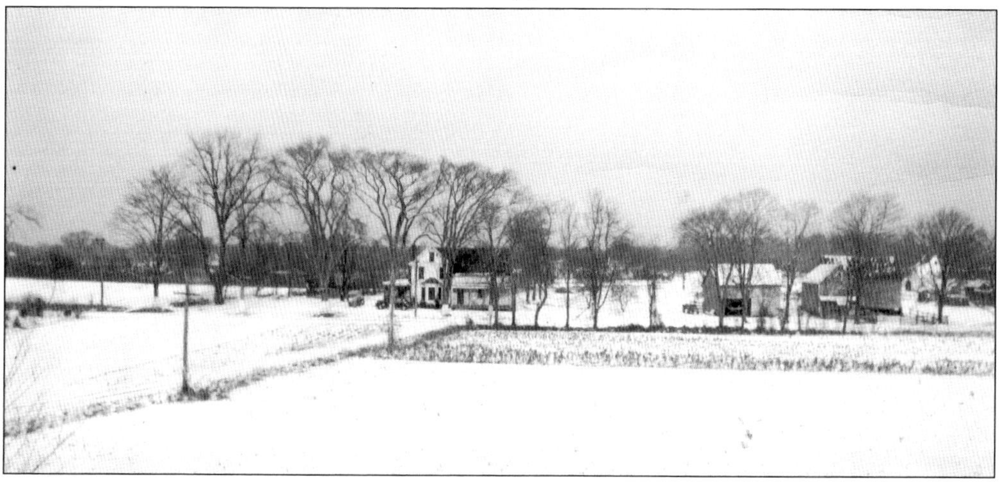

During Prohibition, a truly thirsty East Hanoverian might have stopped by this big old house (center) on Eagle Rock Avenue for a snort. Several stills were also brewing in the township during the government's attempt at temperance. At least one was raided and destroyed by government officials. When Prohibition ended, the building became Ray's Tavern. Fire destroyed Ray's in 1940. Today this is the site of the Hanover Manor. (Courtesy of Herb Johnston.)

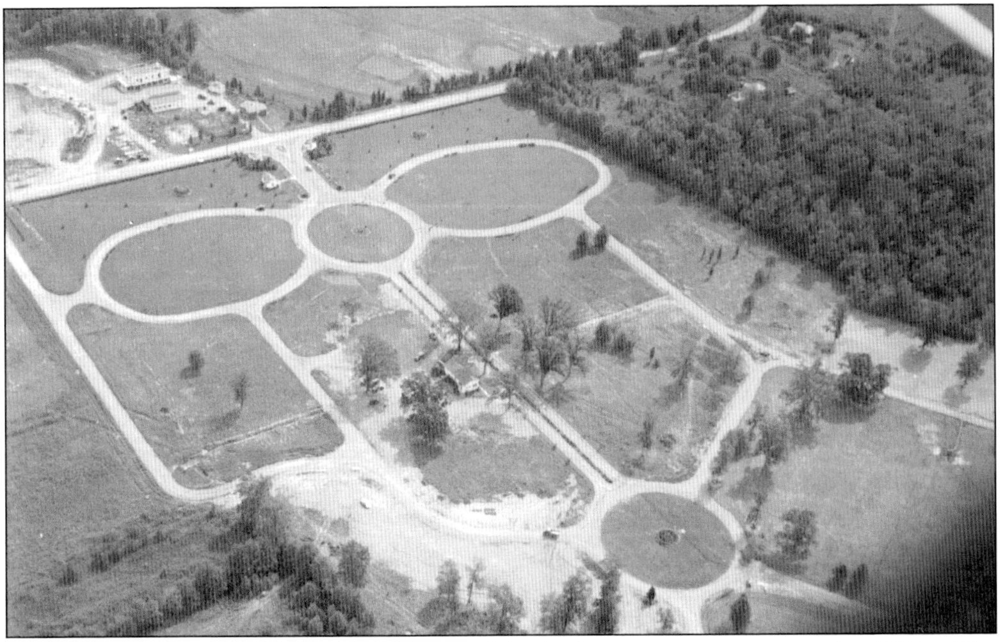

This is an aerial view of Restland Memorial Park during construction in the 1930s. The cemetery was built by the Deskovicks, whose construction company can be seen across Deforest Avenue in the upper left. The chapel (below) is not yet under construction. Everett Rowley Jr. (see page 47) took the photograph. (Courtesy of Everett Rowley Jr.)

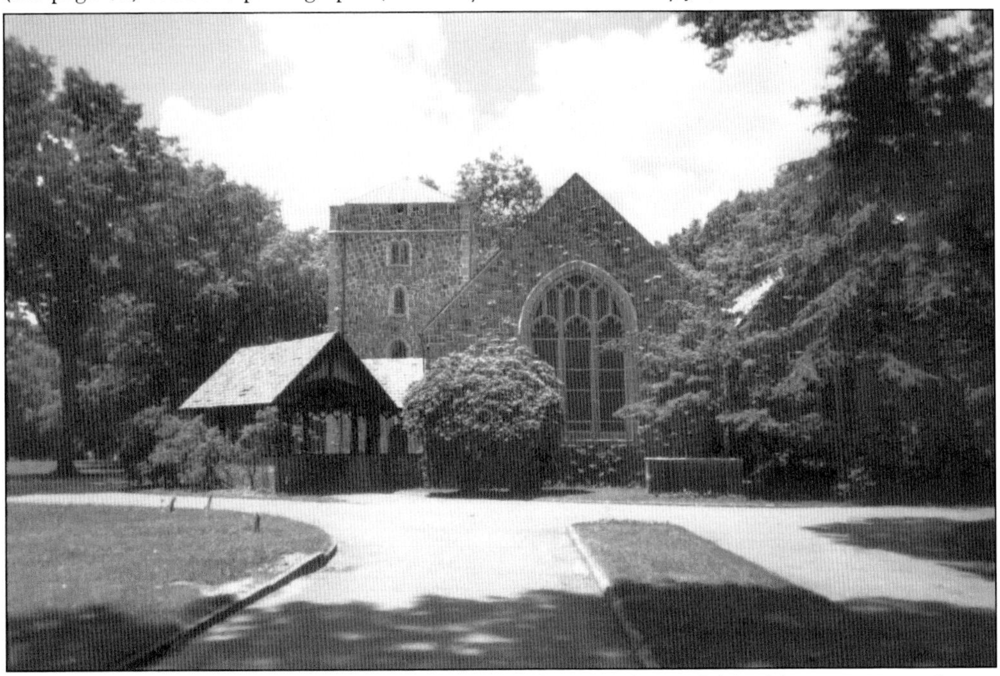

The chapel in Restland Memorial Park is one of the most beautiful buildings in town. It was constructed in 1937 and "dedicated to the everlasting memory of those enshrined here." The medieval-style chapel was inspired by St. Giles Church in Stoke Pogis, England. The English chapel was erected 800 years ago.

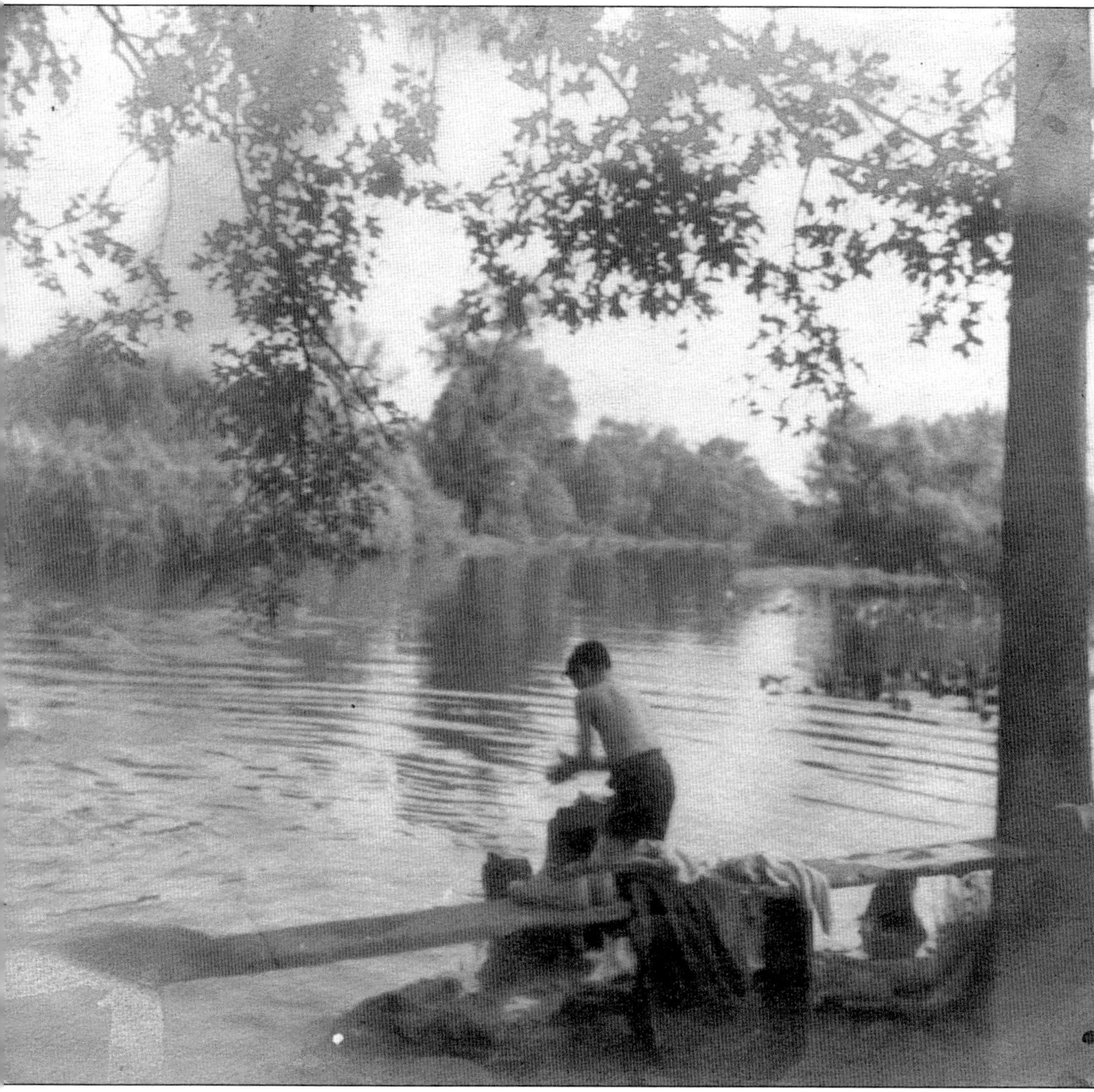

People have been swimming in the Passaic River for thousands of years. The waters were clean and clear until the second half of the 20th century. This photograph was taken *c.* 1935 at a favored swimming spot about one-quarter mile south of Cook's Bridge at Mount Pleasant Avenue. The water was four to five feet deep. At the other end of town, summer cottages enjoyed waterfront views from both sides of the Passaic. A commercial swimming pool and picnic grove called Balyian's opened in the early 1930s next to the Passaic at the northern end of River Road. Passaic River water was used to fill the pool. (Courtesy of the East Hanover Historical Society.)

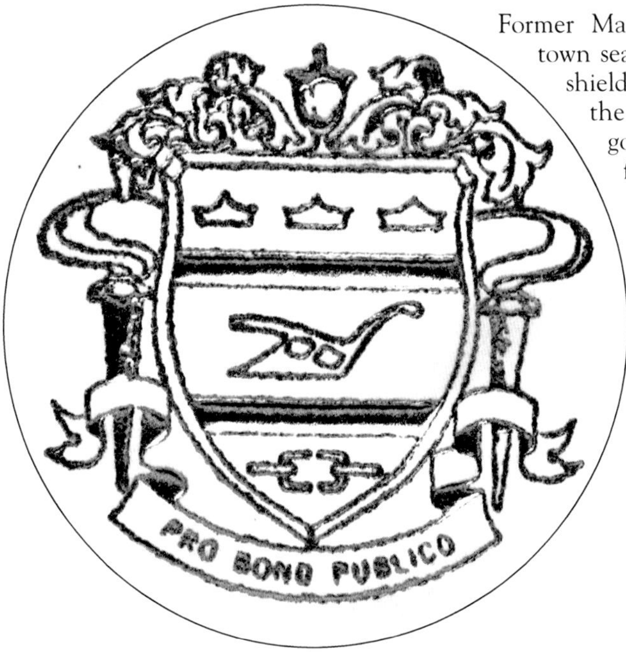

Former Mayor Bob Zakarian designed the town seal in 1962. The symbols include a shield with three crowns representing the three-committeemen form of government; two bands of blue for the rivers; a plow for the agricultural heritage; a broken link for the separation from Hanover Township; twin torches illuminating the past and the future; an urn for the town's cemeteries; and leaf clusters for the town's rural and suburban atmosphere. (Courtesy of East Hanover Town Hall.)

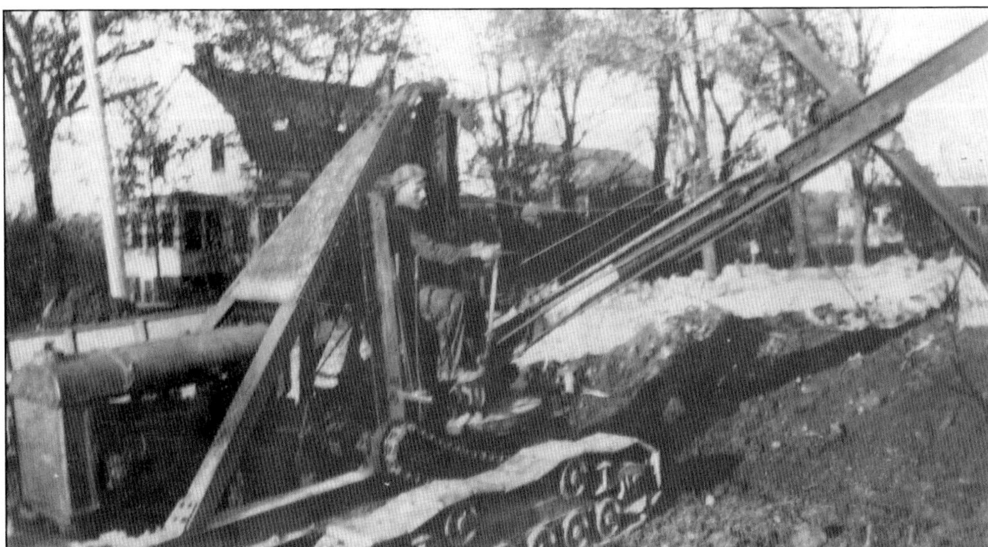

Horace Dixon is shown excavating during construction of Gate of Heaven Cemetery in the early 1930s. He is on a power shovel; Ridgedale Avenue is behind him. Gate of Heaven is a Catholic cemetery affiliated with the Archdiocese of Newark. (Courtesy of Lee Dixon.)

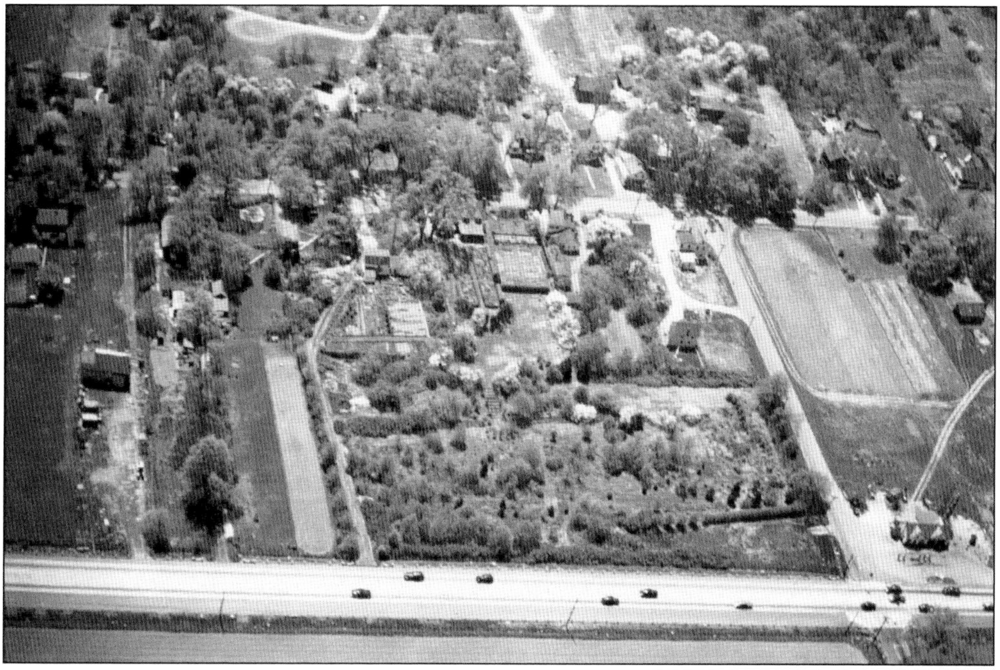

Long before Route 10 became a shopping mecca, this is what it looked like. The cameraman is above Lone Pine Dairy. At the time, Route 10 had three lanes; the center one was nicknamed the suicide lane. The highway was intended to help drivers from eastern New Jersey get to the west more quickly. It worked . . . for a while. (Courtesy of the East Hanover Historical Society.)

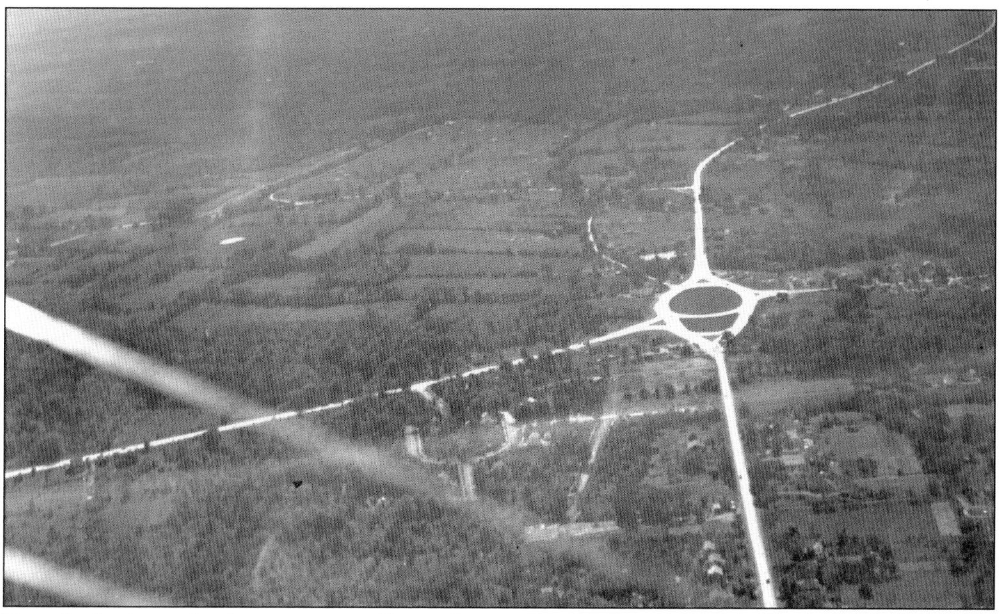

From high above the Livingston traffic circle c. 1936, the camera looks west into East Hanover. Route 10 had been built several years earlier. Originally, it was supposed to follow Mount Pleasant Avenue all the way through town, but homeowners fought that idea. The residents won, and the highway wound up paralleling the main residential stretch of Mount Pleasant Avenue. (Courtesy of the East Hanover Historical Society.)

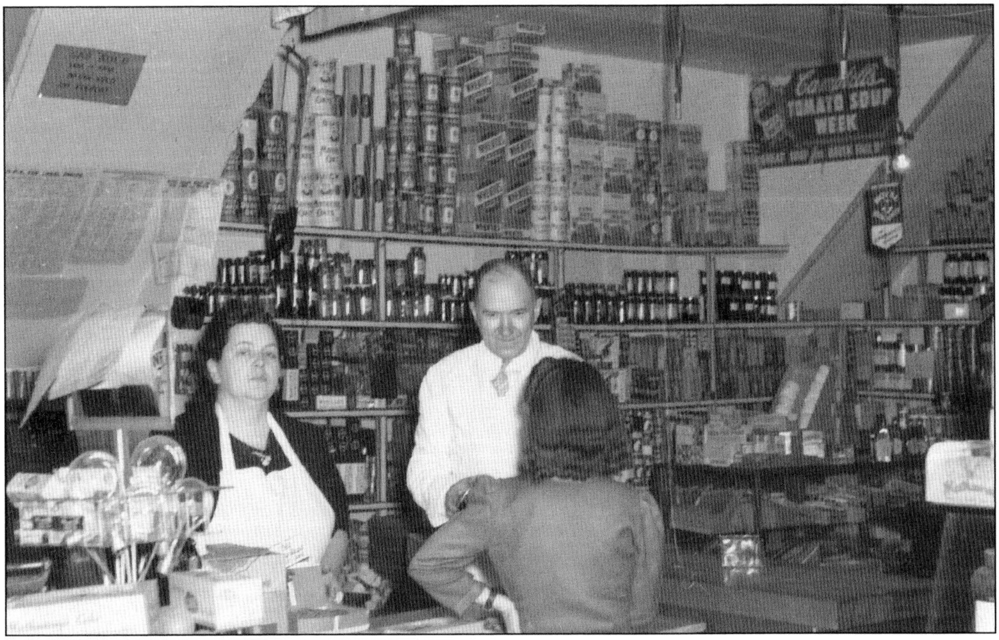

James W. Ross and his wife, Willie Freda (facing the camera), came from North Carolina and opened a small grocery store on Ridgedale Avenue in 1934. They lived above it with their sons Jim and Norwood. Customer Millie Guest (with her back to the camera) shops for dinner in the original store. (Courtesy of Evelyn and Jim Ross.)

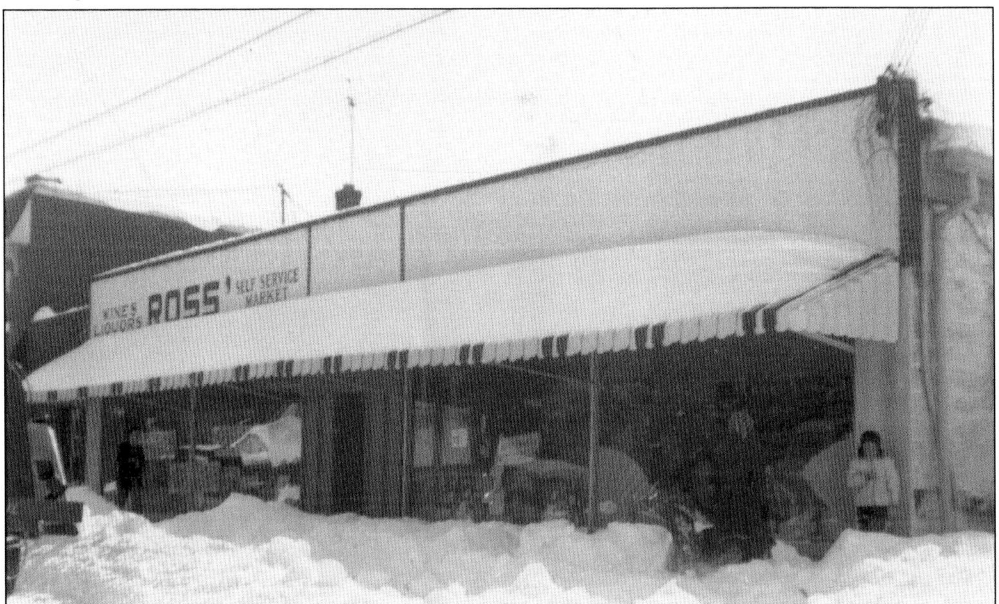

Ross' market became the town's principal grocery store in the 20th century. It had expanded by the time this photograph was taken in 1956, growing along with the town's population. The grocery eventually became Ross' Foodtown. In the early days, chicken coops stood where the parking lot is today. Ross' closed its doors for the last time in August 1999. (Courtesy of Liveria and Norwood Ross.)

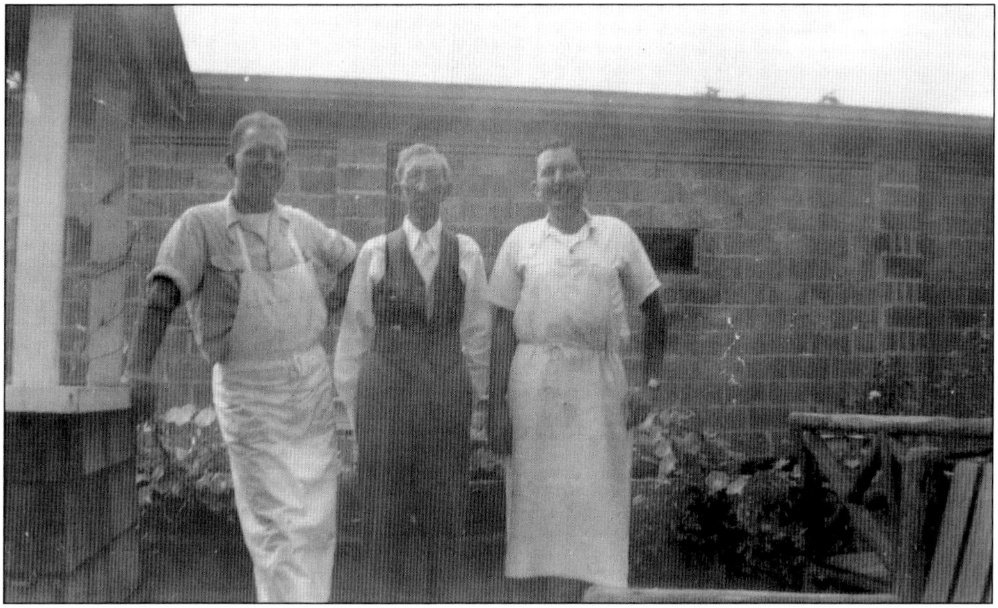

Jim (left) and Norwood Ross stand with their Uncle Guy next to the well behind their market c. 1950. In the old days, Ross' offered home delivery. Jim remembers that homeowners would leave their doors unlocked if they were going to be out. He would bring the order inside and leave it on the kitchen table. Perishables would be put away in the icebox. (Courtesy of Evelyn and Jim Ross.)

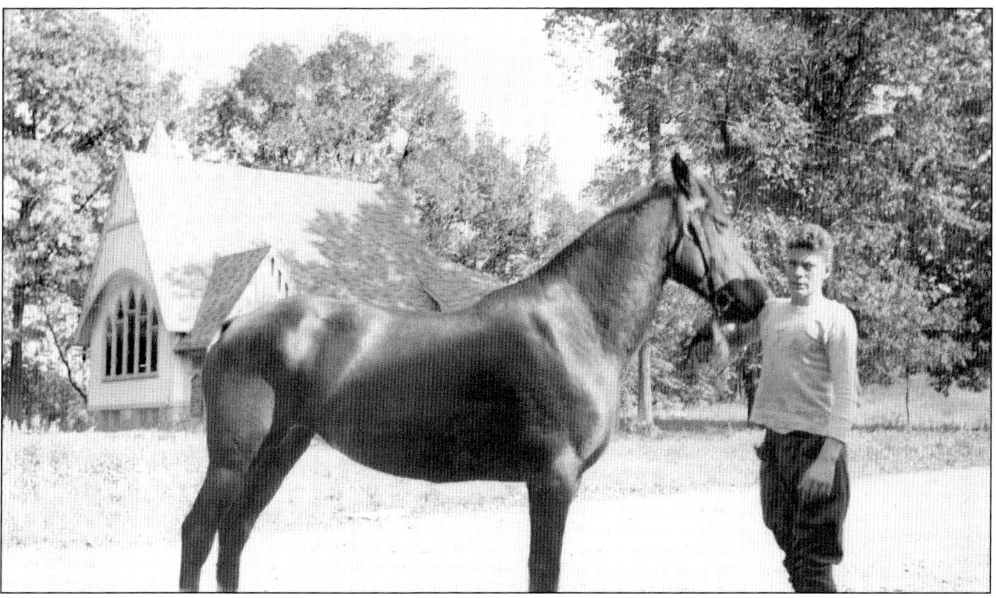

Frank Kent tends to his horse outside of Ross' market. In the 1930s, his family owned a general store with gas pumps on Ridgedale Avenue across from Ross'. Other early general/grocery stores included Hoffman's on Ridgedale and Grove Avenues, Bahr's across from Central School, Whaites' on Mount Pleasant Avenue, and Hopping's at the corner of Ridgedale and Eagle Rock Avenues. (Courtesy of Liveria and Norwood Ross.)

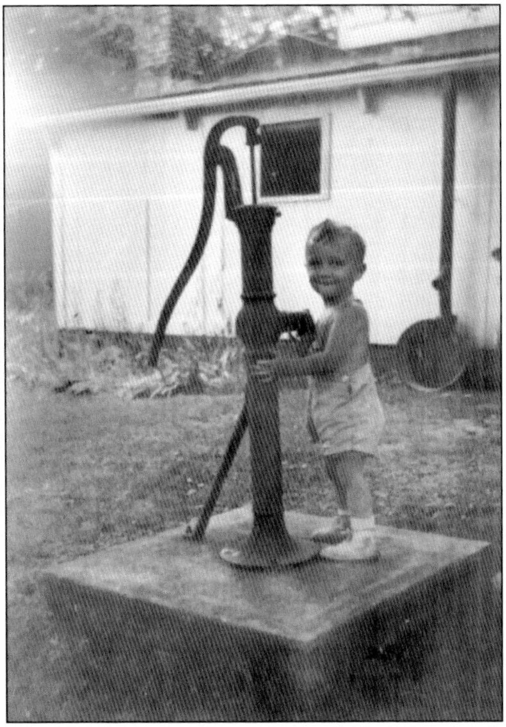

Jack Zaleski mans the pump in his backyard on Mount Pleasant Avenue in 1939. This is how many residents got their water for cooking, drinking, and bathing at that time. Before wells, water came from underground springs and the rivers. (Courtesy of Edna and Henry Zaleski.)

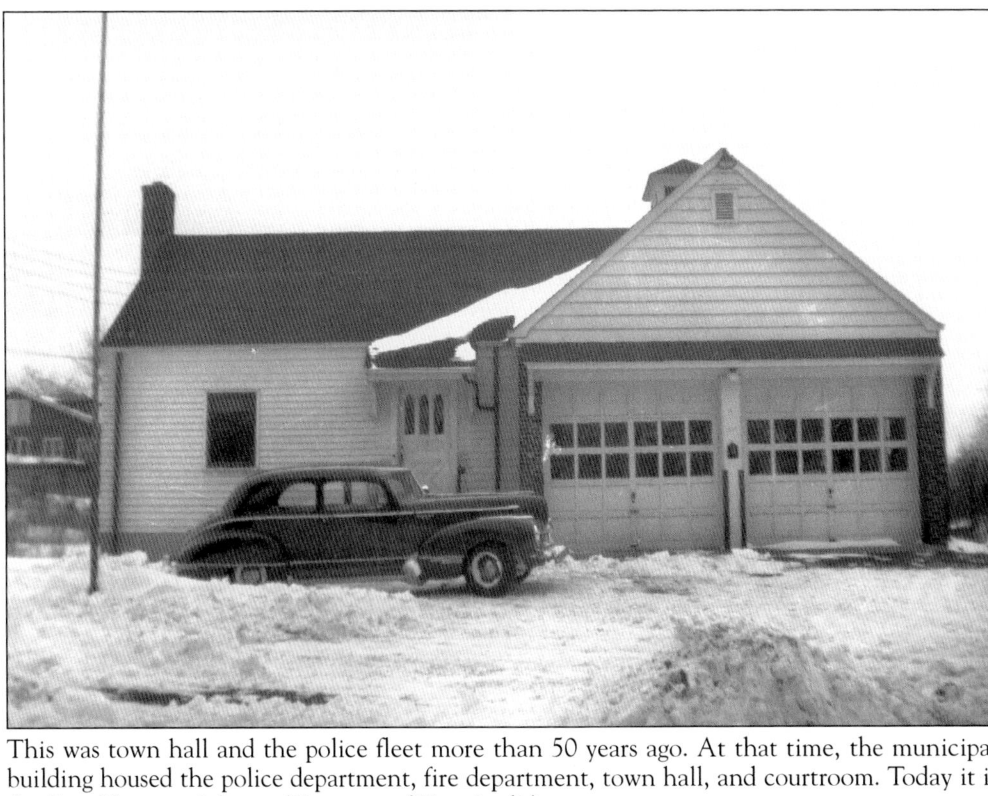

This was town hall and the police fleet more than 50 years ago. At that time, the municipal building housed the police department, fire department, town hall, and courtroom. Today it is the East Hanover Library. (Courtesy of Tom Iradi.)

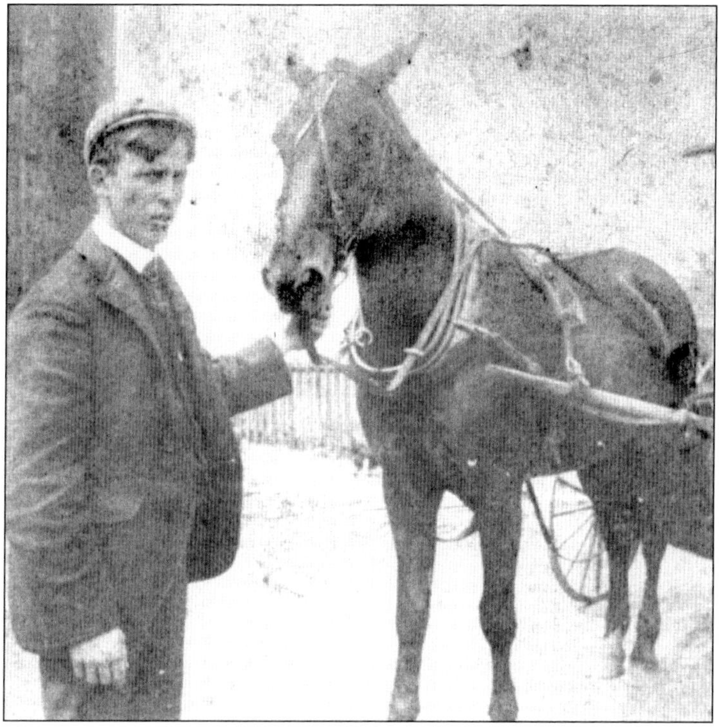

Entrepreneur Charles Little is shown with his horse and laundry wagon in the early 1900s. Charles picked up and delivered laundry in town; his wife, Frances, did the washing. One day while throwing out the wash water, Frances lost her wedding ring. Years later she found it again under a tree. (Courtesy of Helen and James Iradi.)

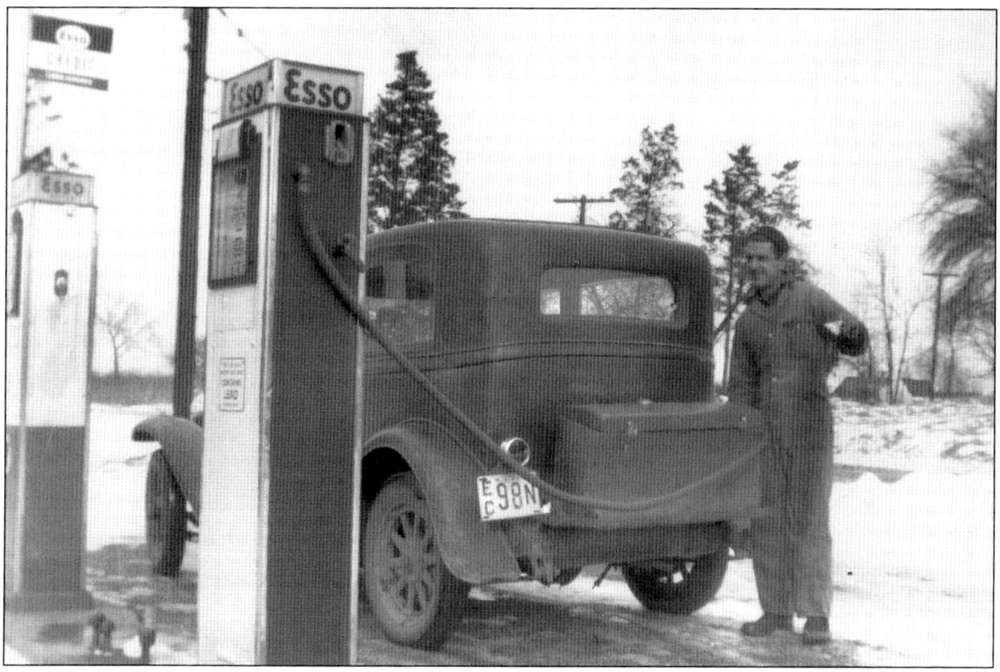

Al Newman fills 'er up in 1946. At that time, the local station was on Ridgedale Avenue; now the site is at the corner of Klinger Road and Ridgedale Avenue West. Ridgedale Avenue used to run behind the Fist Aid Squad, not in front, as it does today. Children from the Ridgedale Park section of town would wait for the school bus inside this gas station when it was cold or rainy. (Courtesy of Tom Iradi.)

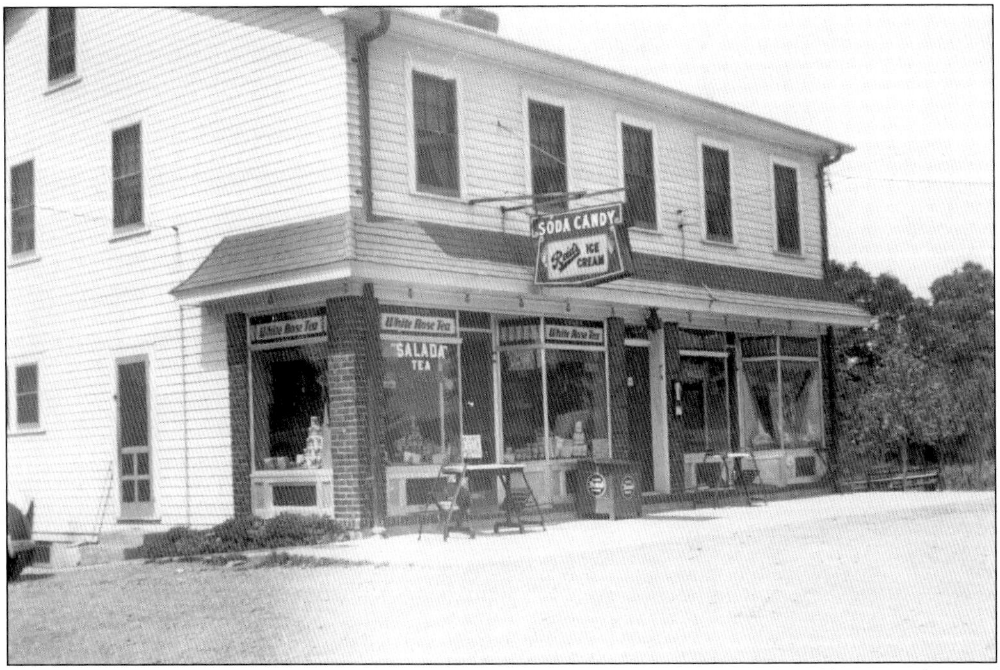

The Pellecchia family expanded their Mount Pleasant Avenue farm stand and beer garden and moved it to nearby Route 10, close to the Passaic River bridge. The family business became the Red Star bar and grill. The grand opening was on June 27, 1936, with free spaghetti and meatballs from 6 to 10 p.m. The Red Star included a general store and restaurant. (Courtesy of Anthony and Anne Pellecchia.)

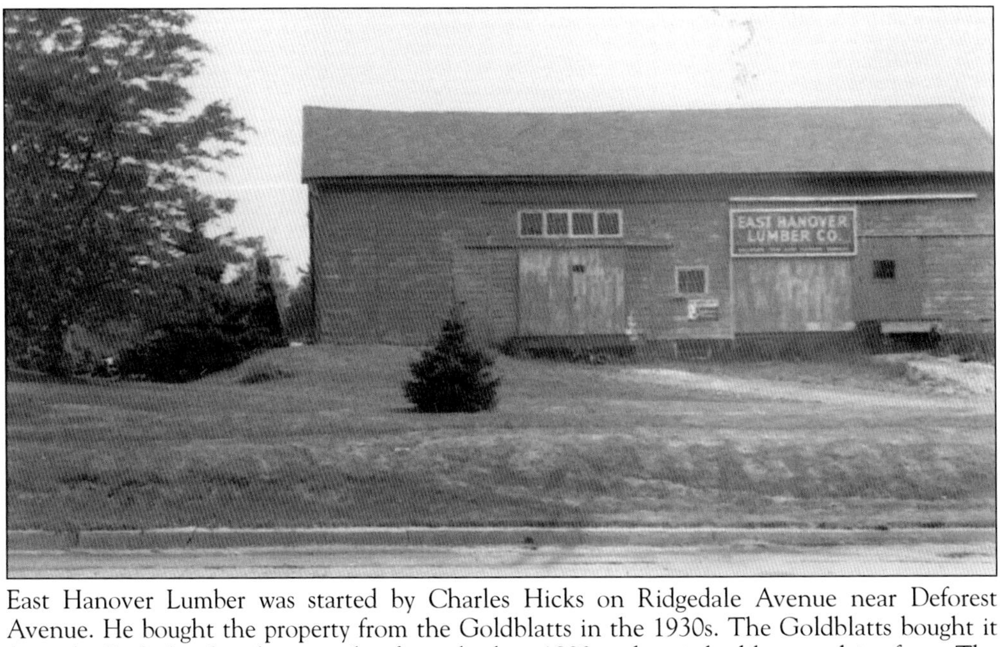

East Hanover Lumber was started by Charles Hicks on Ridgedale Avenue near Deforest Avenue. He bought the property from the Goldblatts in the 1930s. The Goldblatts bought it from the Earls family, who owned it from the late 1800s, when it had been a dairy farm. The lumberyard building, which had been the farm's barn, was moved to make room for railroad tracks. (Courtesy of Catherine Froling.)

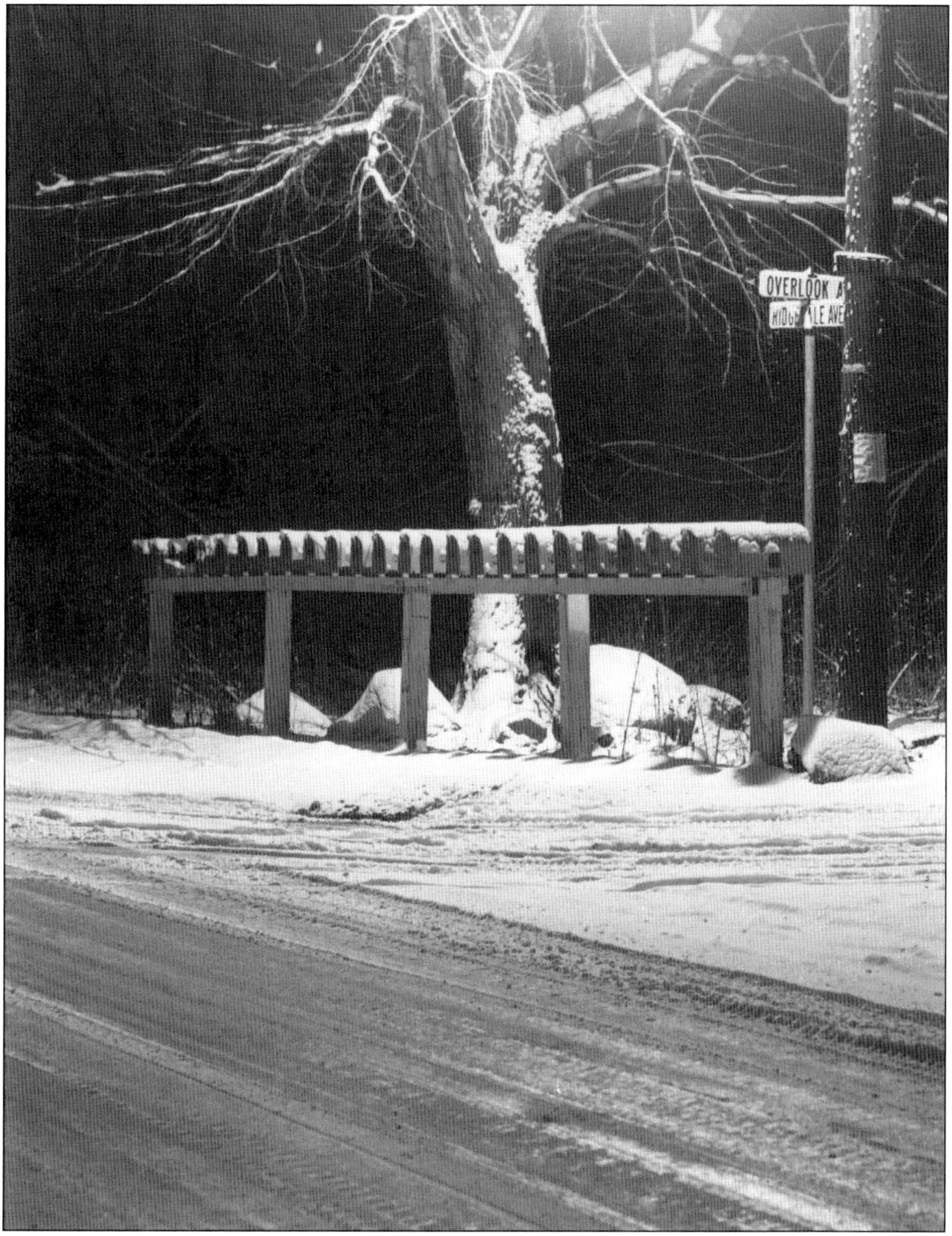

Mail used to arrive at these boxes via rural free delivery (RFD) from the Whippany Post Office. This is what East Hanover RFD looked like on many street corners. Those who preferred could use a post office box at the East Hanover Post Office and pick up their mail there. In the days before faxes and e-mail, people wrote and sent letters to each other much more often. Letters were especially plentiful during times of war. (Courtesy of Bill Schaeffer.)

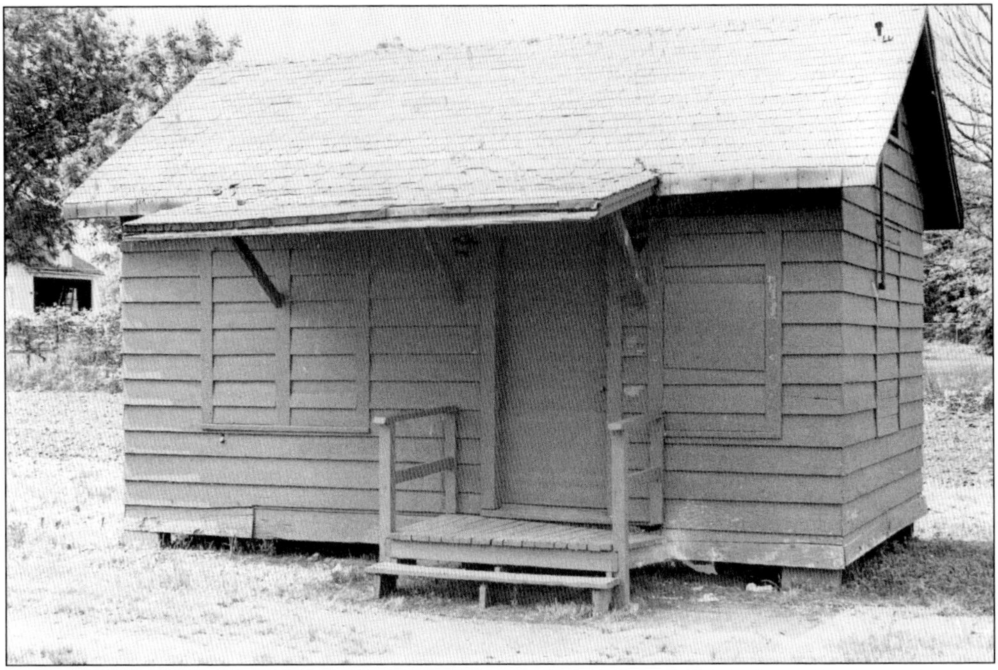

This was the town's first library. The two-room building was donated by Mike Deskovick in the 1950s and stood in the rear of the parking lot adjacent to the present library. It was operated by local volunteers, including a Girl Scout troop. After the library moved to more permanent digs in 1962, this building relocated to Lurker Park. (Courtesy of the East Hanover Department of Public Services.)

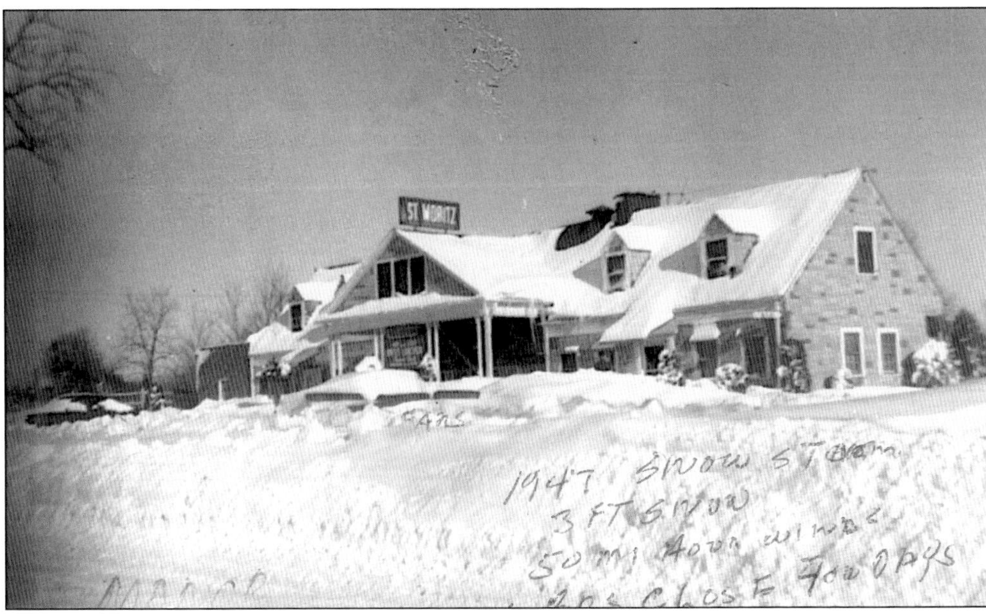

A winter storm packing 50-mile-per-hour winds dumped three feet of snow on the township in 1947, closing some roads for days and keeping customers away from the St. Moritz. On July 11, 1961, fire destroyed the Eagle Rock Avenue restaurant. The site later became Albert's and is now the Hanover Manor. (Courtesy of Herb Johnston.)

Han Herbert Johnston, M.D., opened the first doctor's office in town in the 1920s. Hours were from 9 a.m. to noon and then again from 8 to 9 p.m. In between, Dr. Johnston made house calls. The doctor later moved to California. (Courtesy of Herb Johnston.)

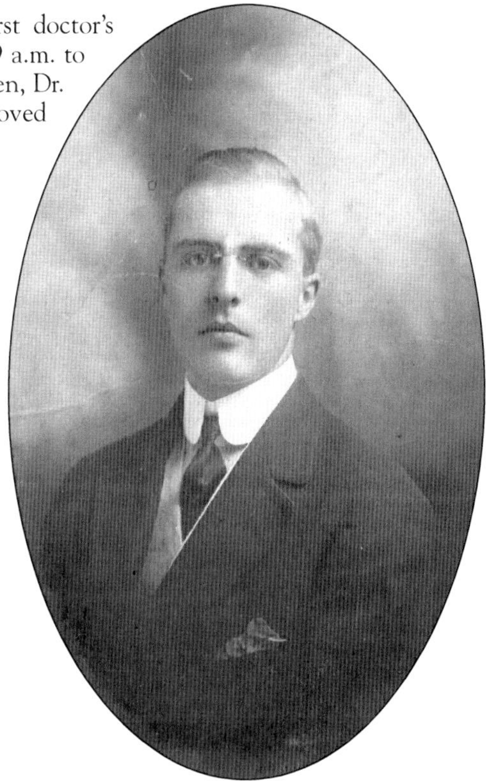

PHONE
MORRISTOWN 2237

1925

HANOVER NECK OFFICE
EAGLE ROCK AVENUE
To 9 A. M. 12-1 NOON 8-9 P. M.

PHONES WHIPPANY 23-F-6
WHIPPANY 23-F-15

DR. H. H. JOHNSTON

WISHES TO ANNOUNCE THAT HE HAS OPENED AN OFFICE TO PRACTICE MEDICINE, SURGERY AND ELECTRICAL THERAPEUTICS AT 154 SOUTH STREET MORRISTOWN, N. J. (NEAR CITY HALL.)

Dr. Johnston had offices on Eagle Rock Avenue (see upper right) and in Morristown. He practiced general medicine and surgery. A March 2, 1928 bill from the doctor to patient William Tuttle showed that doctor visits cost $2 each. (Courtesy of Herb Johnston.)

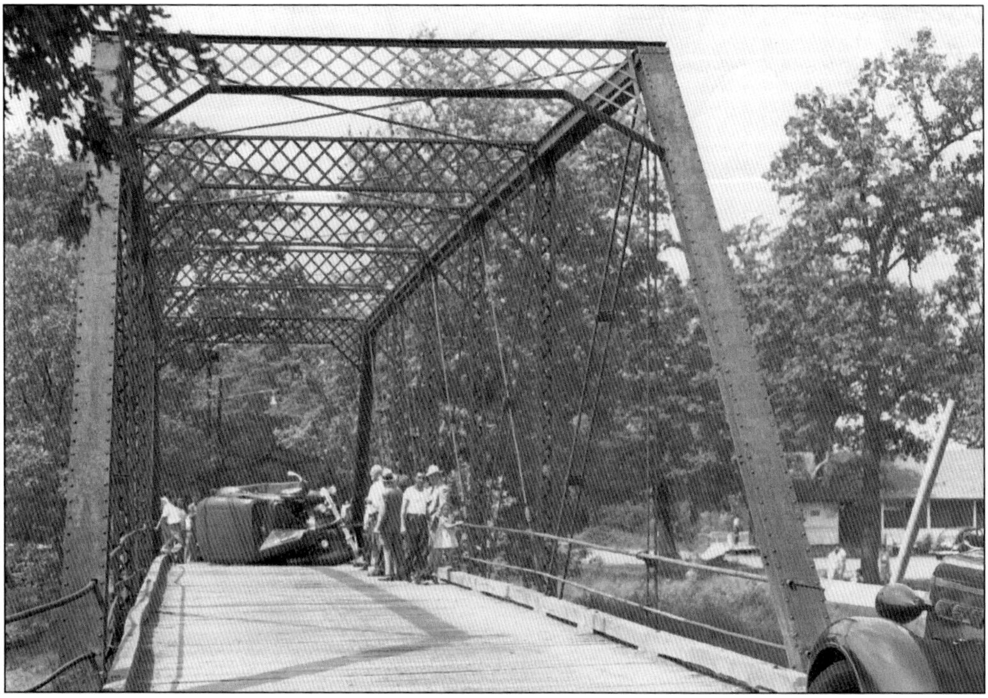

This car did not make it across the Swinefield Bridge on September 4, 1949. The camera is looking from Roseland into East Hanover. River Road is to the left, and Champi's Tavern can be seen on the right. (Courtesy of George and Pamela Schaeffer.)

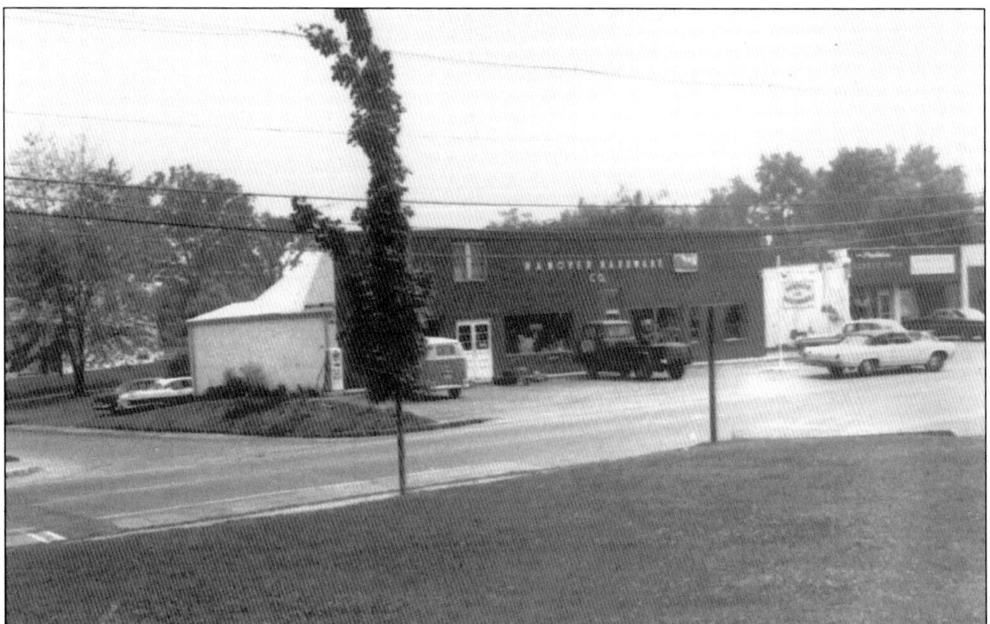

Before Home Depot came to town, the local hardware store was the retailer the average handyman or tradesman patronized. Hanover Hardware Company was across the street from Central School. It carried most of what you needed when something needed fixing. (Courtesy of Catherine Froling.)

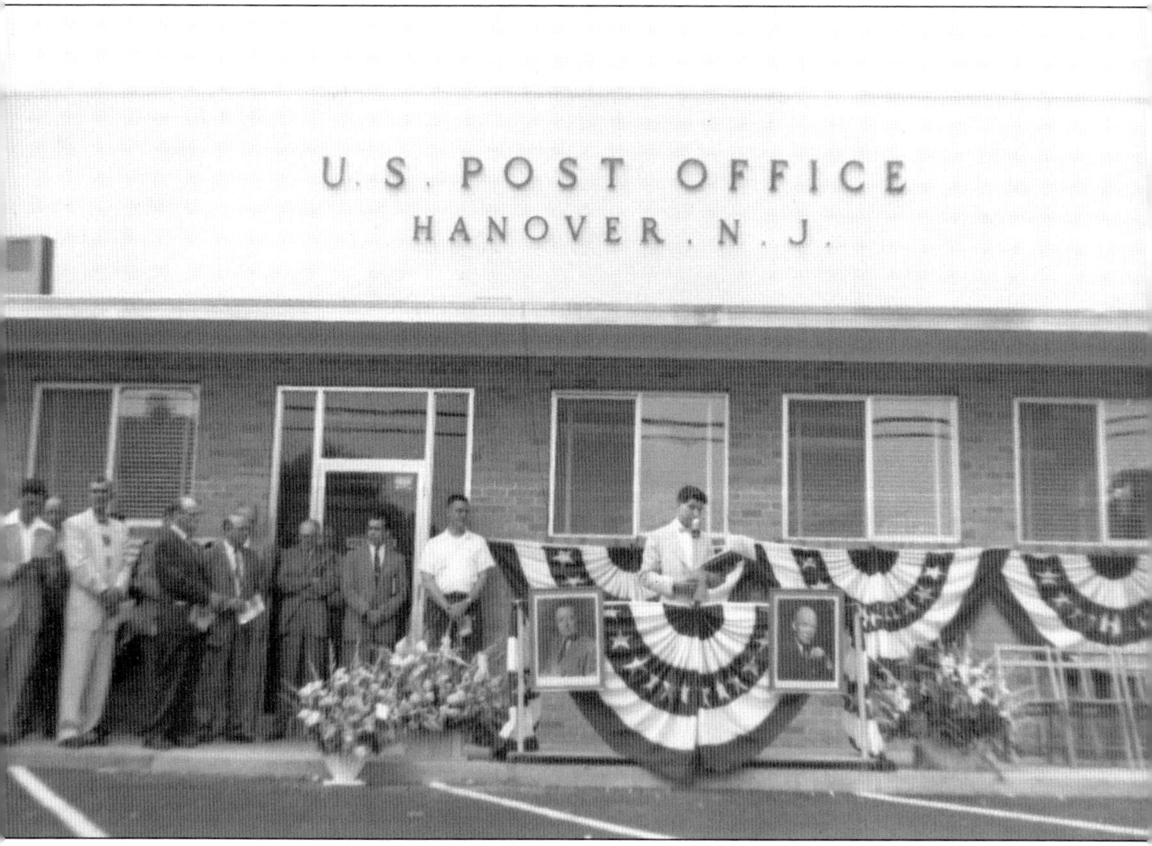

Postmaster Anthony Pellecchia introduces guests at the official dedication of the new post office on Ridgedale Avenue near Barnida Drive on June 13, 1957. The town's first post office had opened on December 12, 1818, in a general store at the corner of Ridgedale and Eagle Rock Avenues. That post office moved to a store at the corner of Ridgedale and what is now Klinger Road in the mid-1800s. Another post office also opened in the Mead Store on Mount Pleasant Avenue c. 1900. Mail was also delivered via RFD from the Whippany Post Office. The name changed from the Hanover Post Office to East Hanover on February 1, 1971. The current post office at Deforest and Ridgedale Avenues opened on August 30, 1974. Early town postmasters included Joshua Perry, Caleb Ely, Moses Beach, James Ely, James R. Mead, Harrison D. Mead, and Orrin Whaites. (Courtesy of Anthony and Anne Pellecchia.)

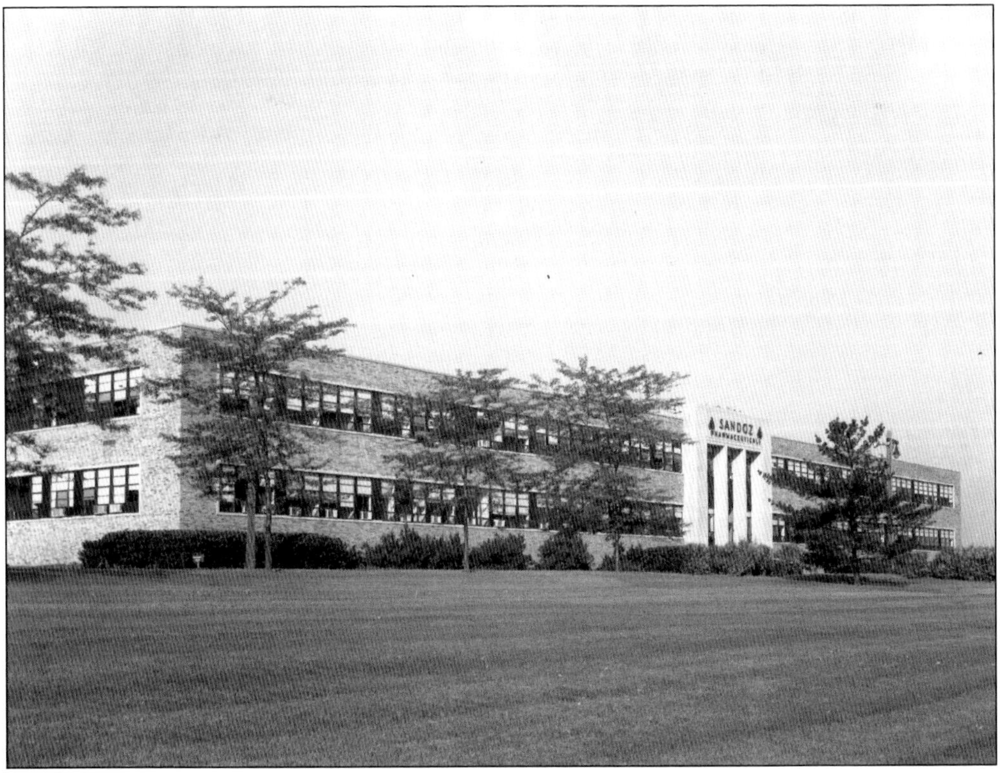

By the mid-1940s, Sandoz had outgrown its New York City facilities and had decided to relocate its pharmaceutical division to Route 10. Centuries earlier, the site had been a Native American settlement perched on high ground close to the Whippany River. As business grew, Sandoz added research, marketing, and administration buildings. (Courtesy of Novartis.)

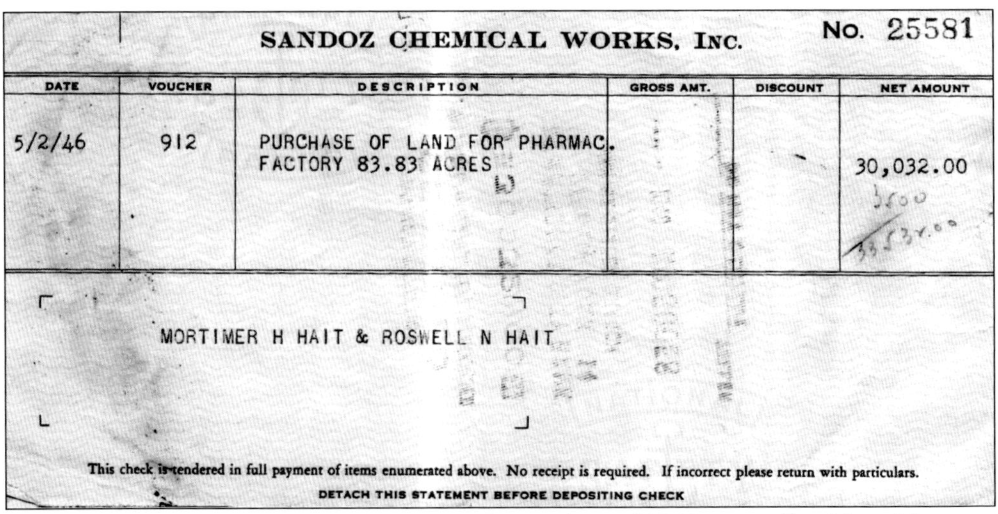
SANDOZ CHEMICAL WORKS, INC. No. 25581

DATE	VOUCHER	DESCRIPTION	GROSS AMT.	DISCOUNT	NET AMOUNT
5/2/46	912	PURCHASE OF LAND FOR PHARMAC. FACTORY 83.83 ACRES			30,032.00 3500 33532.00

MORTIMER H HAIT & ROSWELL N HAIT

This check is tendered in full payment of items enumerated above. No receipt is required. If incorrect please return with particulars.

DETACH THIS STATEMENT BEFORE DEPOSITING CHECK

This Sandoz check stub from 1946 documents the purchase of 83.83 acres of land from Mortimer and Roswell Hait for $30,032. It marked the beginning of the acquisition of 180 acres of land for the company's new pharmaceutical manufacturing plant. (Courtesy of John Esposito.)

Sandoz opened its East Hanover pharmaceutical manufacturing plant in 1954. The parent company had begun in Basel, Switzerland, in 1886 with a small factory that manufactured synthetic dyes. It established an office with four employees in New York City in 1919. The initial business focused on importing dyestuffs for American silk and wool manufacturers. A pharmaceutical division was started in 1925. (Courtesy of Novartis.)

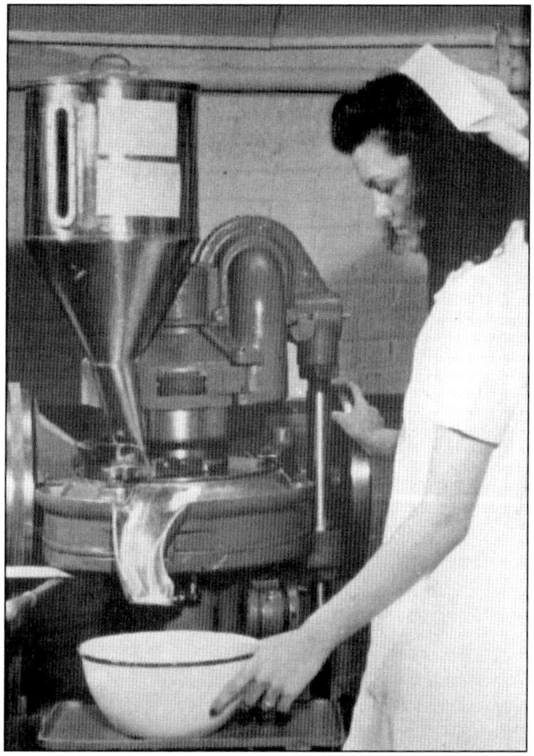

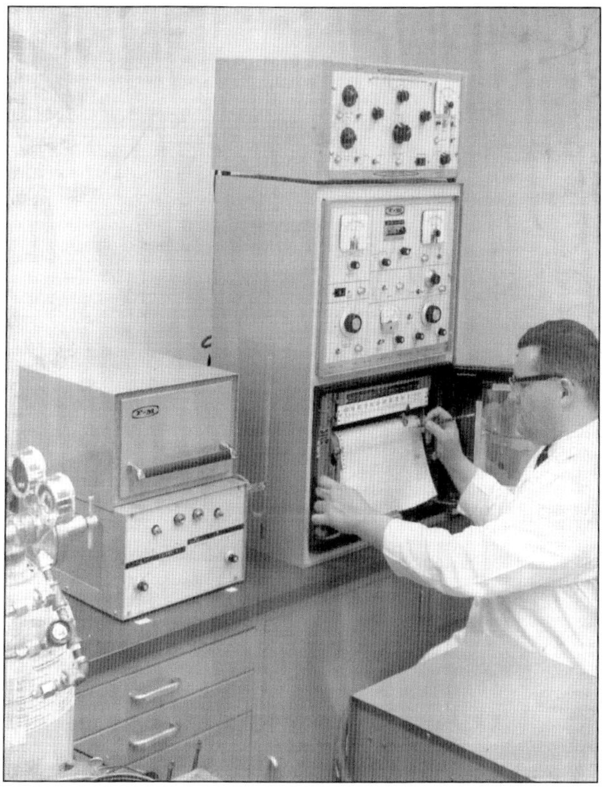

With its scientific and medical innovations over the years, Sandoz made important medical contributions, especially in the areas of organ transplantation, headache management, mental illness, sleep disturbances, geriatrics, allergic/respiratory disorders, and obstetrics. In 1996, Sandoz merged with Ciba-Geigy and became Novartis. (Courtesy of Novartis.)

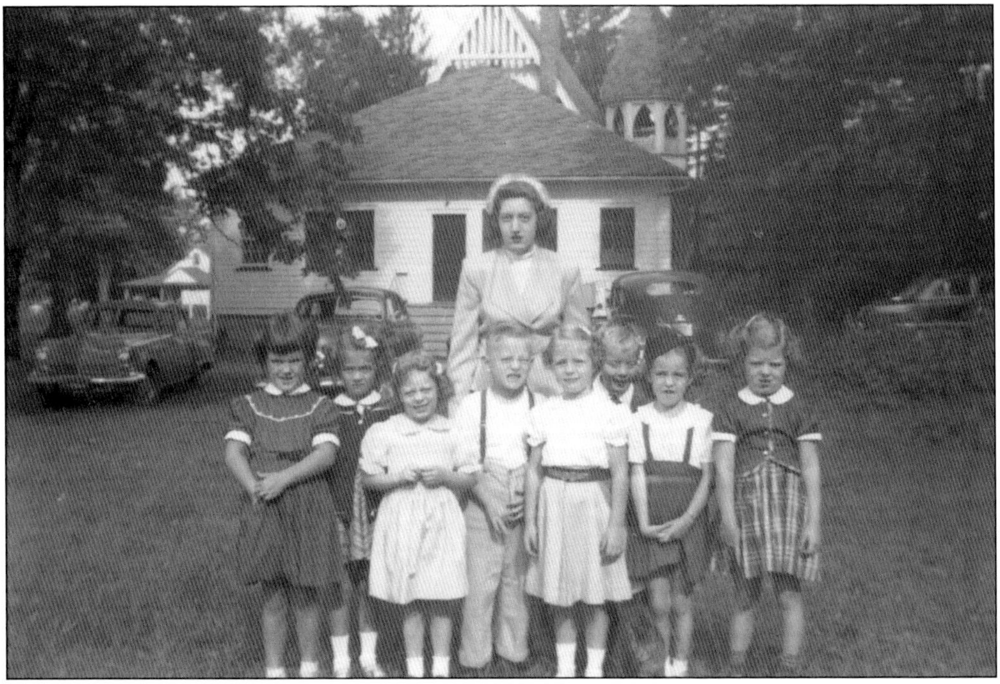

This Sunday school class photograph at Kitchell Memorial Presbyterian Church was taken on September 28, 1952. The church manse was built the next year for the pastor and family. By 1963, Sunday school enrollment had grown to 272. (Courtesy of Liveria and Norwoood Ross.)

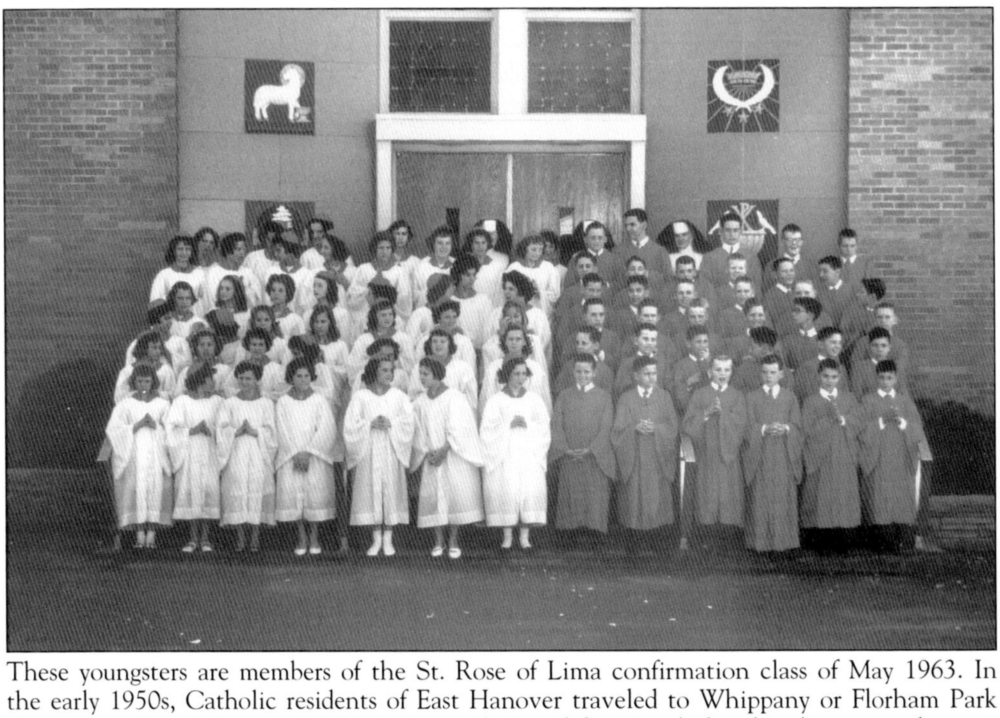

These youngsters are members of the St. Rose of Lima confirmation class of May 1963. In the early 1950s, Catholic residents of East Hanover traveled to Whippany or Florham Park to attend services. As the population grew, the need for a Catholic church in town became evident. (Courtesy of Gus Auermuller.)

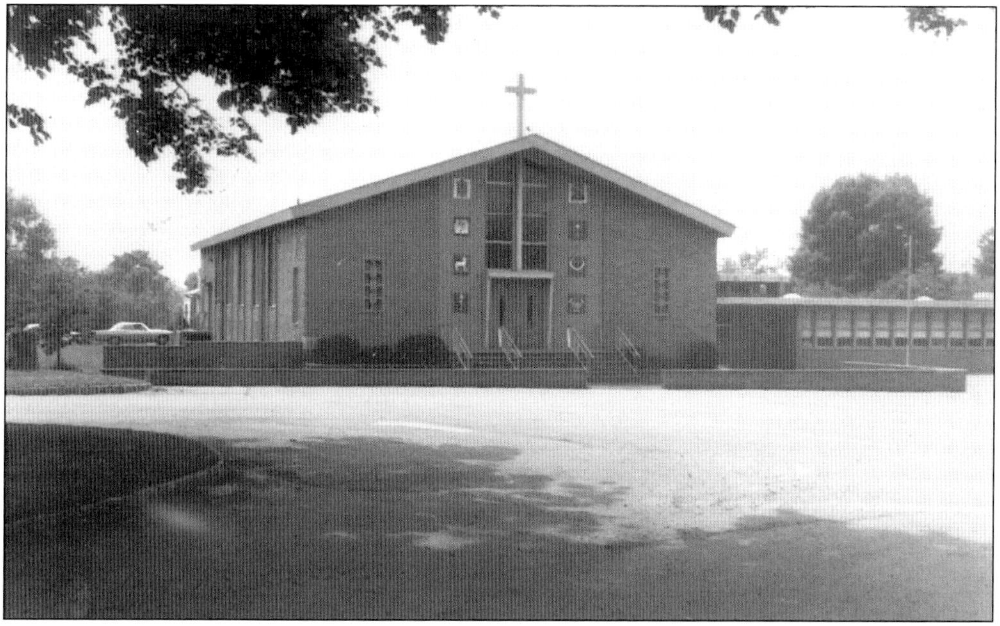

St. Rose of Lima started holding church services at the firehouse on July 21, 1957, and then moved to Central School as demand for space grew. The first service in the new church was celebrated on Christmas Eve 1958, although the building had not yet been completed. The official church dedication took place on June 6, 1959. (Courtesy of Catherine Froling.)

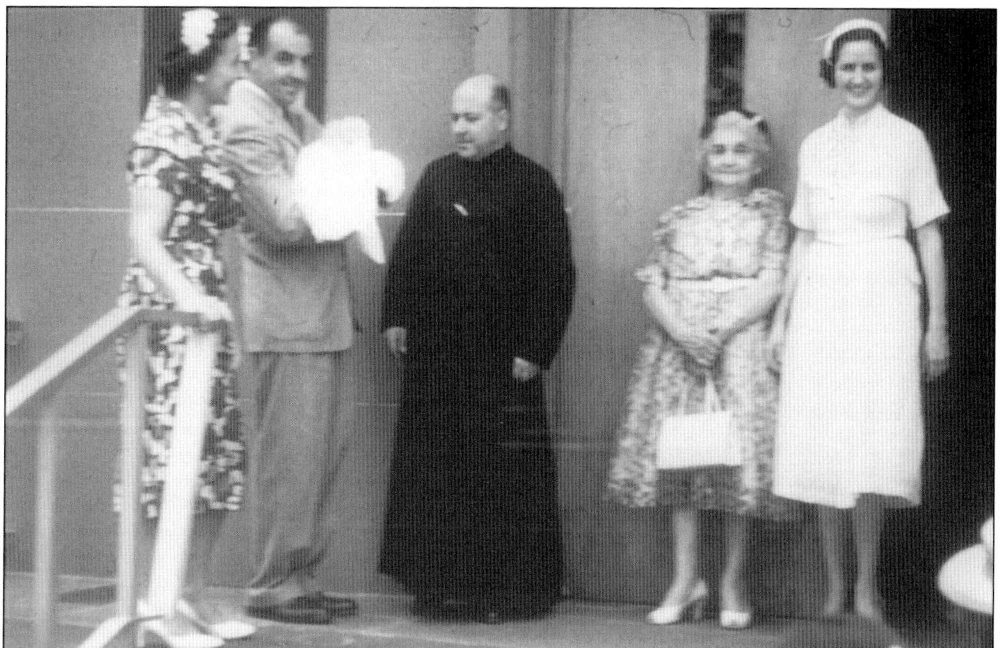

The Reverend Alphonse Tuozzo (center) was the first pastor of St. Rose of Lima Church, serving from 1957 to 1971 and again from 1974 to 1979. He is shown above at the baptism of Terry Wood. Others in the photograph are, from left to right, Marie and Gus Auermuller, the grandmother of Ann Wood, and Ann Wood. (Courtesy of Gus Auermuller.)

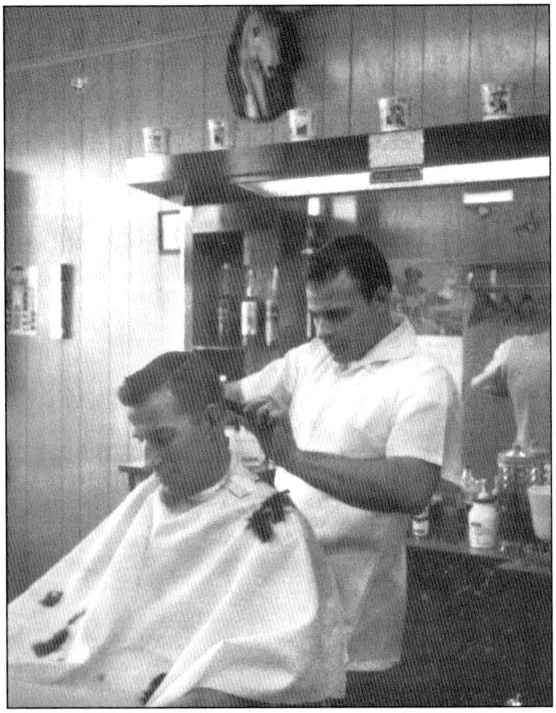

Freddie's Barbershop is one of the oldest retail establishments in town. Fred Costanzo opened his shop in 1960 on Ridgedale Avenue and has been cutting hair for generations of customers ever since. When this photograph was taken, men's haircuts cost $1.75 and children's $1.50. (Courtesy of Fred Costanzo.)

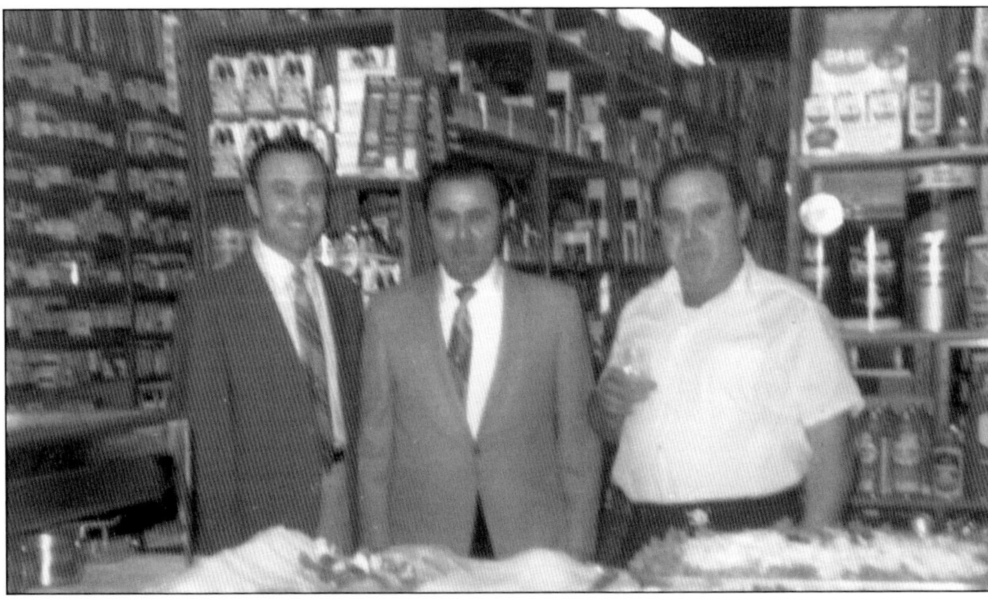

Politi Auto Parts is another retailer that has been around a long time. Brothers Ralph and Americo Politi started the business in 1963 across the street from where it is today. With hard work and some excellent employees, the business outgrew that store and opened across Ridgedale Avenue in a new and larger building. Pictured above during the opening celebration of the new store are, from left to right, Ralph Politi, manager Dan Marcantonio, and Americo Politi. Politi Auto had no choice but to be successful—it supported the 17 children of the two owners. Ralph's family has nine children and Americo's eight. (Courtesy of Ralph and Rita Politi.)

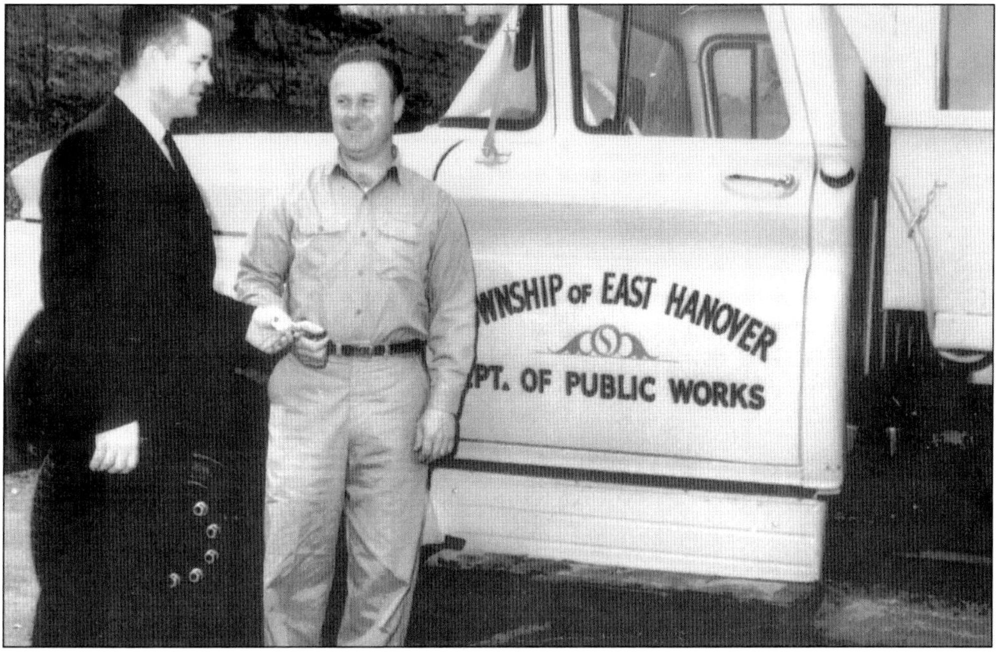

Mayor Barney Flynn (left) hands over the keys to the public works department's first piece of equipment, a 1961 Chevy truck. Accepting the keys is Nick Marcantonio, superintendent of the department and the first and only employee early on. The photograph was taken March 19, 1962, not long after the department was established. (Courtesy of the East Hanover Department of Public Services.)

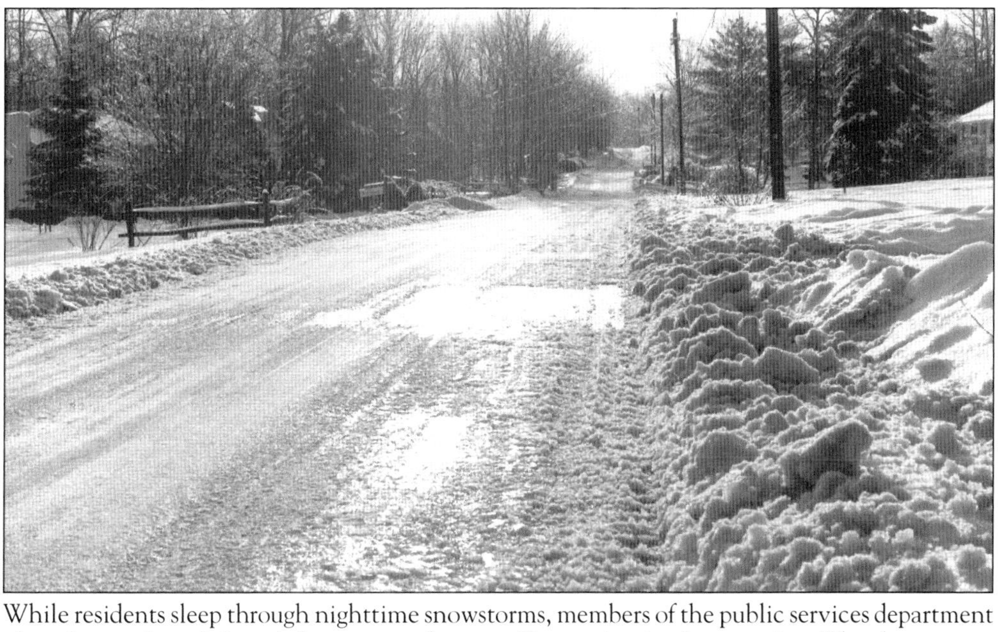

While residents sleep through nighttime snowstorms, members of the public services department plow the roads and shovel the snow to keep traffic moving in the morning. The department grew from one employee in the early 1960s to 32 today. Its responsibilities include maintaining public buildings, grounds, and vehicles, controlling and maintaining the water department and sewers, and parks and recreation. (Courtesy of Bill Schaeffer.)

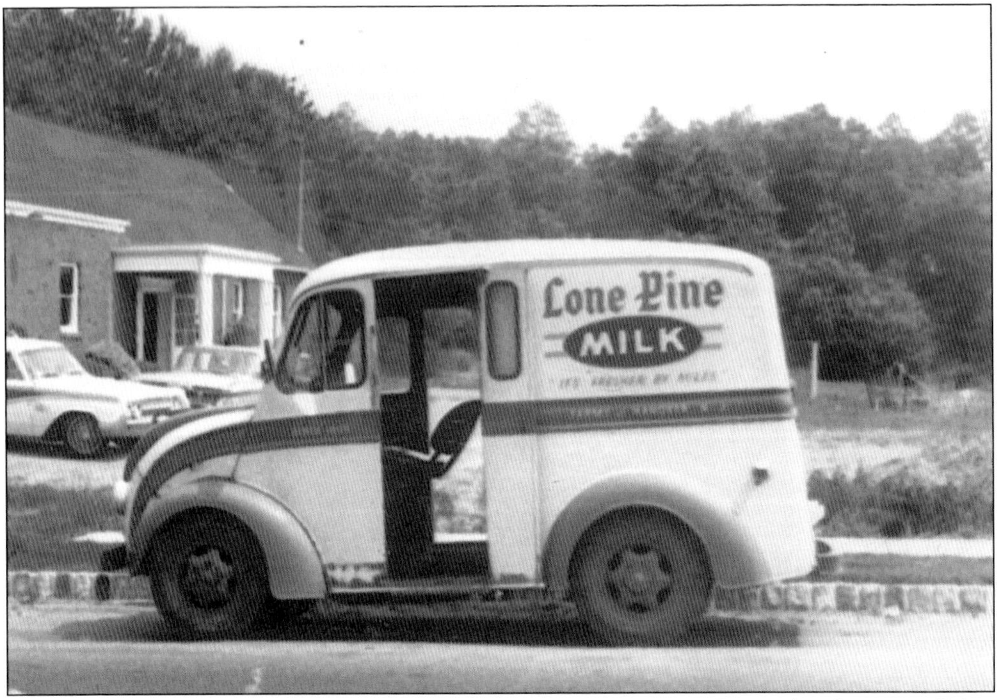

The milkman used to deliver fresh milk early in the morning, right to the doorstep. Other mobile merchants did the same, especially during the 1920s, 1930s, and 1940s, such as the bread man, the produce man, the butcher, and the fish man. (Courtesy of Catherine Froling.)

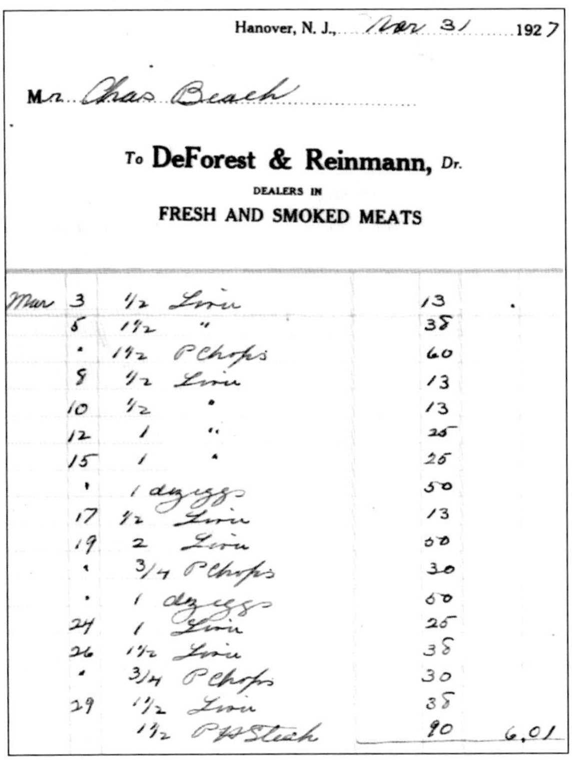
Hanover, N. J., Mar 31 1927

Mr. Chas Beach

To **DeForest & Reinmann,** Dr.

DEALERS IN

FRESH AND SMOKED MEATS

Mar	3	1/2 Liver	13	
	5	1 1/2 "	38	
	"	1 1/2 P Chops	60	
	8	1/2 Liver	13	
	10	1/2 "	13	
	12	1 "	25	
	15	1 "	25	
	"	1 doz eggs	50	
	17	1/2 Liver	13	
	19	2 Liver	50	
	"	3/4 P Chops	30	
	"	1 doz eggs	50	
	24	1 Liver	25	
	26	1 1/2 Liver	38	
	"	3/4 P Chops	30	
	29	1 1/2 Liver	38	
		1 1/2 P H Steak	90	6.01

Charles Beach used the services of the mobile butcher quite often during March 1927. He liked liver a lot. The price was certainly right: 13¢ for a half pound. (Courtesy of Catherine Froling.)

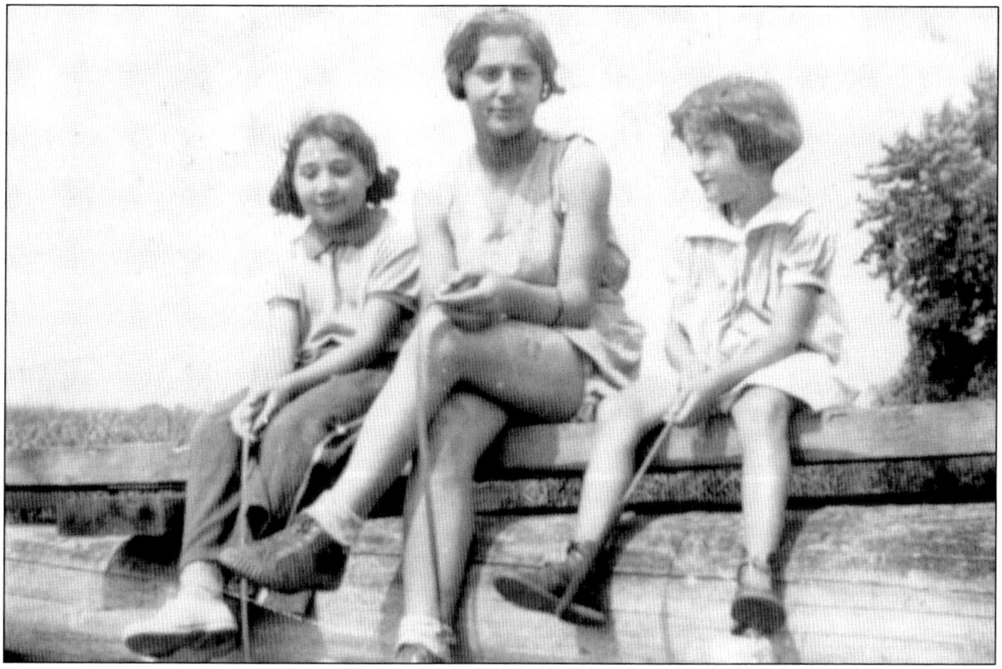

These three young ladies are taking it easy on a lazy summer afternoon in 1937. They are sitting atop an old bridge over the Whippany River at the end of what is now Klinger Road. In the 1800s, Klinger Road and Ridgedale Avenue south of Klinger were one road called Troy Road. Shown in the photograph are, from left to right, Ann Grasso, Eleanor Iradi, and Betty Iradi. (Courtesy of Betty Cardarella.)

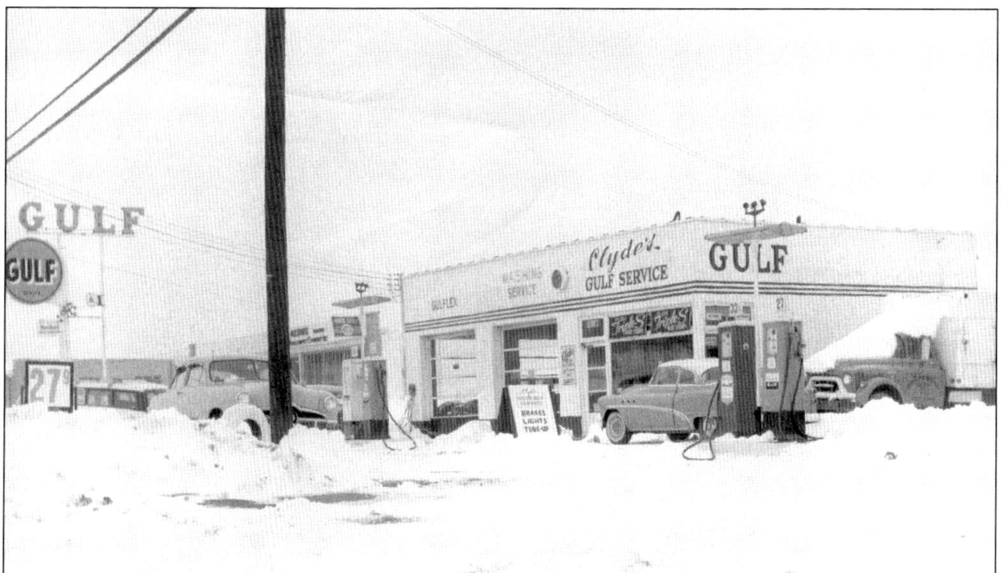

Take a look at the price of gasoline in 1960 at less than 28¢ a gallon. High test was a bargain, too. Clyde Grossmann was the proprietor of this Gulf station on Route 10 where the Ramada Inn is located today. The garbage truck on the right belonged to Charlie Sisco; he had a route in town. (Courtesy of Clyde and Bunny Grossmann.)

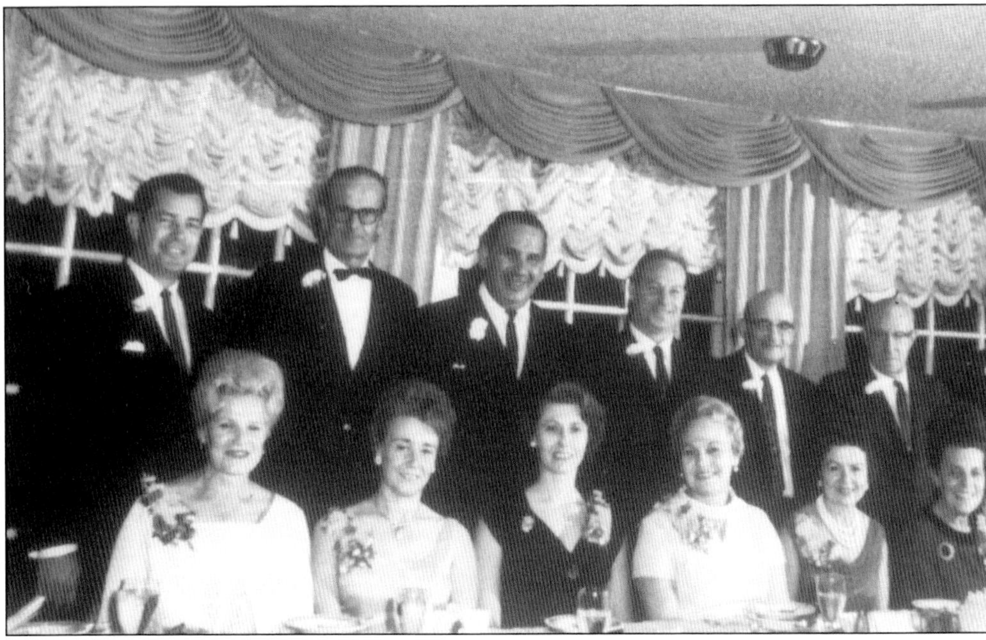

Pictured above are town fathers of yesteryear. They helped govern East Hanover in the 1950s and 1960s. All of the men are former mayors. They are, from left to right, Barney and Helene Flynn, Mike Deskovick and Catherine Froling, Harold and Constance Smith, Bob and Vivian Zakarian, Bill and Grace Hubscher, and Joe and Edith Lurker. (Courtesy of Pete Tamburro.)

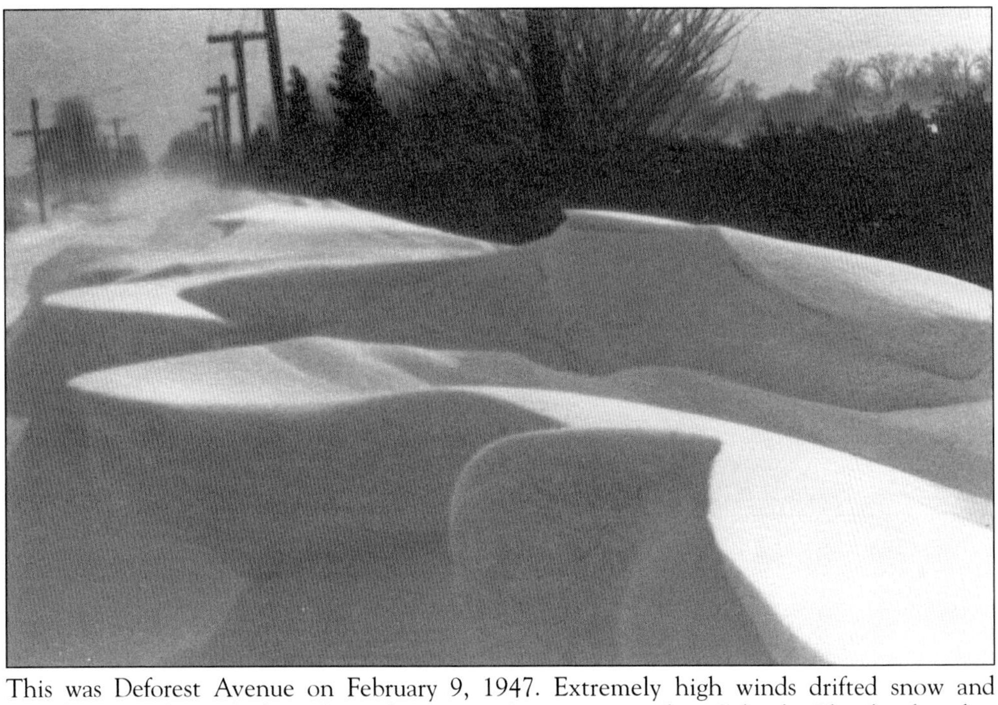

This was Deforest Avenue on February 9, 1947. Extremely high winds drifted snow and closed many side roads throughout the county. It even snowed in Orlando, Florida, that day, for the first time in 29 years. It was a rough winter for much of the country. (Courtesy of Bill Schaeffer.)

Four

PROTECTING THE TOWNSHIP

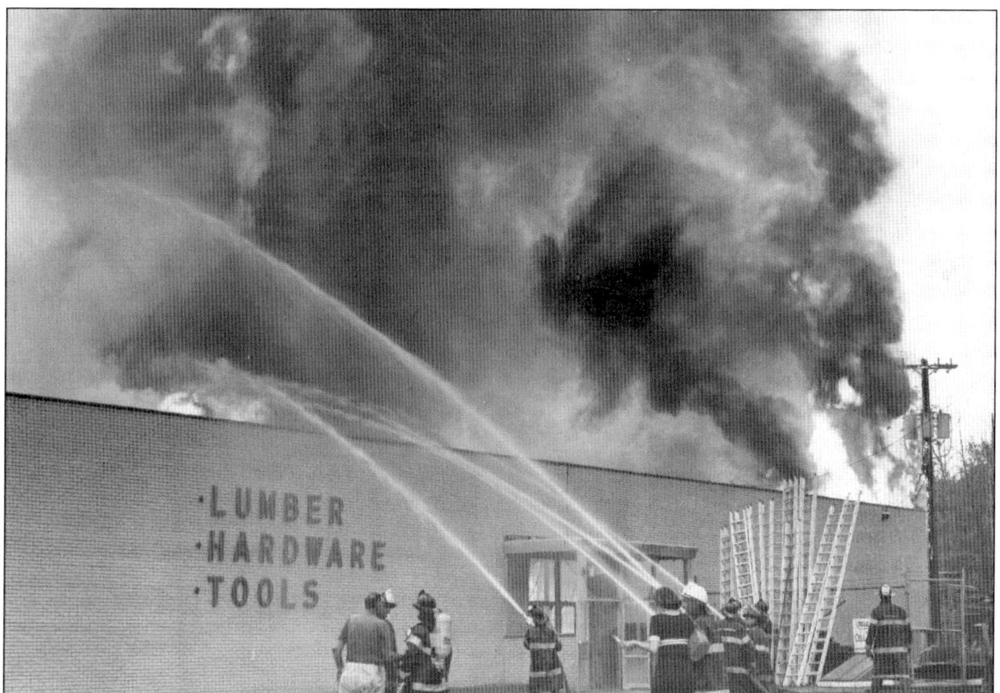

Two Guys' lumber and hardware store on Route 10 was destroyed by fire in the 1960s. Local volunteer firemen are shown fighting the blaze. An aerial truck from the Madison Fire Department was called in to assist. Billowing smoke could be seen miles away. (Courtesy of the East Hanover Fire Department.)

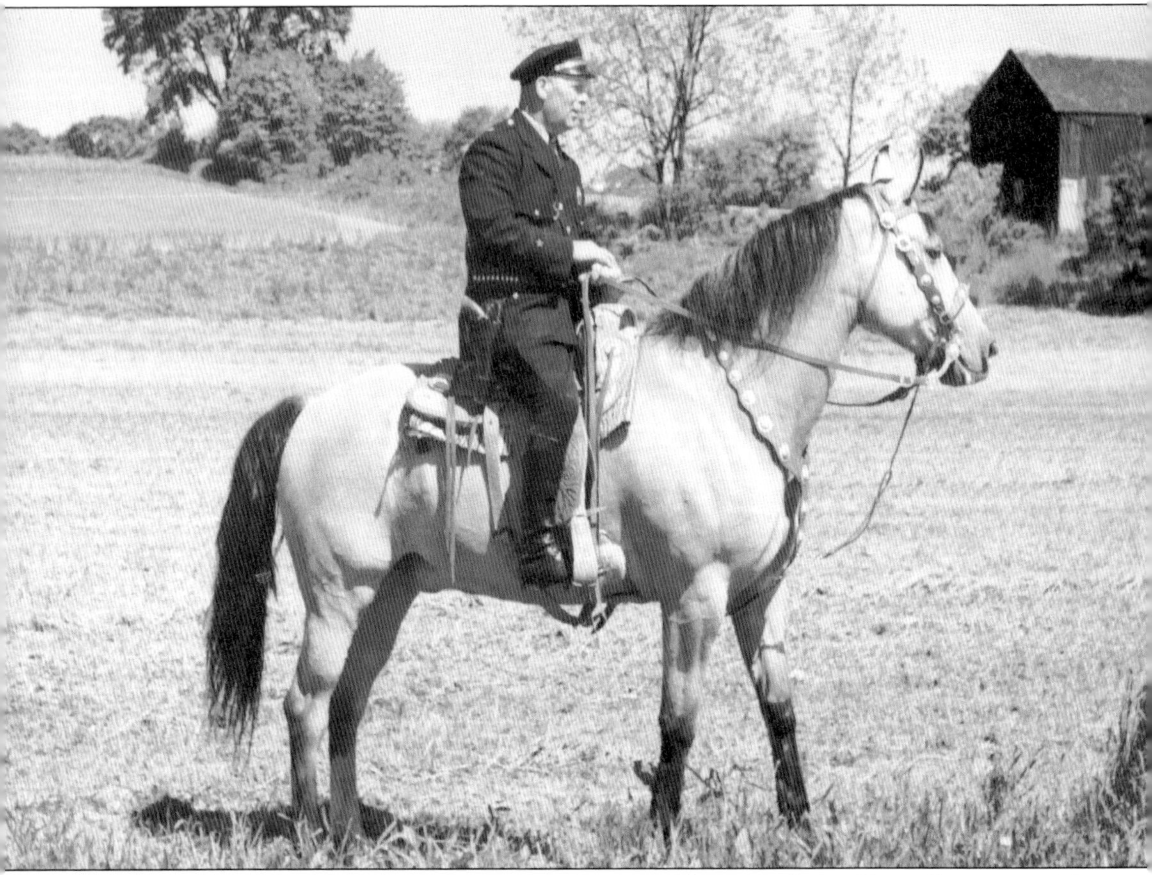

Ralph Shrader was the town's first paid policeman. The second was Harry Davenport. The two comprised the police department in the 1930s, assisted by non-paid special officers. One of the earliest police stations was in a cloakroom at Cobblestone School. The last four digits of the department's telephone number there were 0432, the same as they are today. When both policemen were out on patrol and a call came in, it was routed to Ralph's house. If it were an emergency, Ralph's wife, Ella, would hop in the car and track down the officers. When the town was incorporated in 1928, the township committee appointed Ralph Shrader, Joseph Porter, Norman Smith, Thornton Webb, and William Steckert as special policemen. Each man had to pay a $2.50 deposit for his badge. The deposit was refunded when the badge was returned. Ralph Shrader was also named chief of police, a position he held until 1963. Chief Shrader is shown getting ready for a Memorial Day parade in 1947. (Courtesy of Shirley Shrader.)

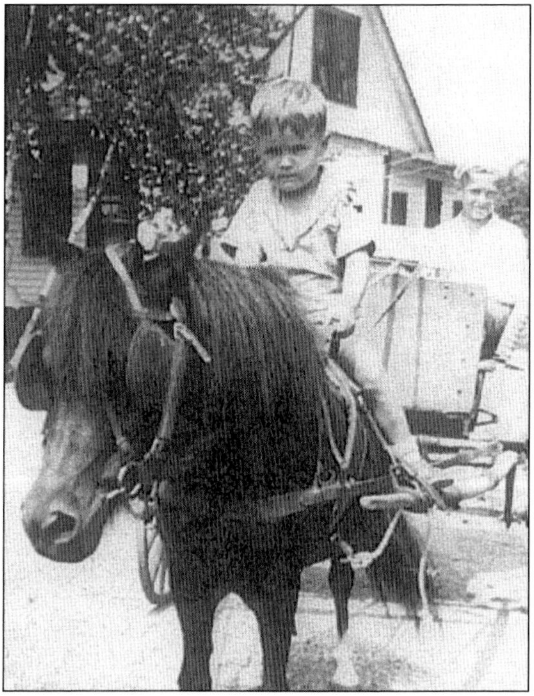

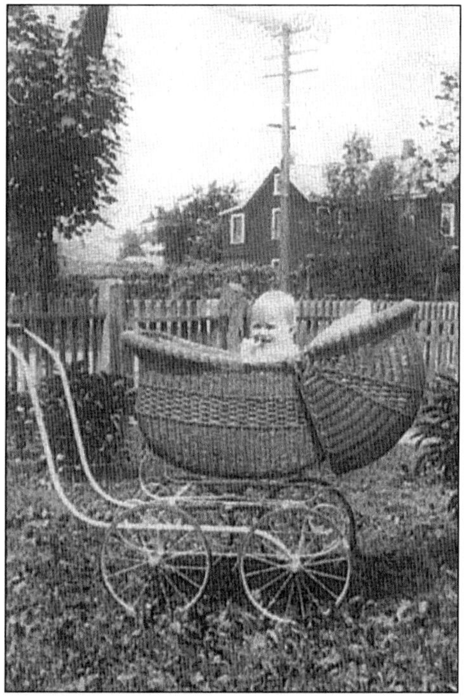

This is Stanley Kalinowski Jr. His parents owned a tavern on Cedar Street. Kalinowski grew up in town, went to school here, and played in local neighborhoods before going off to fight in World War II. He never made it home. He lost his life in Europe so that other children could play peacefully and freely in the backyards and ball fields around town. (Courtesy of Tom Iradi.)

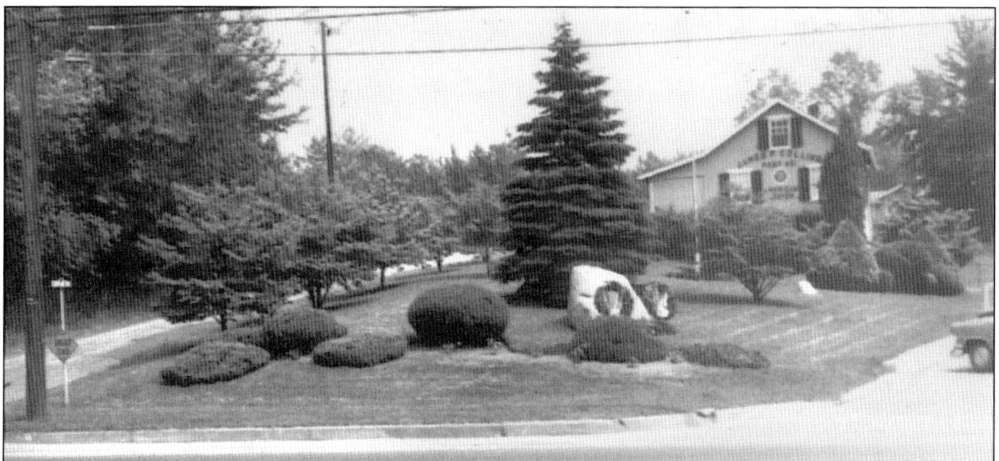

The James P. Collins American Legion Post headquarters was located at the corner of Ridgedale and Cleveland Avenues. It has since been razed. A stone monument is still there, though, with the names of the young men from town who gave their lives in World Wars I and II, the Korean War, and Vietnam. They are James Casey, Richard Eddy, Ruban Feiler, Frederick Horning, Stanley Kalinowski Jr., Walter Klinger, Charles Little, John Massa, Irving Petry, Alfred Schaeffer, Michael Spagnolo, Raymond Tuttle, Walter Van Ness, Ronald L. Nussbaum, and Gary J. Allen. (Courtesy of Catherine Froling.)

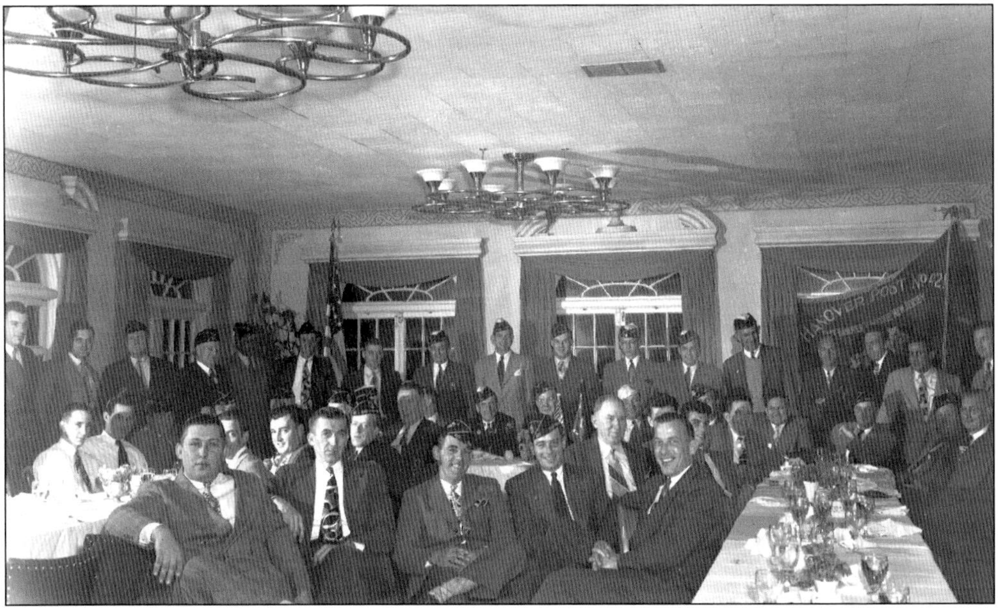

These local men are members of the newly formed American Legion Post 421. The photograph was taken in 1946 or 1947. Most of the men had recently returned home from duty in World War II. The name of the post was later changed to the James P. Collins Post. (Courtesy of Anthony and Anne Pellecchia.)

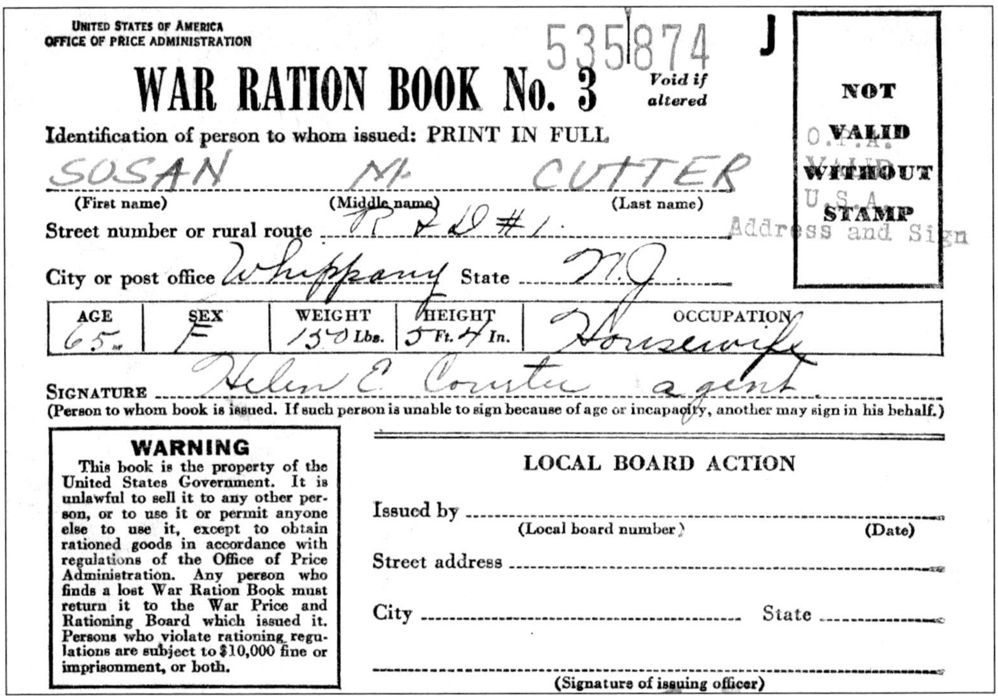

UNITED STATES OF AMERICA
OFFICE OF PRICE ADMINISTRATION

535874 J

WAR RATION BOOK No. 3 *Void if altered*

NOT VALID WITHOUT STAMP

O.P.A. VALID U.S.A. Address and Sign

Identification of person to whom issued: PRINT IN FULL

SOSAN M. CUTTER
(First name) (Middle name) (Last name)

Street number or rural route RFD #1

City or post office Whippany State N.J.

AGE	SEX	WEIGHT	HEIGHT	OCCUPATION
65	F	130 Lbs.	5 Ft. 4 In.	Housewife

SIGNATURE Helen E. Courter agent
(Person to whom book is issued. If such person is unable to sign because of age or incapacity, another may sign in his behalf.)

WARNING
This book is the property of the United States Government. It is unlawful to sell it to any other person, or to use it or permit anyone else to use it, except to obtain rationed goods in accordance with regulations of the Office of Price Administration. Any person who finds a lost War Ration Book must return it to the War Price and Rationing Board which issued it. Persons who violate rationing regulations are subject to $10,000 fine or imprisonment, or both.

LOCAL BOARD ACTION

Issued by .... (Local board number) (Date)

Street address ....

City .... State ....

.... (Signature of issuing officer)

In an age of considerable prosperity, rationing is all but forgotten. During World War II, however, it was very real. Susan Cutter's ration book instructs that stamps inside authorize the bearer to purchase rationed goods in quantities and at times designated by the government. The rule was "If you don't need it, don't buy it." (Courtesy of Don Courter.)

Members of the 1961 police department pose on the front steps of the old police station on Ridgedale Avenue. They include, from left to right, the following: (front row) Joe Schuler and Ralph Shrader; (middle row) Larry Bode, George Schaeffer, and Don Brower; (back row) Alan Schweitzer, Bill Scioscia, and Conrad Rittweger. (Photograph by Bill Schaeffer; courtesy of George and Pamela Schaeffer.)

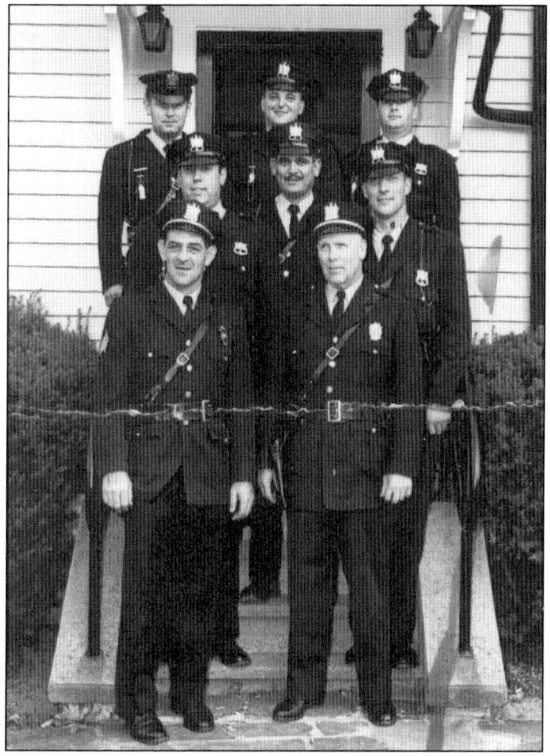

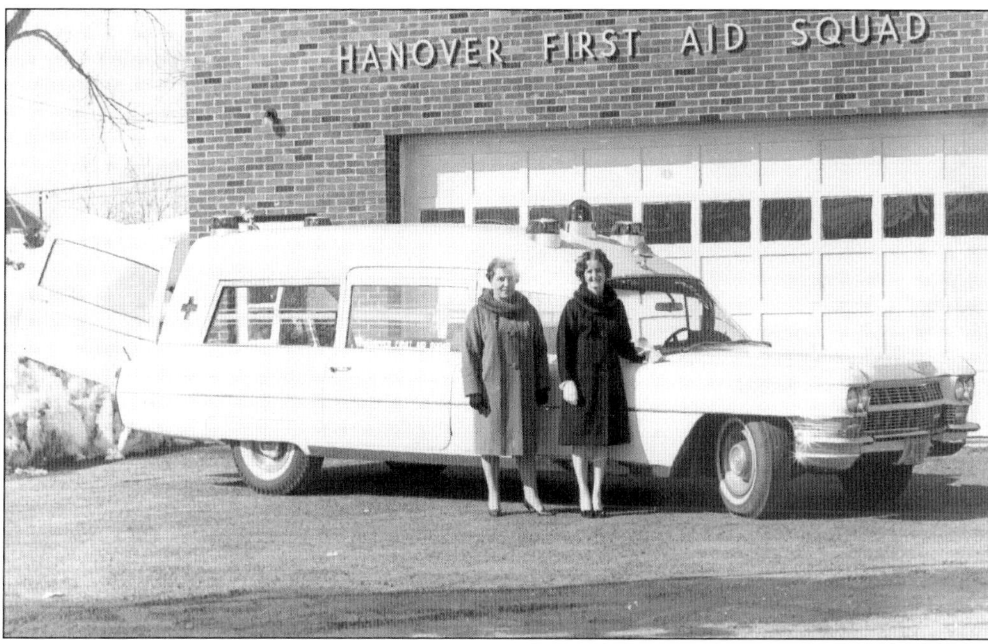

The town's volunteer first-aid squad was incorporated in 1955. Its first ambulance was a 1948 Buick. Construction began on the squad building on Ridgedale Avenue in 1961, with many of the squad members volunteering to help build the facility. Shown above with a newer rig in 1964 are, from left to right, Capt. Weetona Hobby and Pres. Estelle Schwenke. (Courtesy of Weetona Hobby.)

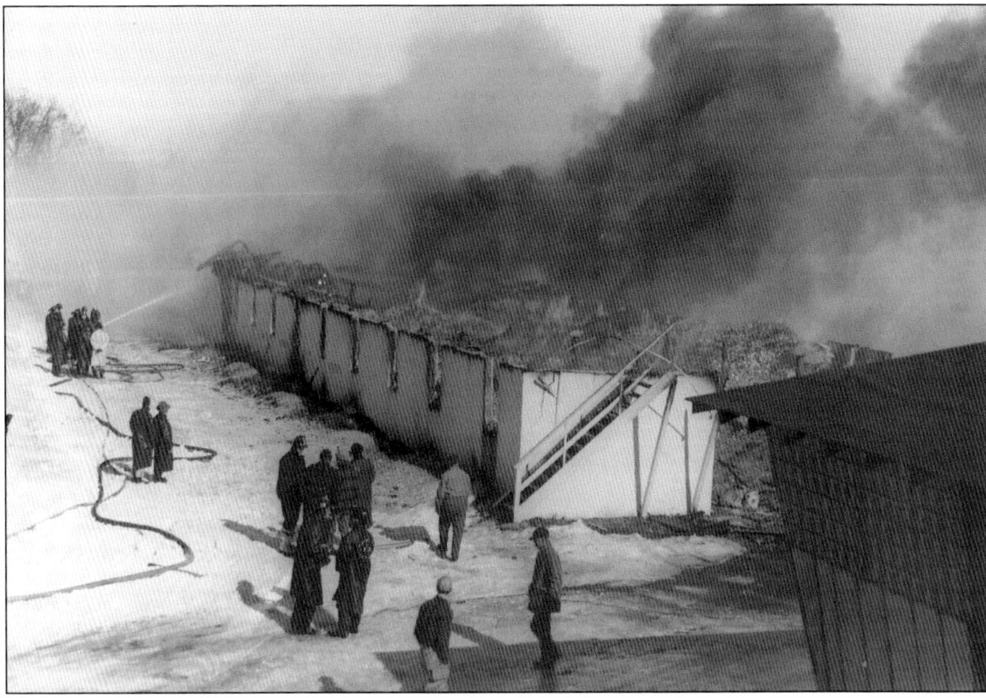

The Norda fire that started on February 15, 1948, burned for 22 hours. At times, drums of lemon oil and alcohol exploded, endangering firefighters. One Florham Park fireman was injured when he was blown off a ladder. The fire destroyed a 250-foot warehouse on Route 10 where Costco is today. (Courtesy of Nichols Photo Service and the East Hanover Fire Department.)

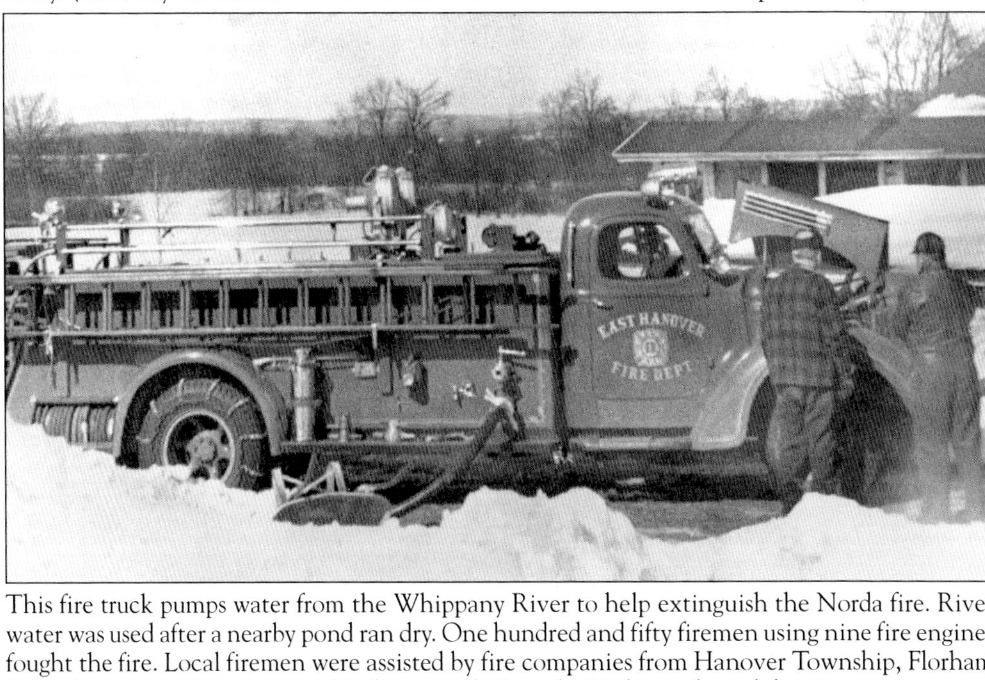

This fire truck pumps water from the Whippany River to help extinguish the Norda fire. River water was used after a nearby pond ran dry. One hundred and fifty firemen using nine fire engines fought the fire. Local firemen were assisted by fire companies from Hanover Township, Florham Park, Livingston, Morristown, Madison, and Newark. High winds and freezing temperatures after dark hampered the effort. (Courtesy of the East Hanover Fire Department.)

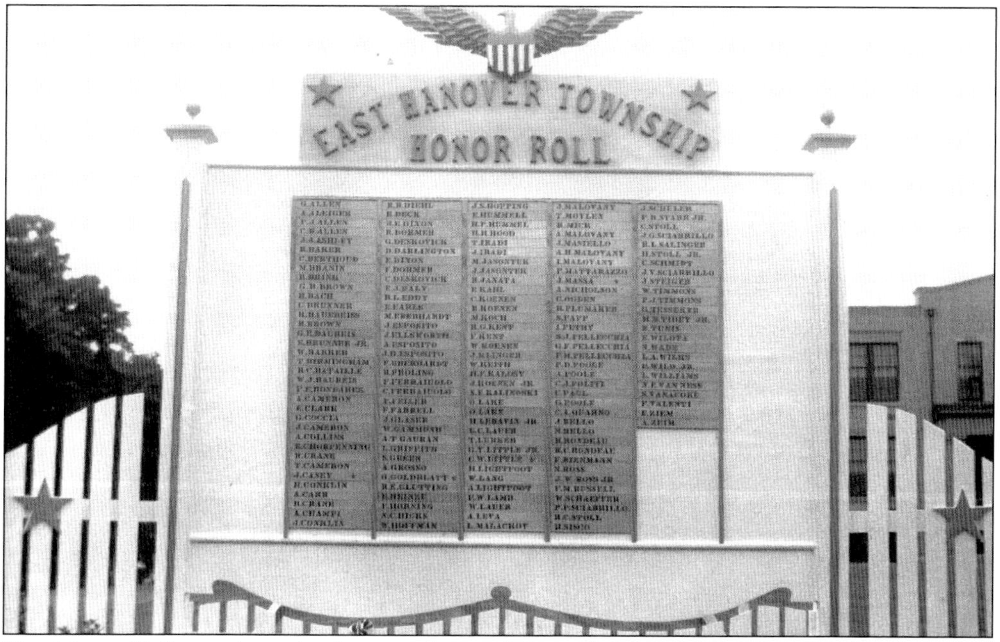

The Honor Roll stood on the lawn in front of Central School during World War II, listing the young people from town who were serving in the armed forces. A star next to the name indicated that the soldier had lost his life. (Courtesy of Tom Iradi.)

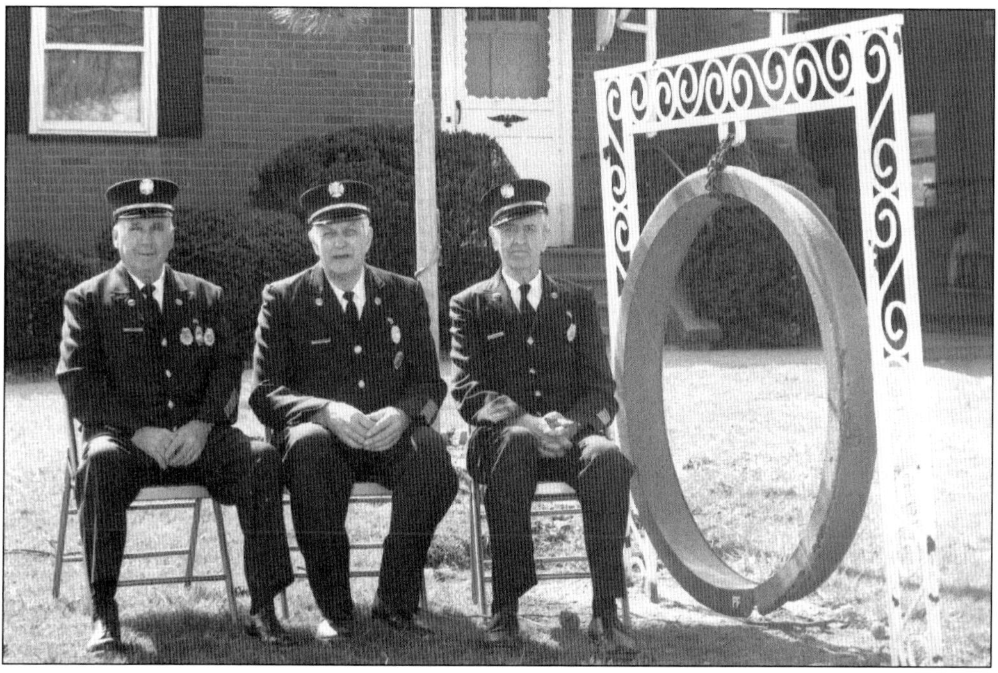

Shown in front of the old firehouse on Ridgedale Avenue are senior volunteer firefighters, from left to right, Jack Munther, Howard Palmer, and Ray Poppendieck. They are sitting next to a fire ring, which was once a train wheel. Three of these rings were placed throughout town on July 9, 1930, and used as an alarm system. The rings were hammered vigorously to alert other volunteers when there was a fire. (Courtesy of the East Hanover Fire Department.)

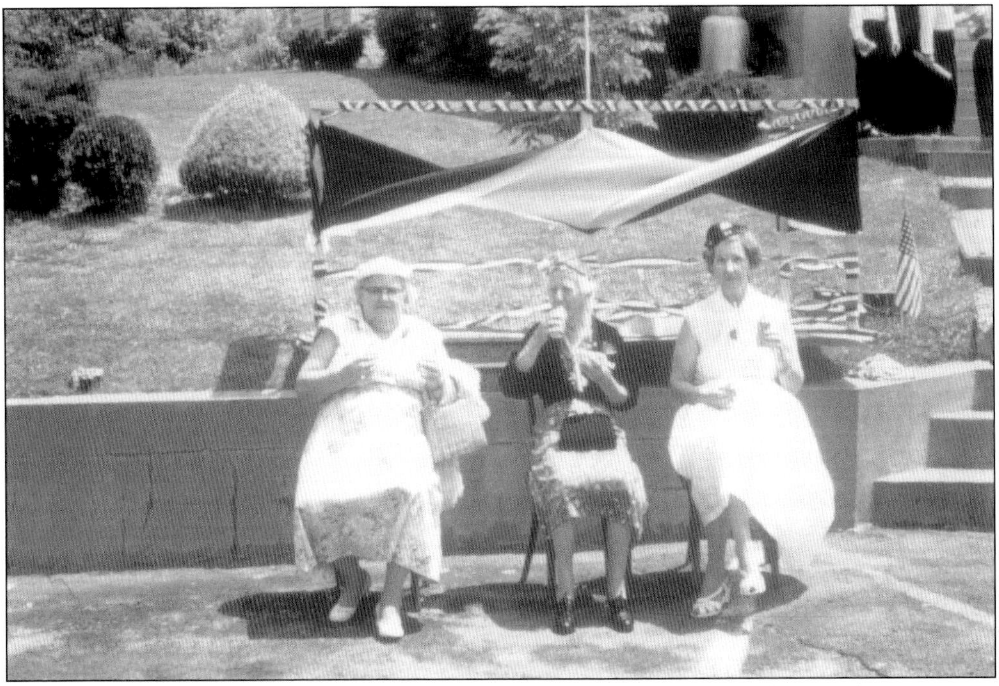

Three Gold Star Mothers from town are recognized at a Memorial Day observance in 1957. They are mothers of young men who died in World War II. Pictured above are, from left to right, Bessie Petry, Frances Little, and Florence Kalinowski. (Courtesy of Helen and James Iradi.)

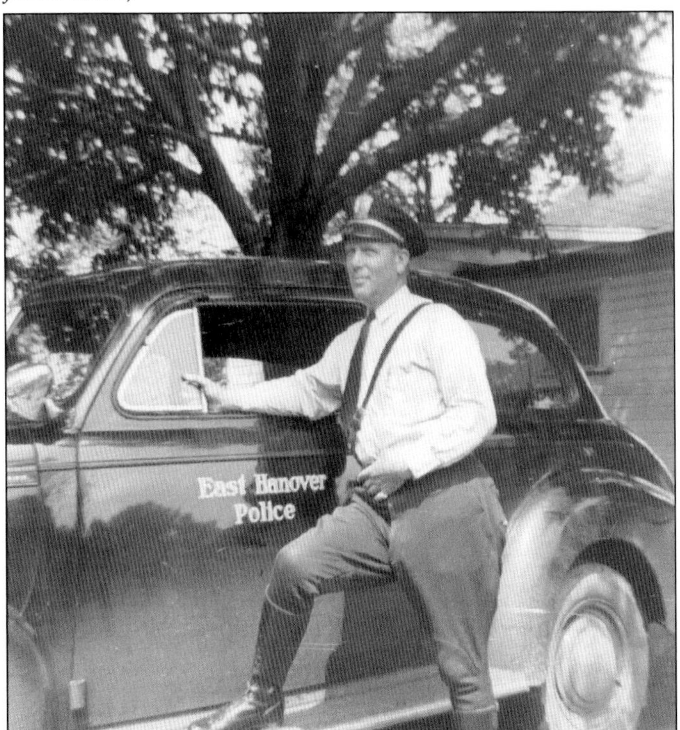

Police chief Ralph Shrader shows off the town's first police car in 1940. Patrol cars today are equipped with sophisticated computers. (Courtesy of Bill Shrader.)

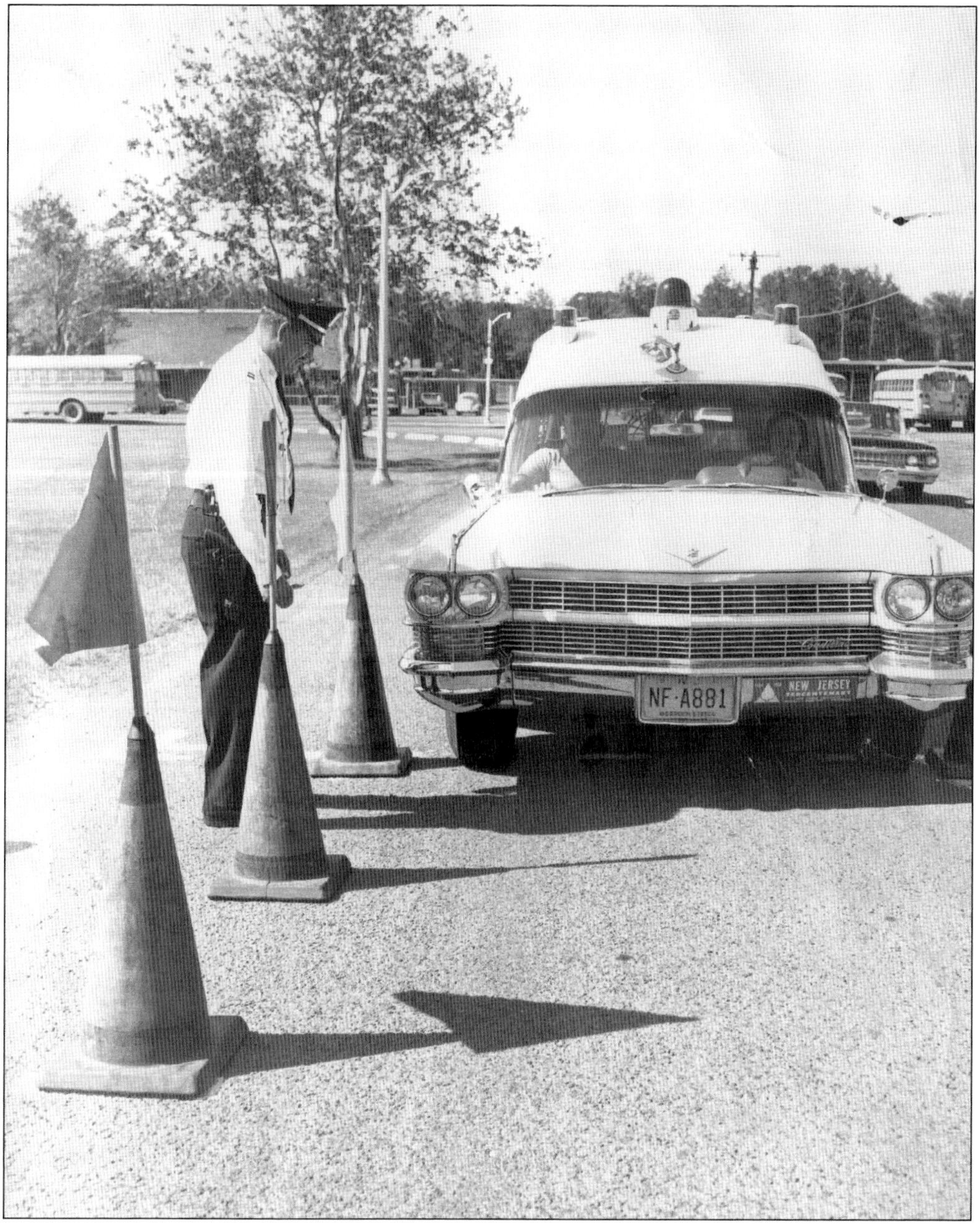

First-aid squad members took driving tests in 1964 to make sure they could handle a new $20,000 ambulance. The tests were administered by the driver education department at Hanover Park High School. Drivers were rated by police captain George Schaeffer (shown above), Thomas Langon, a driver education instructor at the high school, and William Baker, who was in charge of bus transportation at the school. (Courtesy of George and Pamela Schaeffer.)

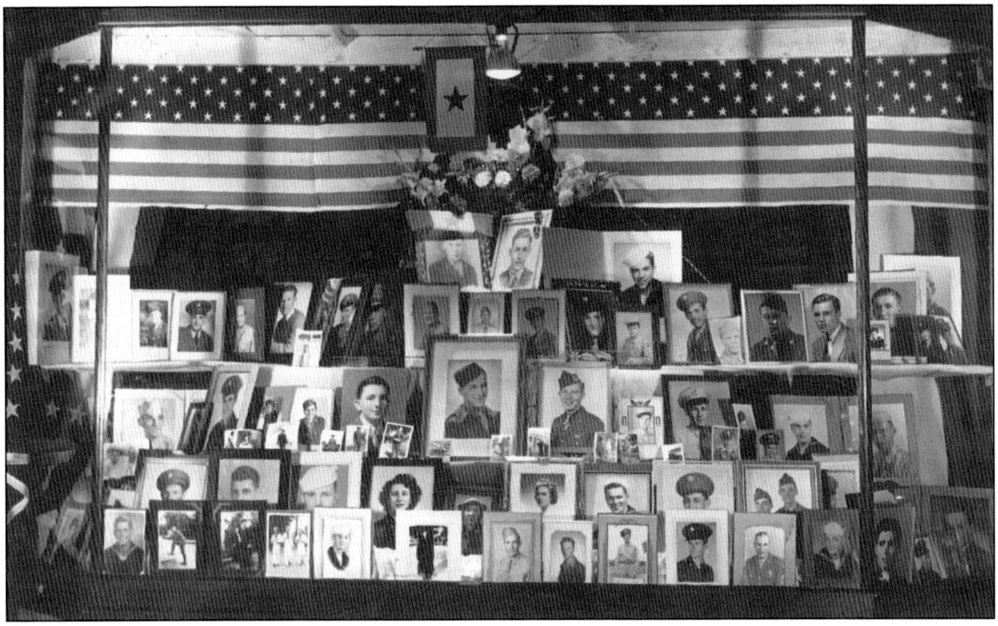

This corner window display at Ross' grocery store in 1943 included photographs of men and women from town who were serving in the armed forces during World War II. Willie Freda Ross started the display when her two boys, Jim and Norwood, went off to serve. (Courtesy of Liveria and Norwood Ross.)

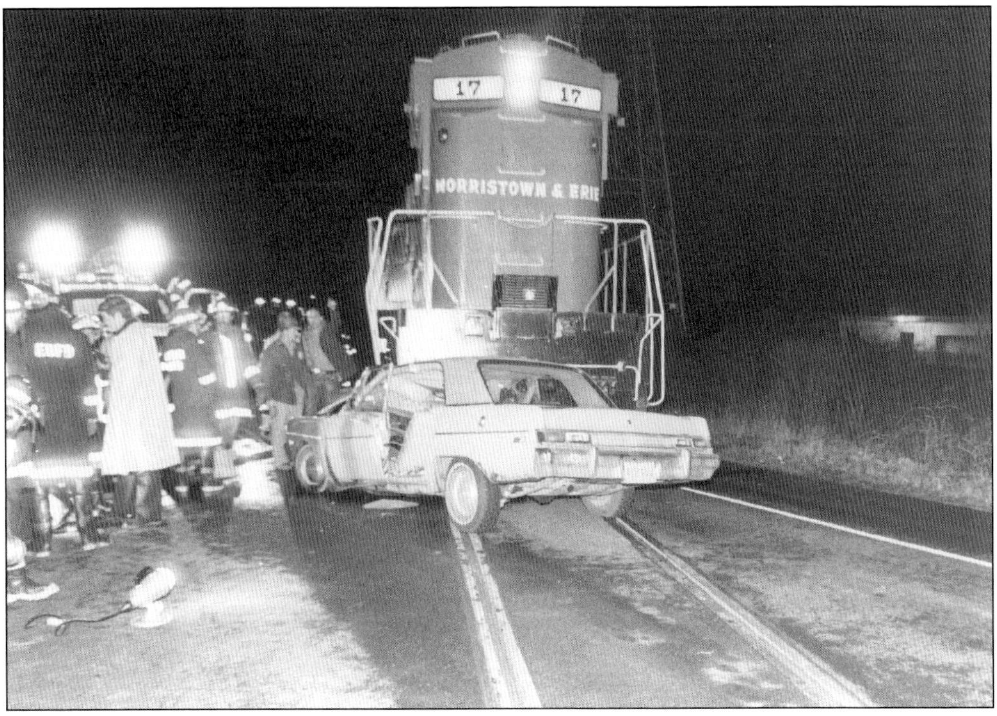

More than one car and train have collided at railroad crossings in town. Some of the accidents have been serious, like this one on Ridgedale Avenue. (Courtesy of the East Hanover Fire Department.)

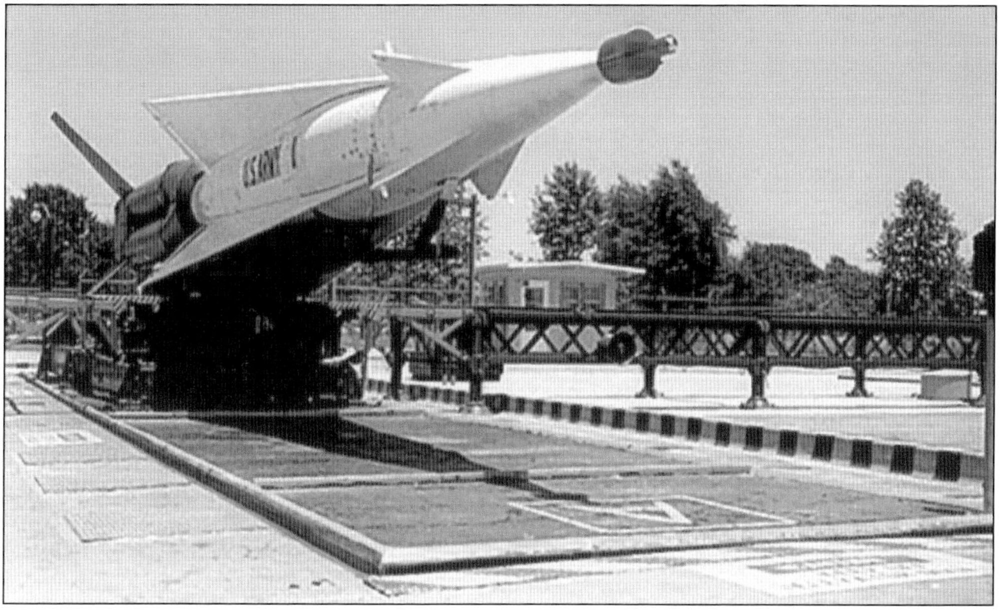

This gave new meaning to "Protecting the Township." East Hanover had its own supersonic, guided surface-to-air missile base. Nike site NY-80L (below) operated off River Road from 1954 to 1974. Built by the army, its purpose was to help defend the metropolitan area against the possibility of an air attack by long-range Soviet bombers. East Hanover stored the missiles and launch equipment; the operations center was located in Livingston. There were six underground missile magazines at the Nike launcher site in town. Each magazine could store either 10 Ajax missiles or six Hercules missiles. (An example of a Nike Hercules missile on its launcher is shown above, as it would have looked at the site, although this photograph was not taken in East Hanover.) The facility was patrolled 24 hours a day by armed guards. To everyone's good fortune, no missile was ever launched from East Hanover. (Above courtesy of the U.S. Army; below courtesy of Catherine Froling.)

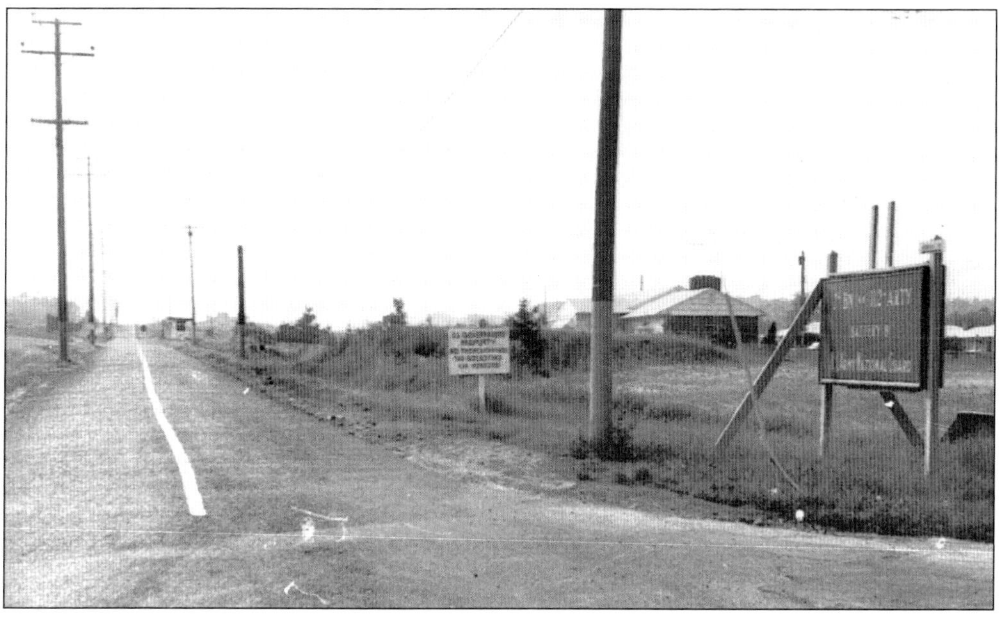

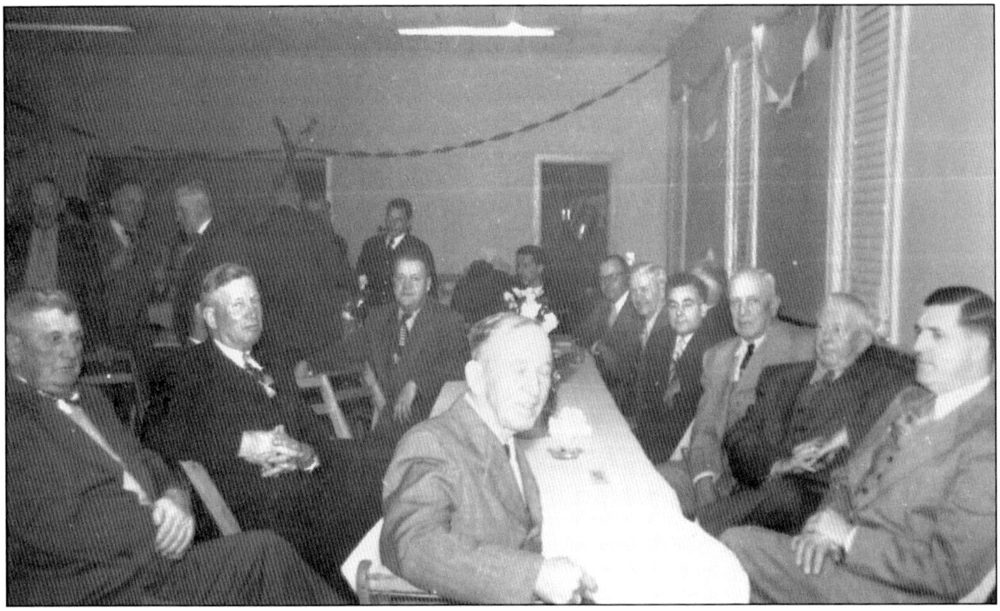

These are some of the volunteer firemen who helped protect East Hanover in the first half of the 20th century. They gathered for an old-timers' day celebration in 1949. Some of them had helped out in 1948 when a bad sleet storm knocked out power in town from January 2 through 10. Trees were down, roads blocked. The nursing home needed heat. (Courtesy of the East Hanover Fire Department.)

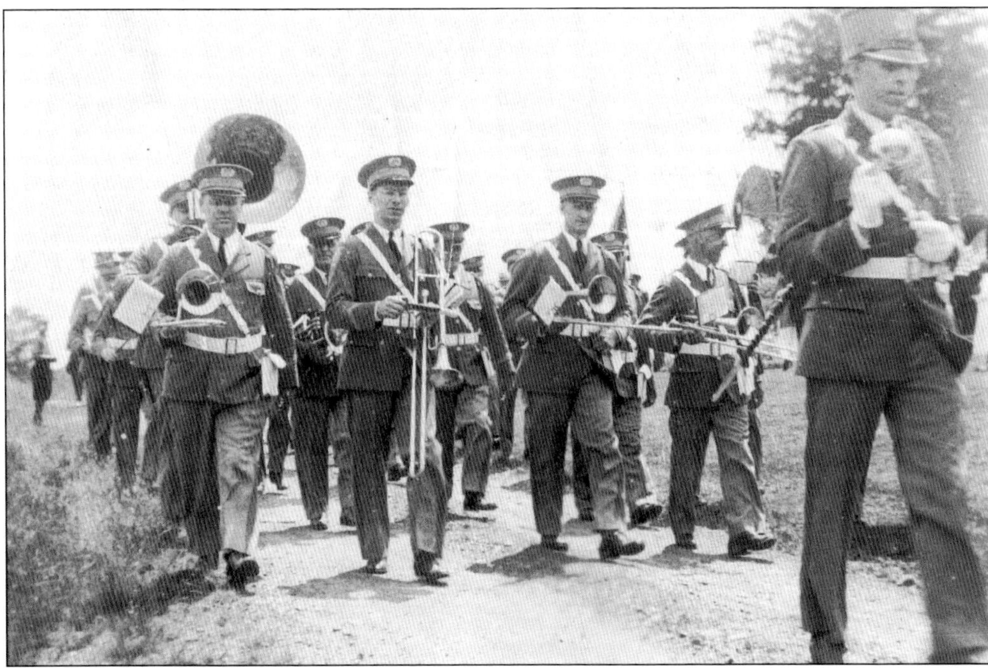

Some town parades long ago took a different route than they do today. They started at the Hanover Cemetery on Hanover Road, headed to Mount Pleasant Avenue, then to River Road. From there they traveled to Deforest Avenue and then north on Ridgedale Avenue to Central School. (Courtesy of Tom Iradi.)

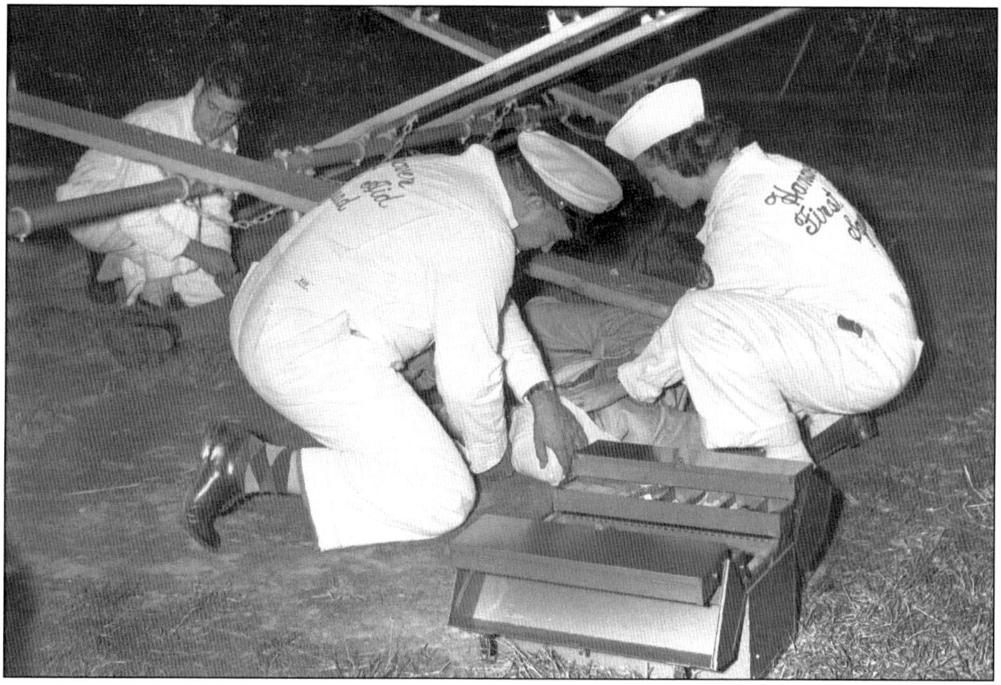

First-aid squad volunteers have donated their time and expertise since before this photograph was taken in October 1956. Drills like this one keep members up to date on life-saving techniques. Emergency calls have increased significantly over the years with the population and business growth of the town. (Courtesy of Lyla Brumbaugh and the East Hanover First Aid Squad.)

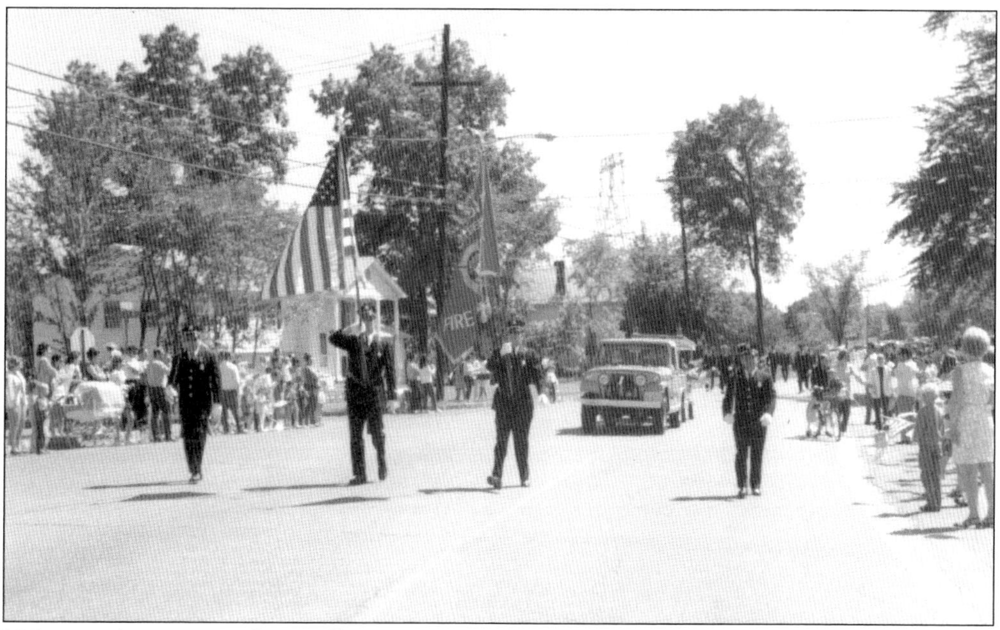

Volunteer firemen march proudly in a Memorial Day parade along Ridgedale Avenue. Parades in these days started near Chicjon Lane, marched south on Ridgedale, and ended at Central School. (Courtesy of the East Hanover Fire Department.)

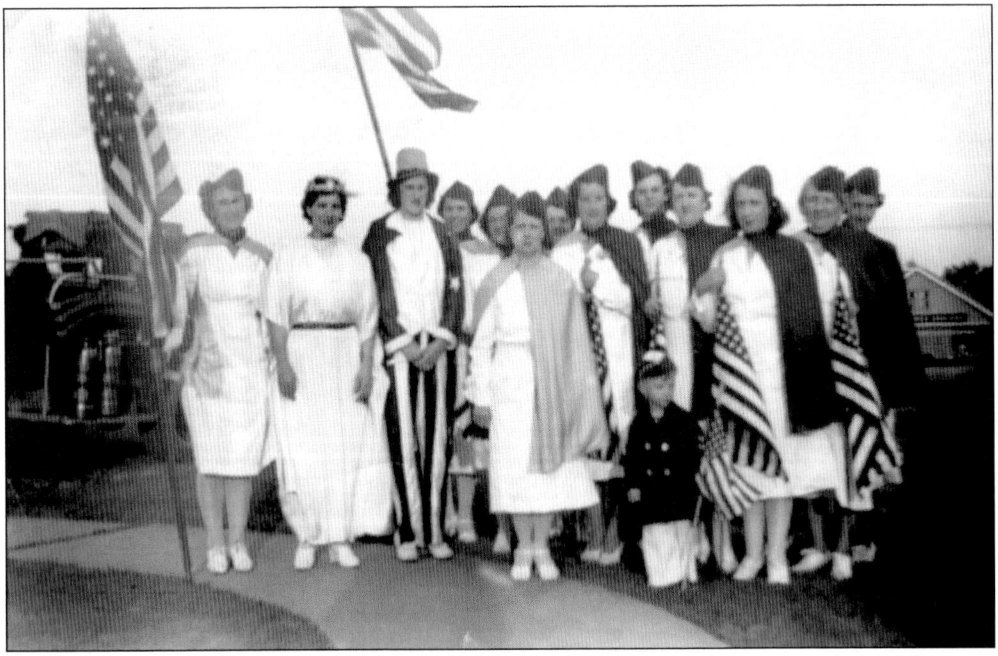

Members of the Daughters of America, a women's civic organization, are shown during a Memorial Day parade on Ridgedale Avenue. Many different groups have participated in the annual parade over the years. (Courtesy of Lee Dixon.)

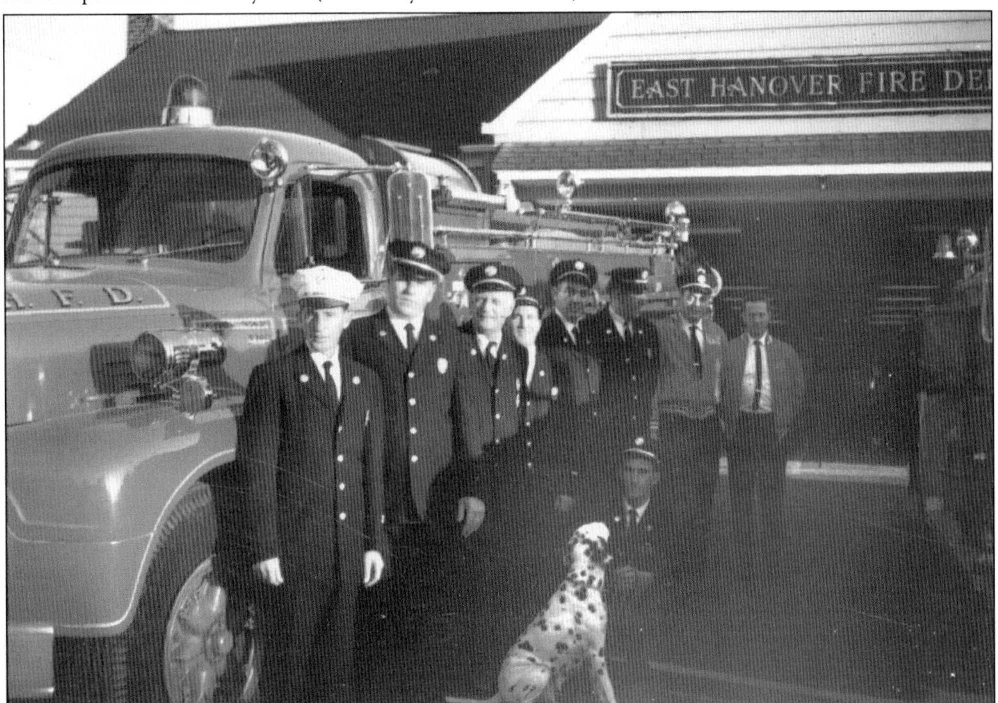

Fire department volunteers show off a new truck at the old firehouse. The department has since purchased increasingly sophisticated equipment to keep up with the needs of the growing township. (Courtesy of the East Hanover Fire Department.)

Five

GOING TO SCHOOL

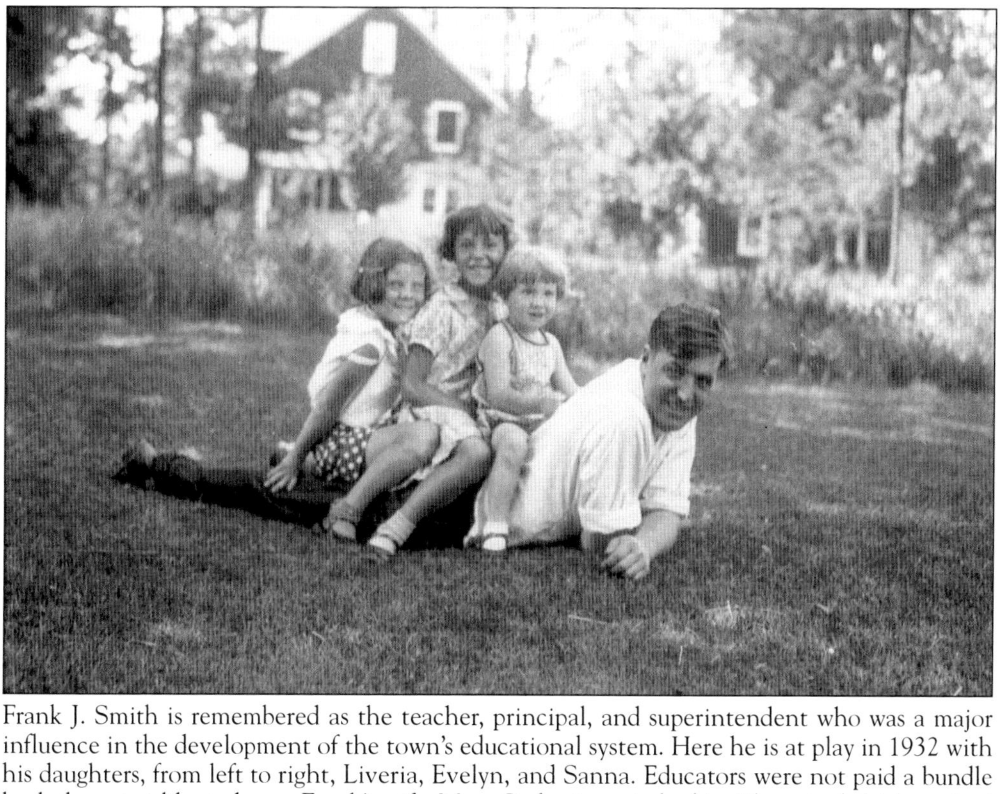

Frank J. Smith is remembered as the teacher, principal, and superintendent who was a major influence in the development of the town's educational system. Here he is at play in 1932 with his daughters, from left to right, Liveria, Evelyn, and Sanna. Educators were not paid a bundle back then, just like today, so Frank's wife, Mary Catherine, pitched in. She raised chickens, had an egg route, and grew flowers to help support the family. (Courtesy of Evelyn and Jim Ross.)

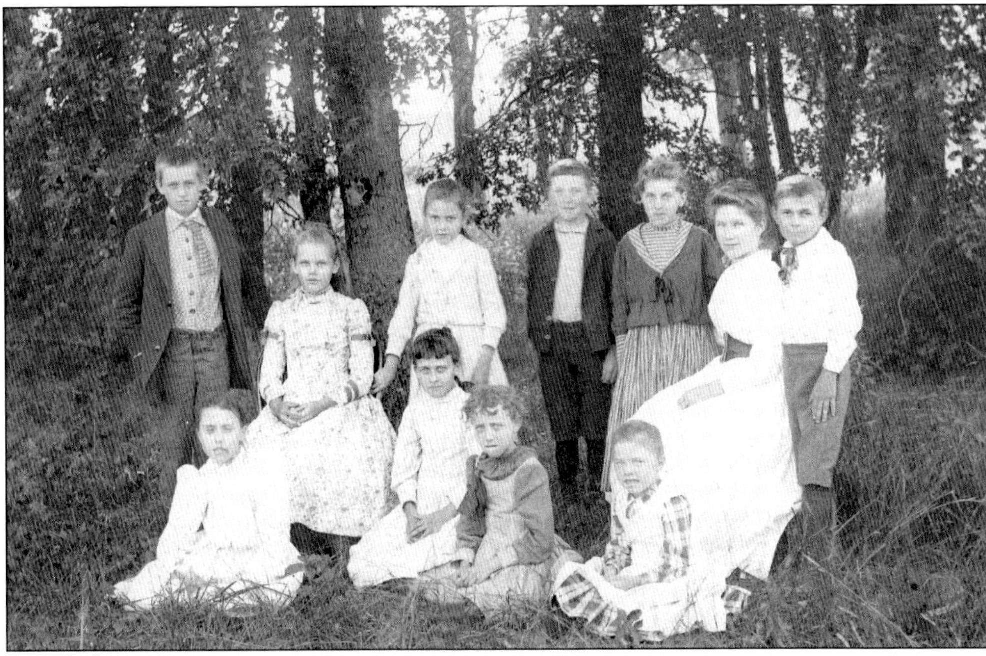

These students would soon be studying geography, writing, spelling, arithmetic, and grammar after this class photograph from the Hanover Neck School was taken in 1890. Shown, from left to right, are the following: (sitting) Lottie Young, Susan Cutter, Lorena Rickey, Frances Hicks, and Sarah Sisco; (standing) Harry Pruden, Lizzie Hicks, Vance Sisco, Ada Dixon, Miss Mutchler, and Wallace Hendy. (Courtesy of Don Courter.)

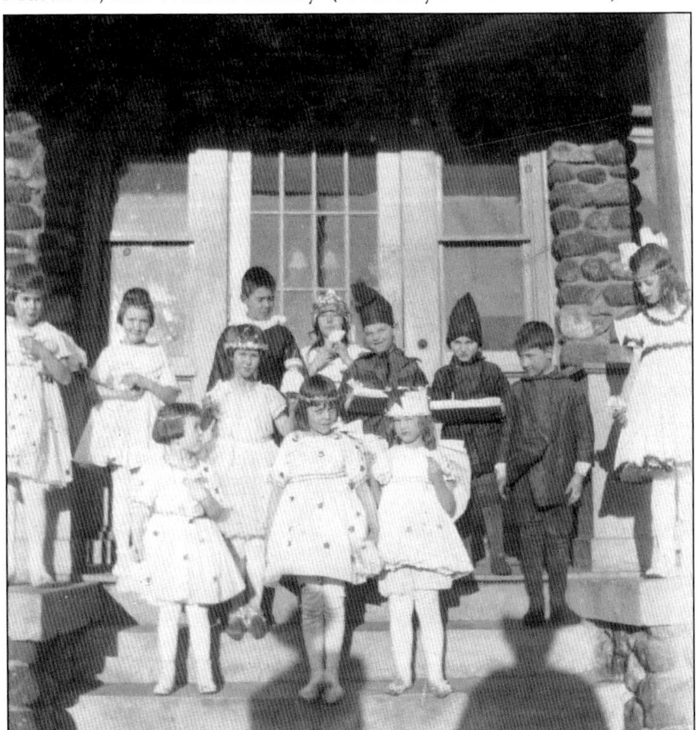

Teachers made the costumes for this class play at Cobblestone School *c.* 1922. The school had been built seven years earlier. (Courtesy of Edna and Henry Zaleski.)

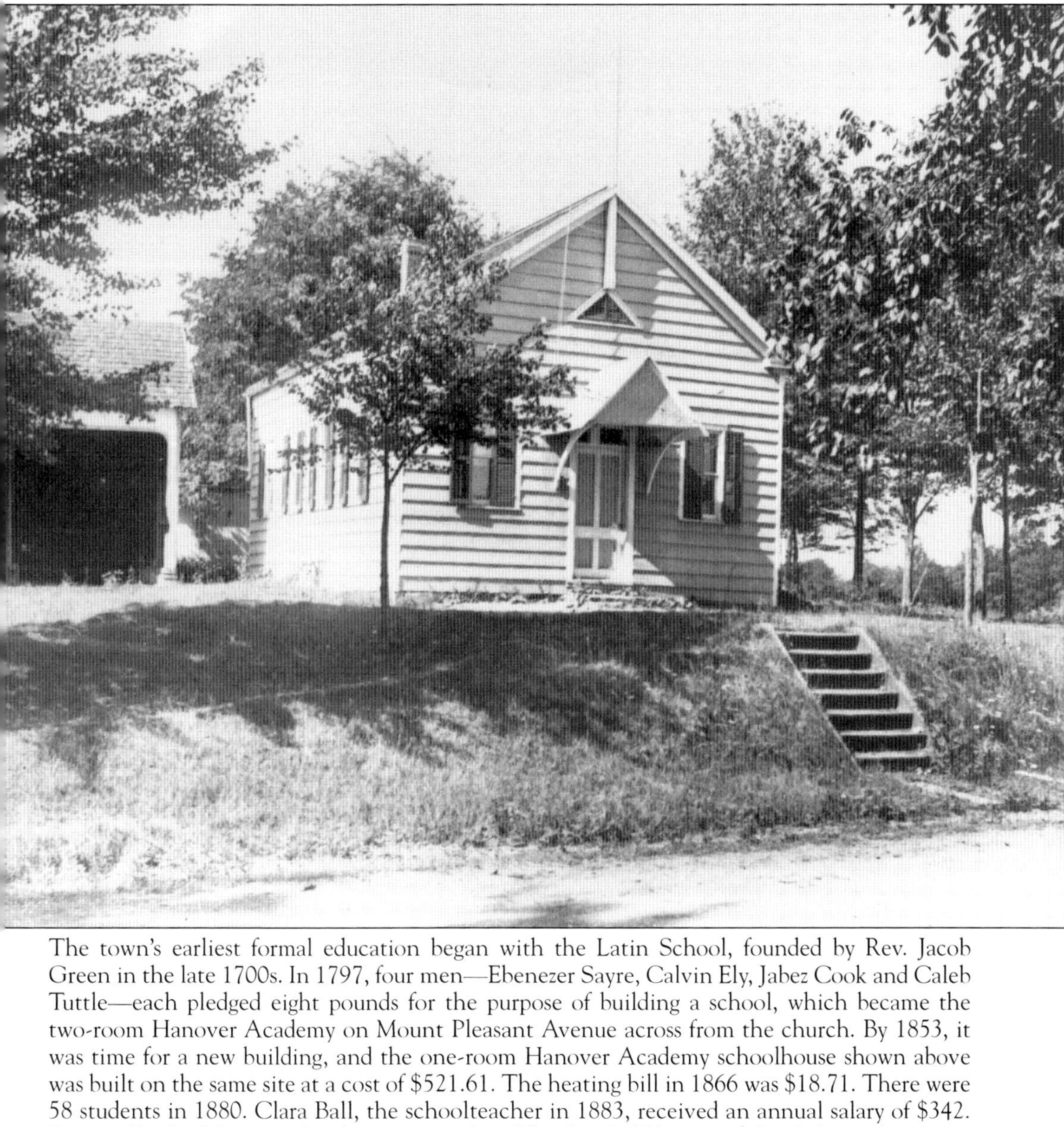

The town's earliest formal education began with the Latin School, founded by Rev. Jacob Green in the late 1700s. In 1797, four men—Ebenezer Sayre, Calvin Ely, Jabez Cook and Caleb Tuttle—each pledged eight pounds for the purpose of building a school, which became the two-room Hanover Academy on Mount Pleasant Avenue across from the church. By 1853, it was time for a new building, and the one-room Hanover Academy schoolhouse shown above was built on the same site at a cost of $521.61. The heating bill in 1866 was $18.71. There were 58 students in 1880. Clara Ball, the schoolteacher in 1883, received an annual salary of $342. Eventually the Hanover Academy was replaced by the Cobblestone School down the street. (Courtesy of the East Hanover Historical Society.)

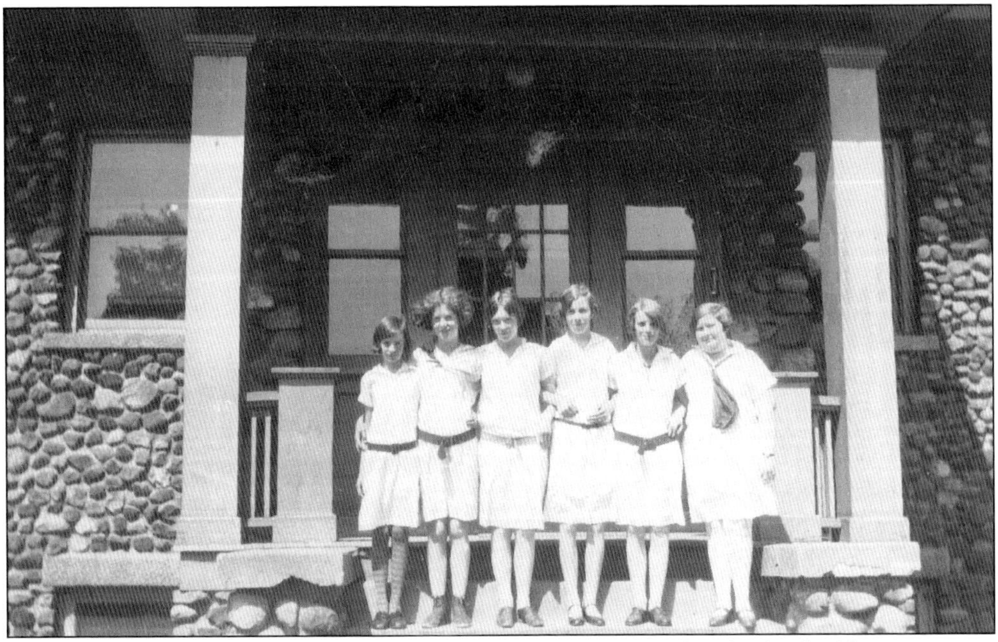

This is an early photograph of students at the Cobblestone School. The building is unique in that most of the exterior is made from the naturally rounded stones. It is now home to the town's senior citizen's club. (Courtesy of Don Courter.)

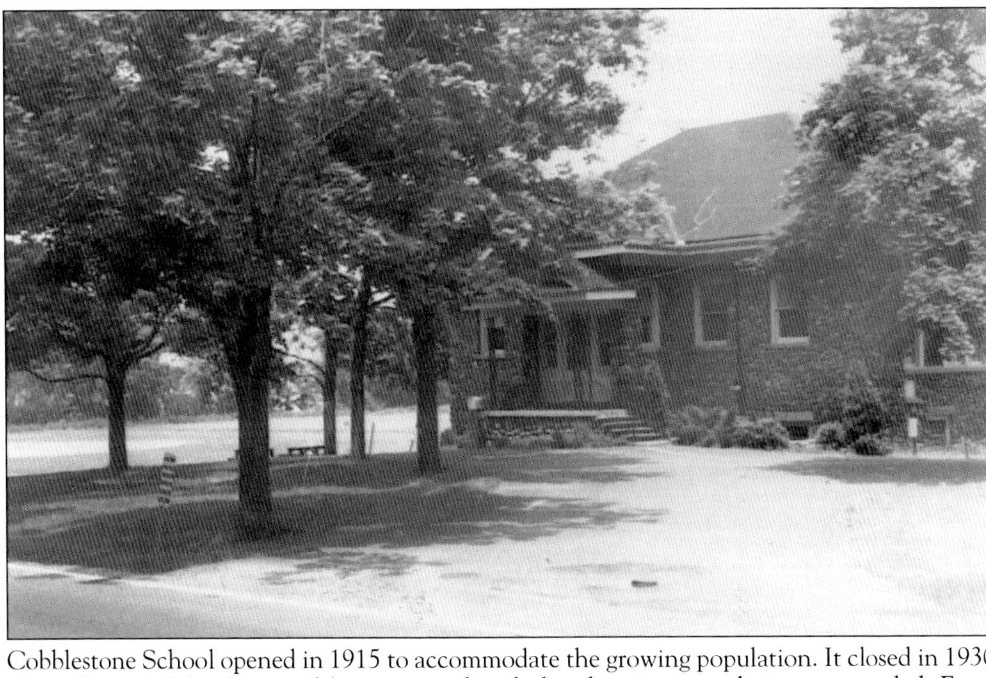

Cobblestone School opened in 1915 to accommodate the growing population. It closed in 1930 when Central School opened but reopened and closed again several times as needed. For a time in the 1930s, it was rented to the Florham Park School system. Later it became the Helen Kingsley School. (Courtesy of Catherine Froling.)

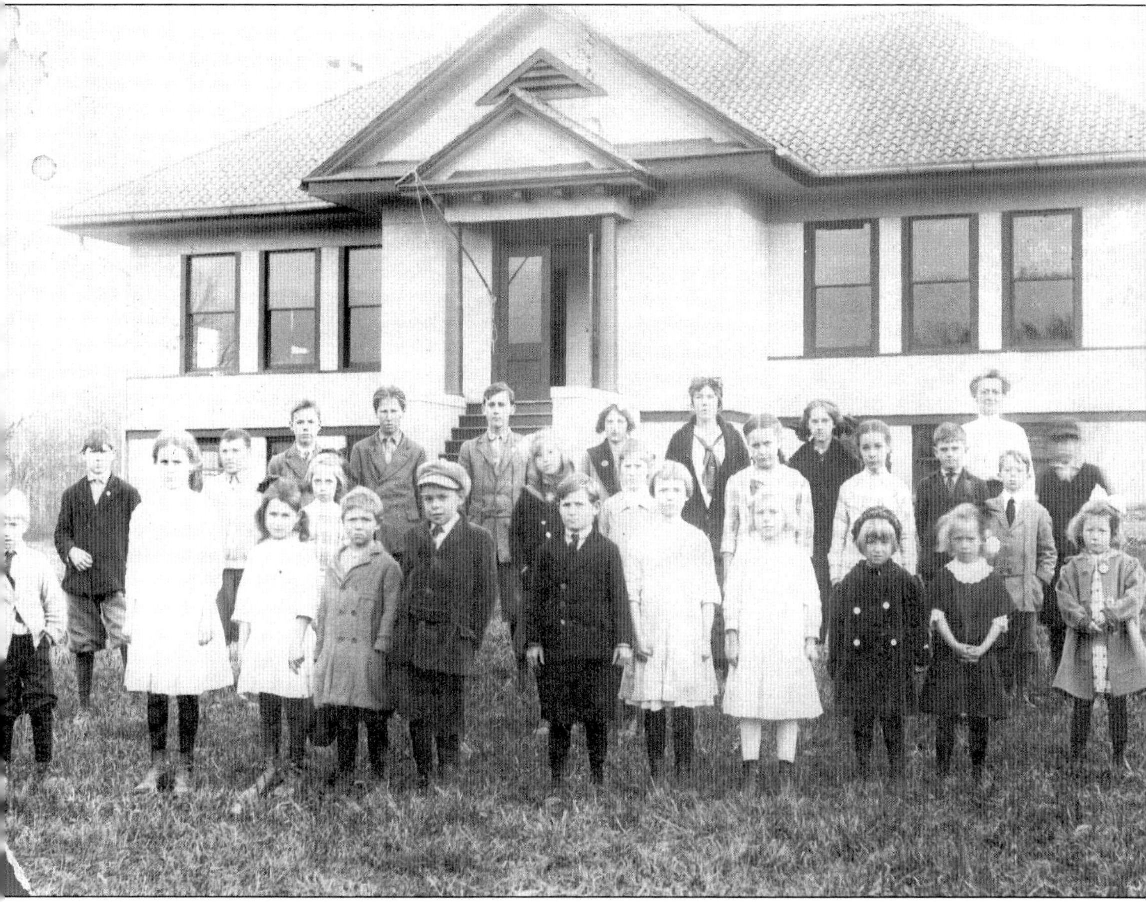

Students at the then-new Hanover Neck School pose in front of the schoolhouse that was built in 1911. The first Hanover Neck School was built on Ridgedale Avenue near Dixon Place in the early 1800s. People in the neighborhood donated the materials and built the 24- by 30-foot structure. A wood-burning fireplace heated the school in the winter. Desks were arranged facing the walls. The seats were planks with no backs. Children in the northern portion of town attended Hanover Neck. Some had to walk several miles to get there. Around 1840, a new owner of the property where the school stood was bothered by its presence, so the school was moved away from his house and closer to where this building is on School Avenue. There were 49 students by 1880. The school's hip roof with oriental-inspired broad flaring eaves is an architectural design more often found on train stations in that time period. (Courtesy of Don Courter.)

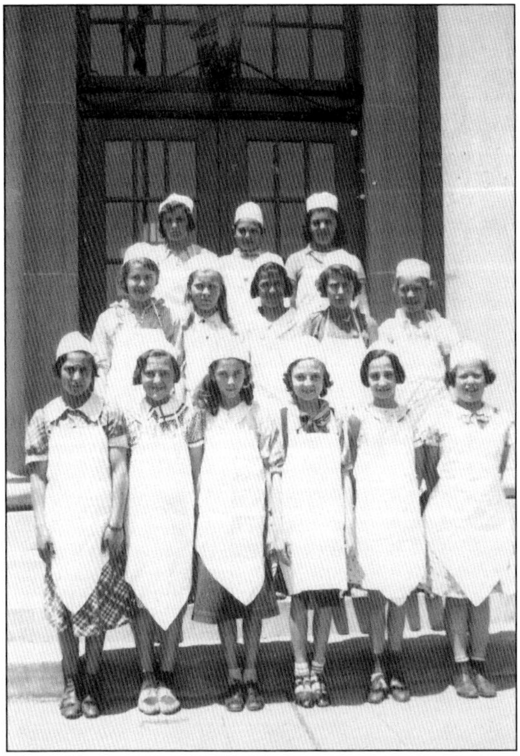

These culinary artists in training are students in the 1936 or 1937 cooking class at Central School. Class was held in the morning. Sometimes the students would help cafeteria personnel prepare the day's lunch for the school. (Courtesy of Evelyn and Jim Ross.)

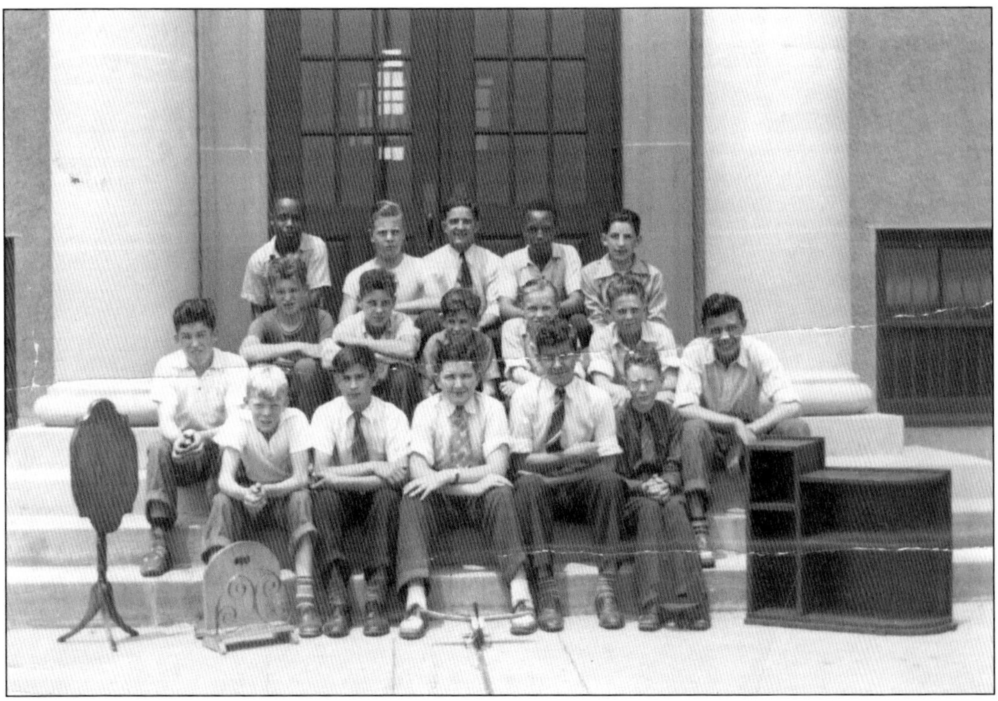

Students in the industrial arts class at Central School *c.* 1939 show off several of the projects they worked on during the year. They are sitting on the front steps of the school. (Courtesy of Evelyn and Jim Ross.)

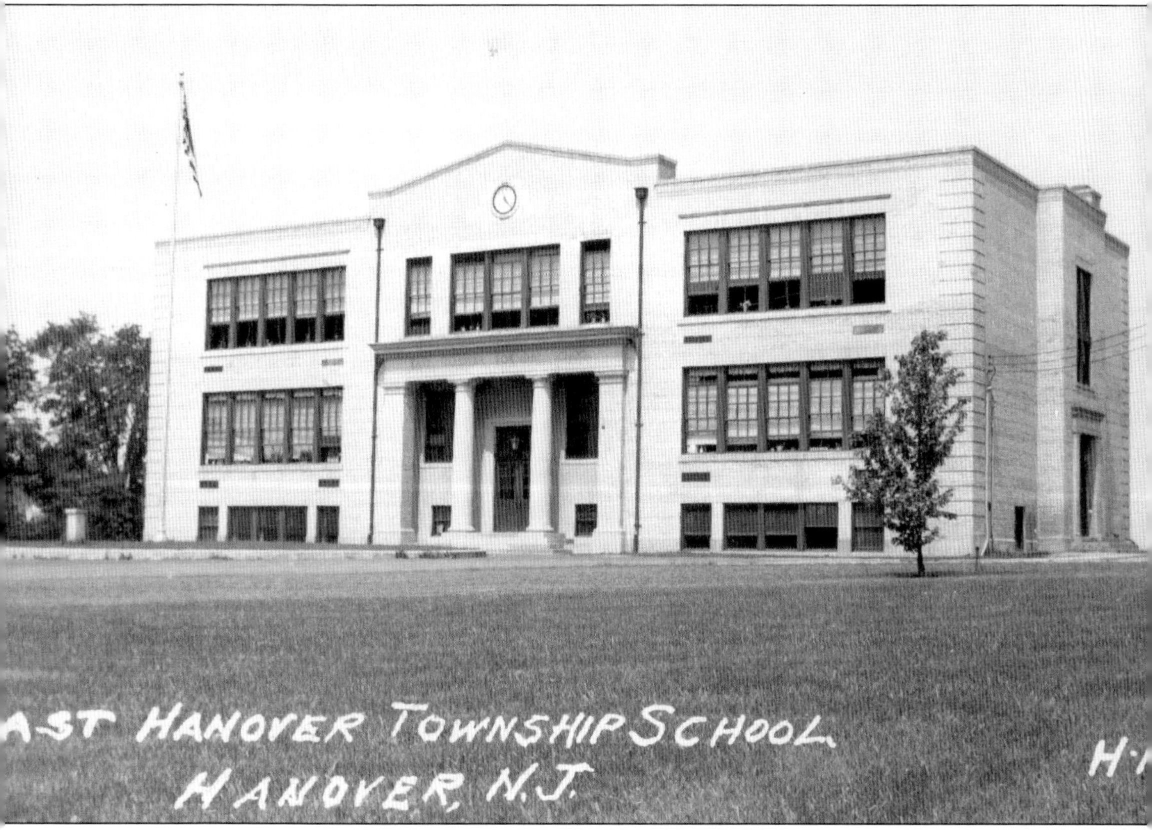

Construction on Central School began a year after the township was incorporated, and the one-story school opened in 1930. A second story was added in 1939, as shown in this postcard. More additions to the school came later. For a time, Central School included kindergarten through the ninth grade, but the ninth-grade class did not last long. Early school rules were clear on how students should behave: "Every pupil is expected to attend school punctually and regularly; to conform to the regulations of the school, and obey promptly all the directions of the teacher; to observe good order and propriety of deportment, to be diligent in study, respectful to teachers, kind and obliging to classmates; to refrain from the use of profane and vulgar language, to be clean in person and clothing." (Courtesy of Evelyn and Jim Ross.)

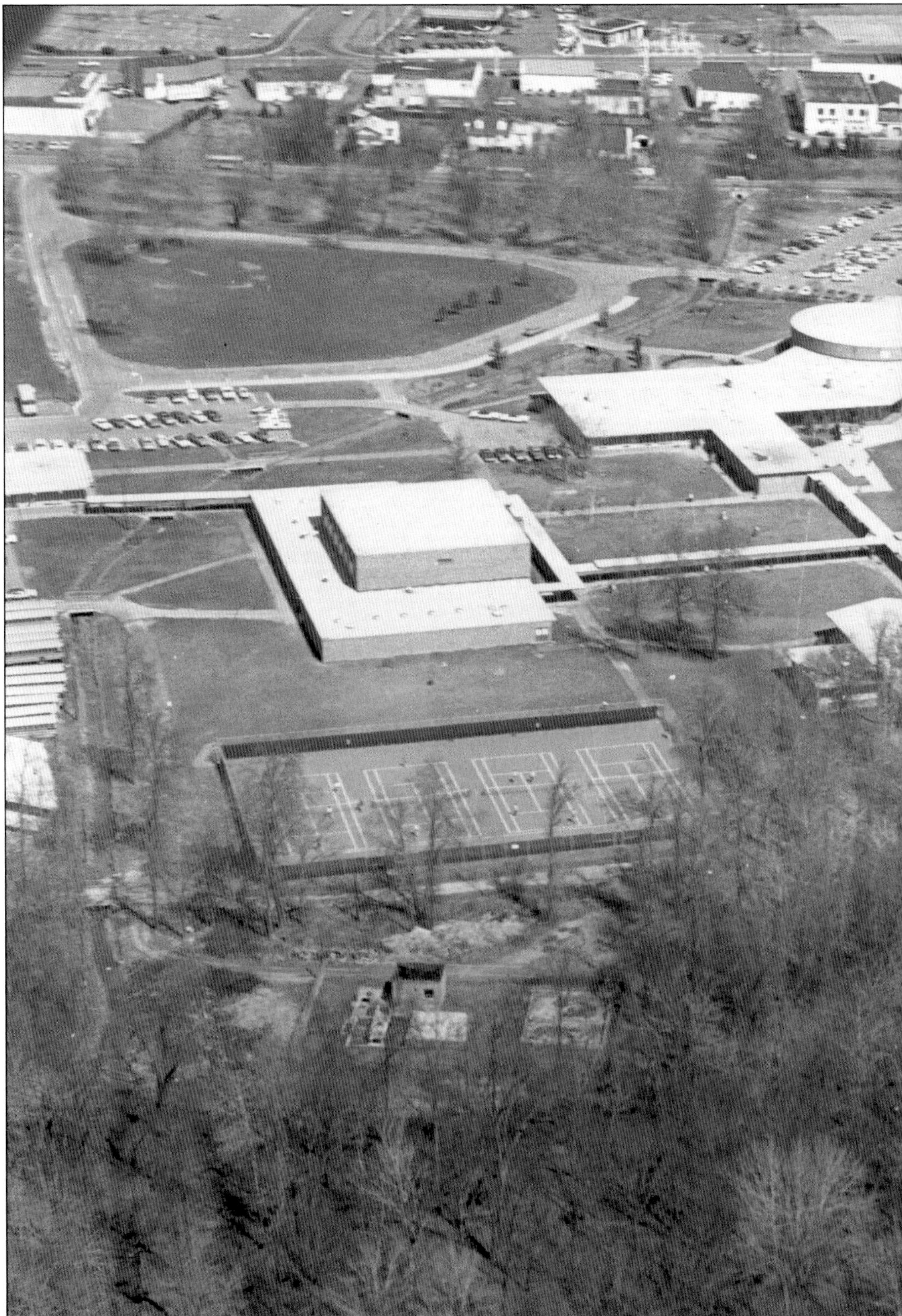

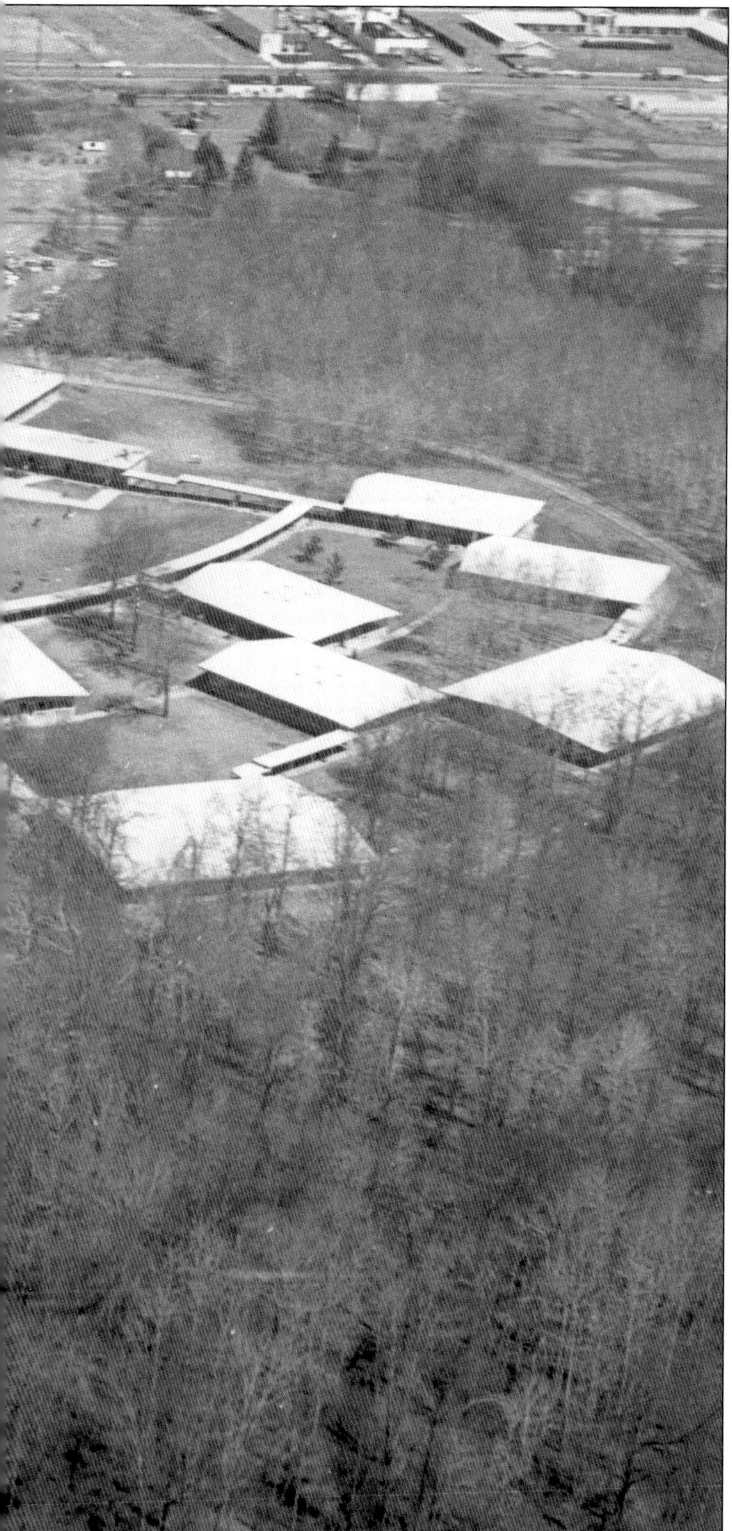

The Hanover Park Regional High School District commenced December 11, 1953, when voters from East Hanover, Hanover Township, and Florham Park elected to join as a region. The first day of school on the campus of Hanover Park was November 24, 1956. For the first few months of that term, students temporarily went to school at Madison High School and the Ridgedale School in Florham Park. Before Hanover Park was built, East Hanover high school students had gone to Madison, and before that some attended in Caldwell. Construction of Hanover Park's innovative campus-style buildings began on June 25, 1955, and was completed in February 1958. The inaugural graduating class of 99 students accepted their diplomas in 1958. (Courtesy of the East Hanover Fire Department.)

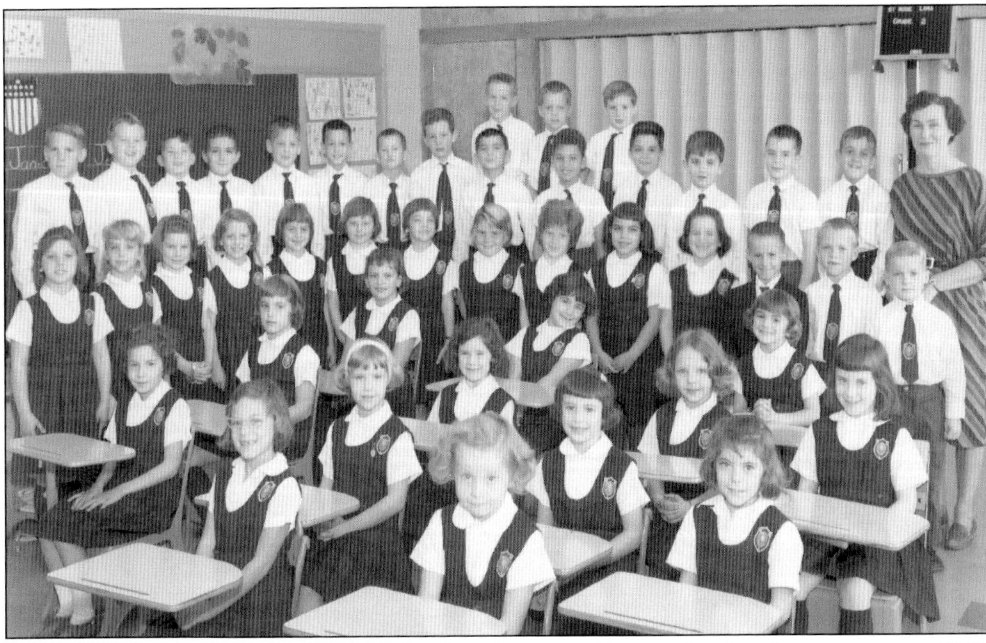

Second-graders at St. Rose of Lima School enthusiastically pose for the photographer in 1965. Sisters from St. Joseph of Newark staffed the new school in 1961. Sister Regina Agnes, Superior, was originally assigned to the parish along with Sisters Augustine and Camille. (Courtesy of Anthony and Anne Pellecchia.)

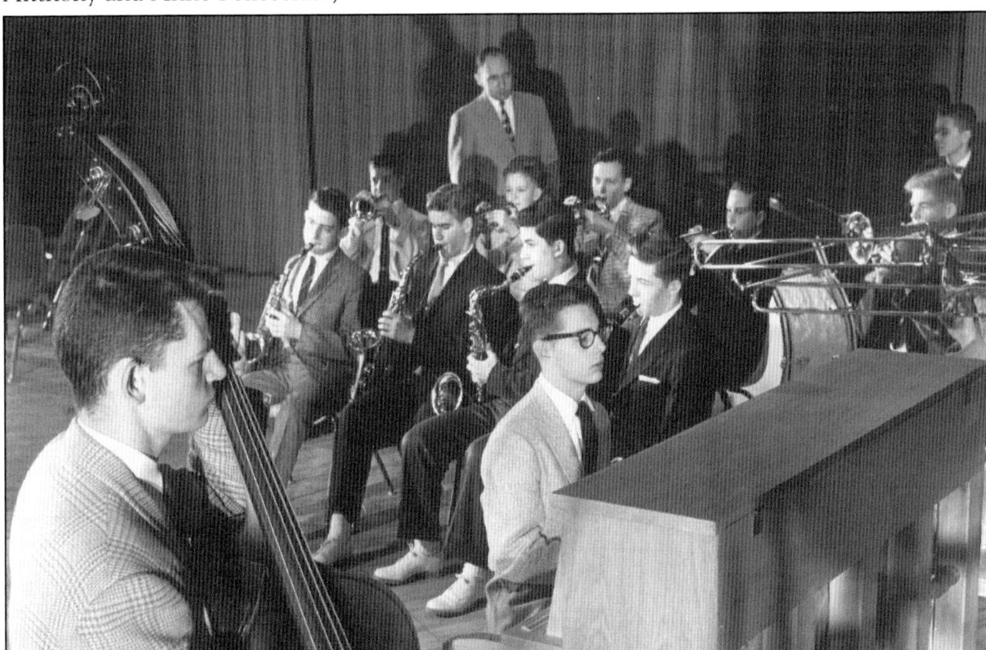

Hanover Park's 1957–1958 dance band included B. Daly (bass violin); L. Chegwidden (piano); C. Sharpe, G. Beach, B. Cestone, and B. Livingston (saxophone); B. Mottram, G. Allen, D. Kreck, and R. Pojedenic (trumpet); C. Weis, R. Goodenow, and D. Kitchell (trombone); and A. Motter (drums). Mr. Kreutzer is the teacher. (Courtesy of Hanover Park High School.)

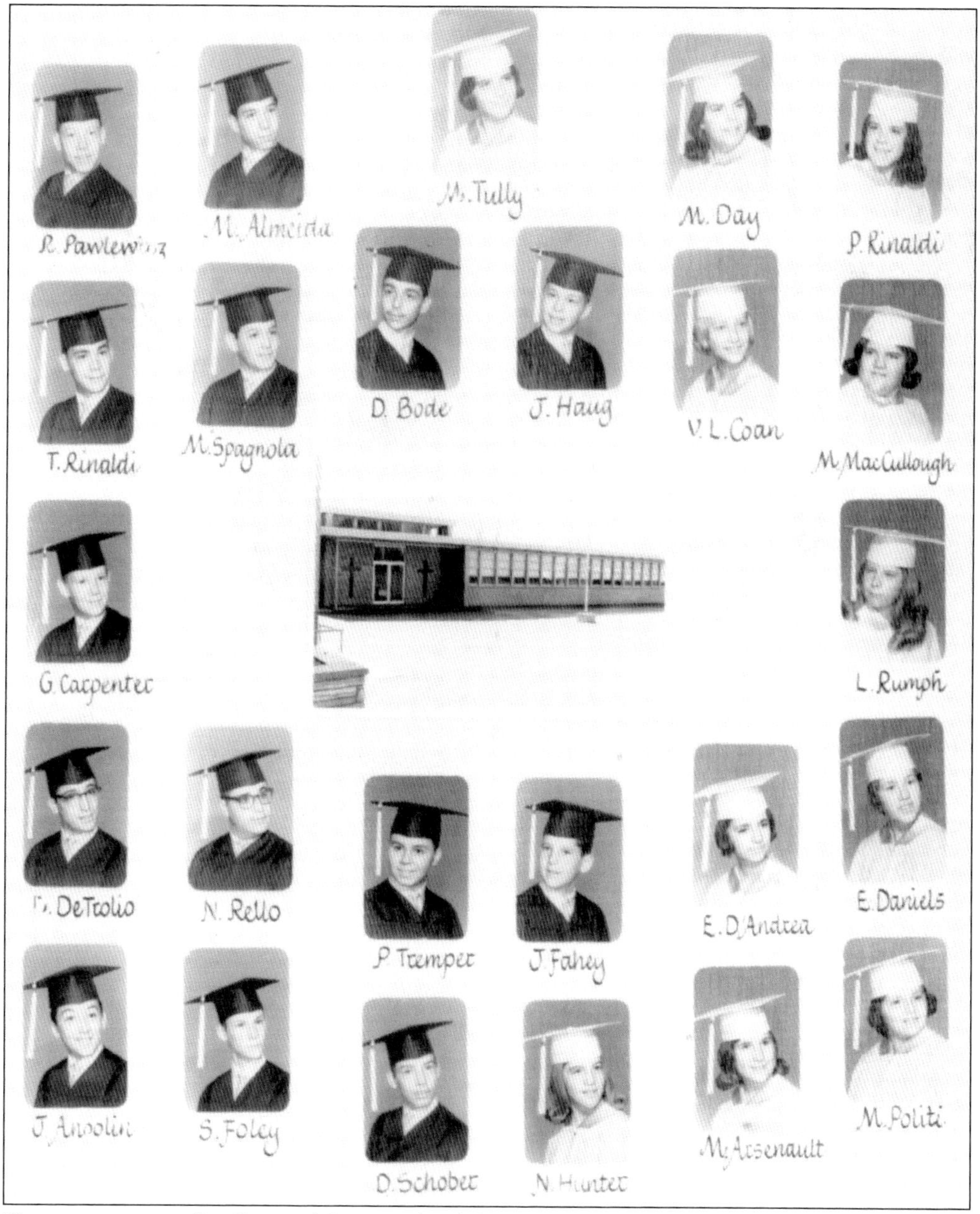

Construction on St. Rose of Lima School began in June 1961. When school started in September, the building was not yet completed, so classes were held in the church basement. By December, the construction was finished and the school opened one week before Christmas 1961. Shown is the St. Rose of Lima School graduating class of 1967. (Courtesy of St. Rose of Lima Academy.)

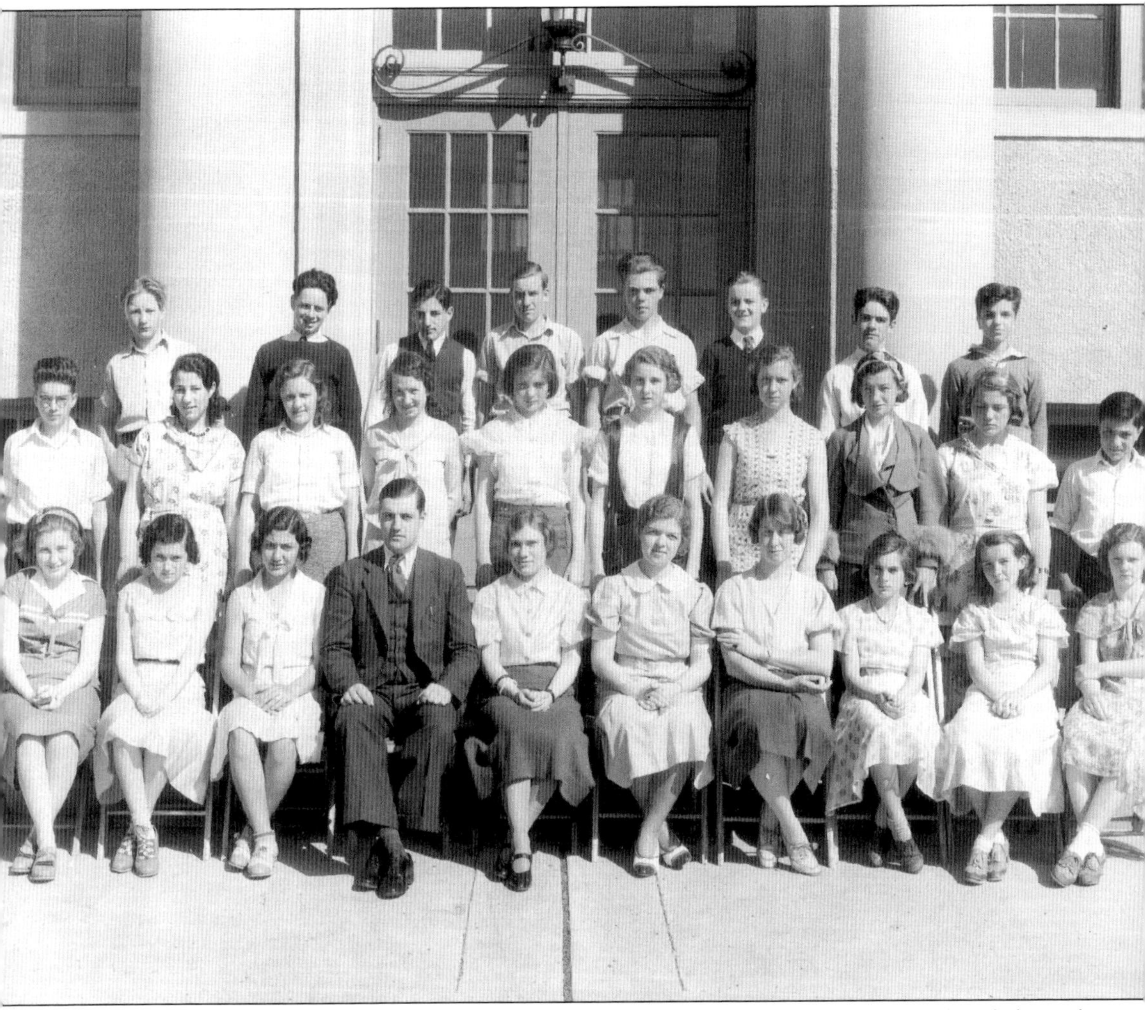

Principal Frank J. Smith is seated in the front row of the 1933 Central School eighth-grade graduating class. Pictured above are, from left to right, the following: (front row) Helen Horton, Marie Wingard, Lucille Iradi, Frank J. Smith, Phyllis Klinger, Lucille Claus, Elizabeth Van Suan, Jane Munther, Mildred Lake, and Lillian Gray; (middle row) Robert Smith, Ida Vanacore, Lettie Hansen, Anna Timmons, June Hiller, Florence Sorg, Frances Stenger, Helen Boehm, Weetona Kredel, and Anthony Grasso; (back row) Joe Hoffman, Richard Diehl, Frank Ferraiuolo, George Baureis, Ted Dixon, Charles Teats, George Brown, and Robert Busto. (Courtesy of Weetona Hobby.)

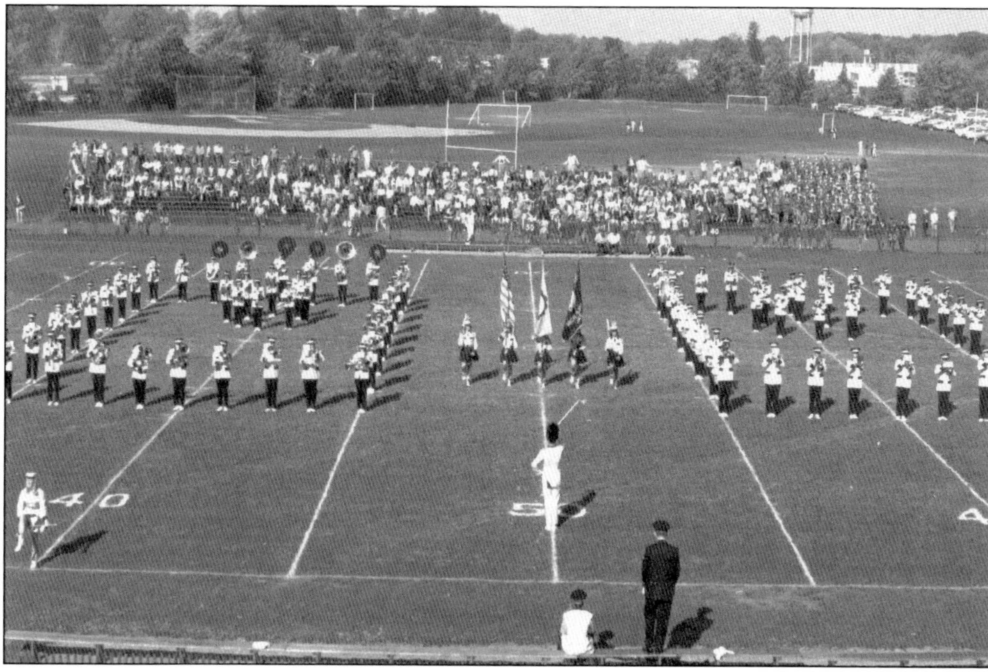

The 1961–1962 Gold Hornets Marching Band and Color Guard perform on the high school football field as spectators look on from the visitors' bleachers. Band and chorus members practiced during workshop period. Other students used workshops as a study hall. (Courtesy of Hanover Park High School.)

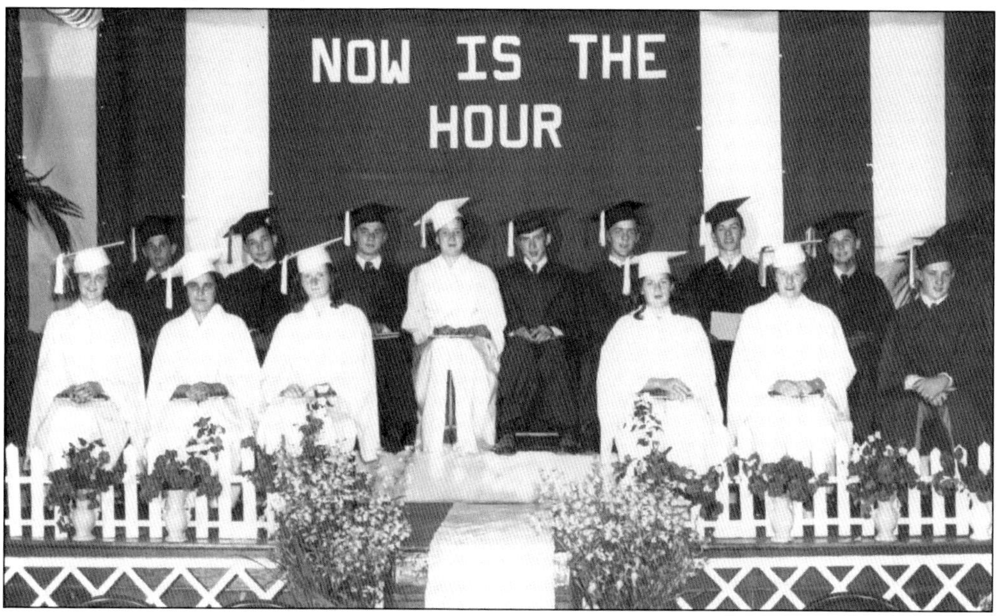

"Now is the Hour" was the motto for the 1948 graduating class of Central School. The graduates included, in alphabetical order, Janet Louise Brunner, Ronald John Hadley, Mary Ann Hetterly, Charles Lods, Mila Malackov, Mary Marcantonio, James Arthur Miller, Richard Nicholson, Francis Eric Norman, Jeffery Graham Norman, Daniel O'Neill, Henry Poole, Sylvia Jean Poole, Ellen Doris Schuler, and Gerald Witwick. (Courtesy of Ken Hadley.)

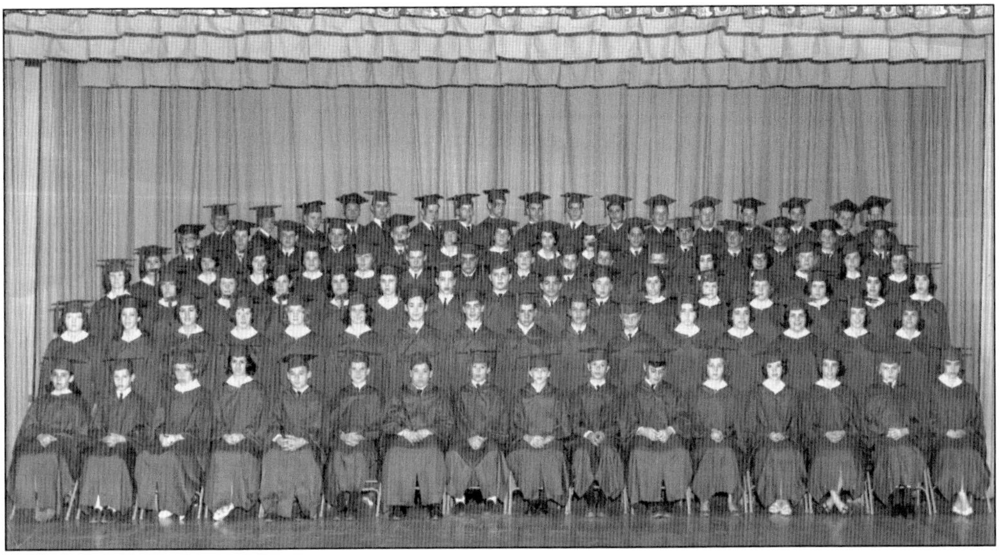

These eighth-graders were getting ready to sing "I Believe" at their Central School graduation in 1964. This class went on to be the 1968 graduating class of Hanover Park High School, the last class to include students from East Hanover, Florham Park, and Hanover Township. (Courtesy of Jack Horner Studios.)

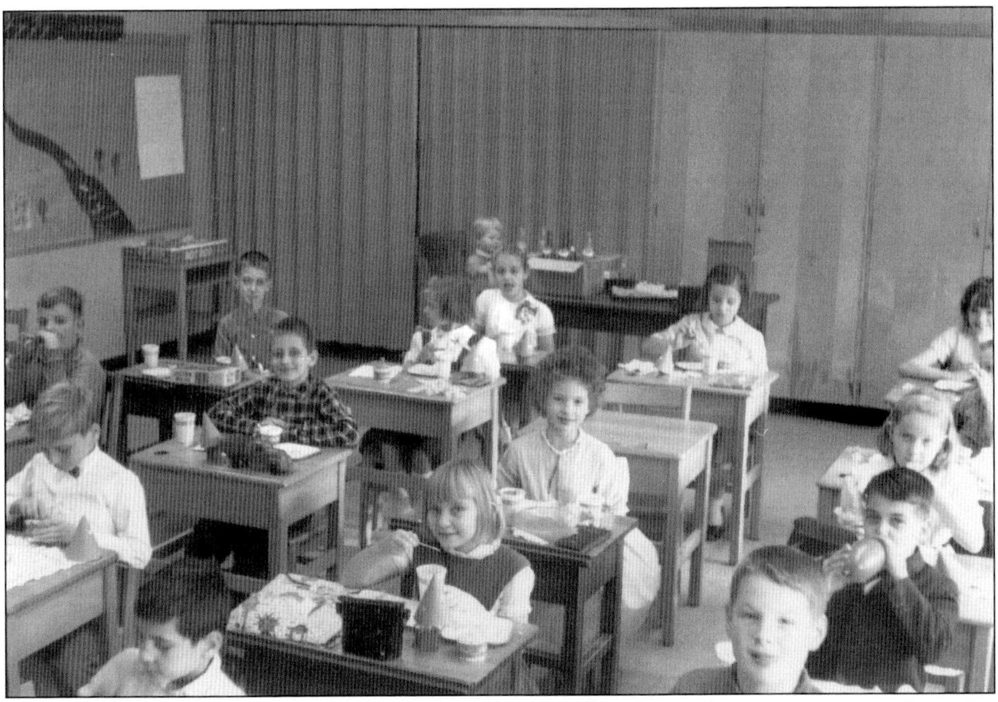

Their desks are filled with materials as these local students wait for an assignment from the teacher during a class c. 1960. Some of the desks had holes in the upper corners where ink bottles were placed long, long ago. (Courtesy of Bill Shrader.)

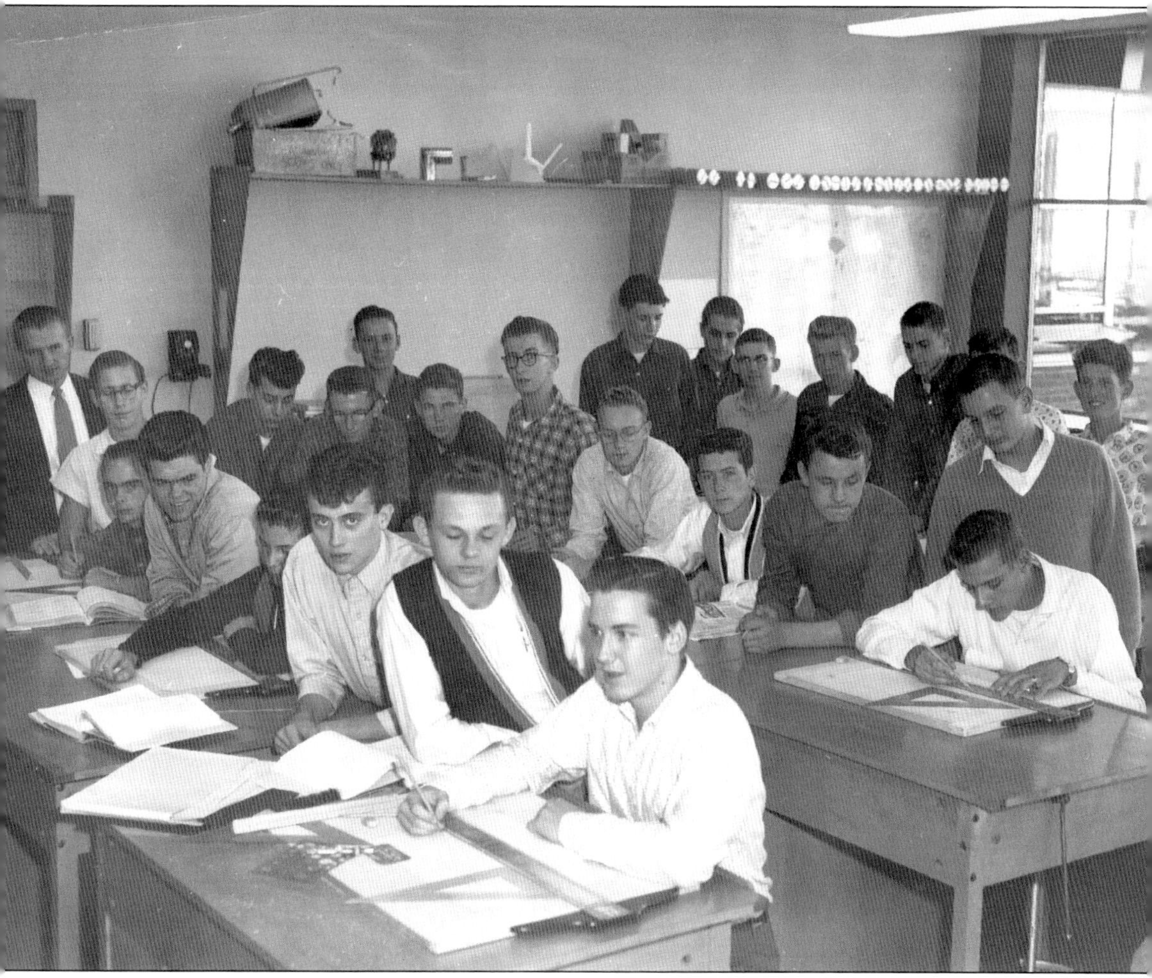

Adrian Vanderdoes keeps an eye on these appropriately dressed mechanical drawing students at Hanover Park. The original dress code for boys included: "Only the collar button of a shirt may be unbuttoned. Socks must be worn at all times. Sandals may be worn provided they are worn with socks. No shorts, work pants or dungarees with rivets may be worn. No T-shirts or sweatshirts may be worn as outer garments. Hair must be will groomed and neat." Girls' rules included: "No slacks, shorts or overskirts while classes are in session. Skirts and dresses are not to be worn more than two inches above the top of the knee cap. [Administrators were known to carry rulers to measure the length.] Culottes may be worn but must conform to the above length and must look like a skirt or dress while standing. Hair must present a neat, well groomed appearance." The general rules were: "Students should not indulge in unusual haircuts or styles and should not wear jewelry or ornamentation in bad taste." (Courtesy of Hanover Park High School.)

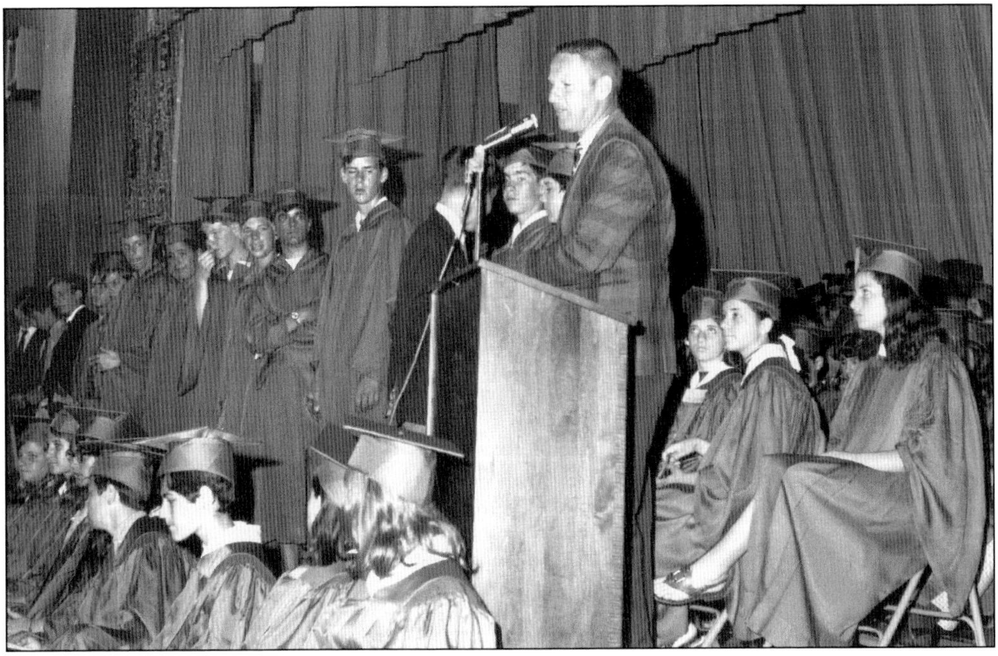

Bill Shrader helped countless local boys begin developing their athletic skills and start getting into shape. He was the boys' gym teacher and coach at Central School and then Middle School from 1955 to 1984. Shrader is shown presenting athletic awards during a graduation ceremony at Central School. (Courtesy of Bill Shrader.)

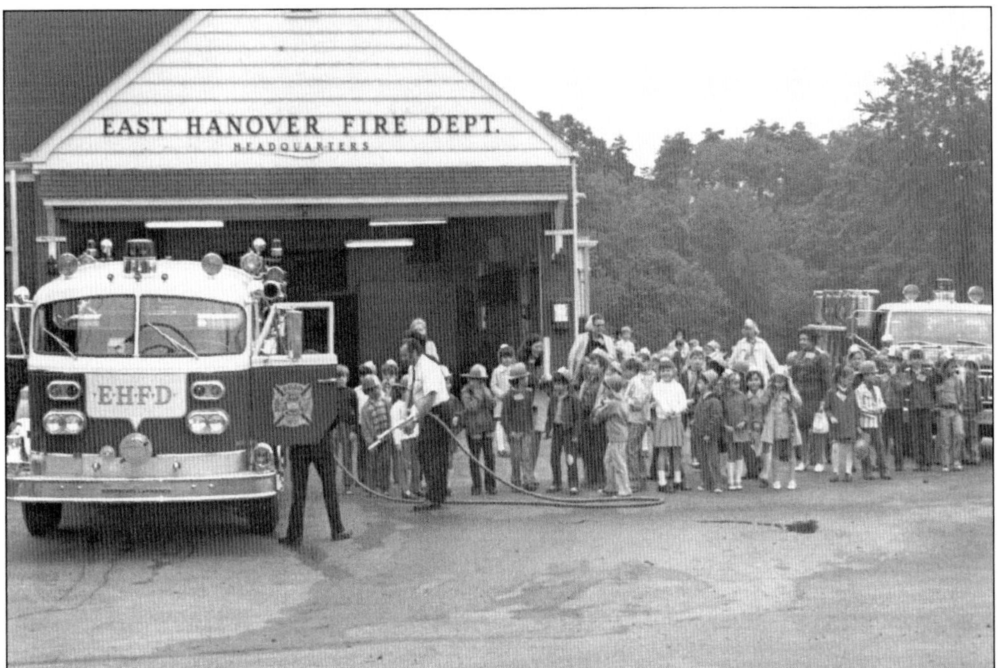

Students line up during a field trip to the former fire headquarters during Fire Prevention Week. Firemen have offered this important instruction to youngsters at the schools and the station for many years. (Courtesy of the East Hanover Fire Department.)

Six

SPORTS AND LEISURE

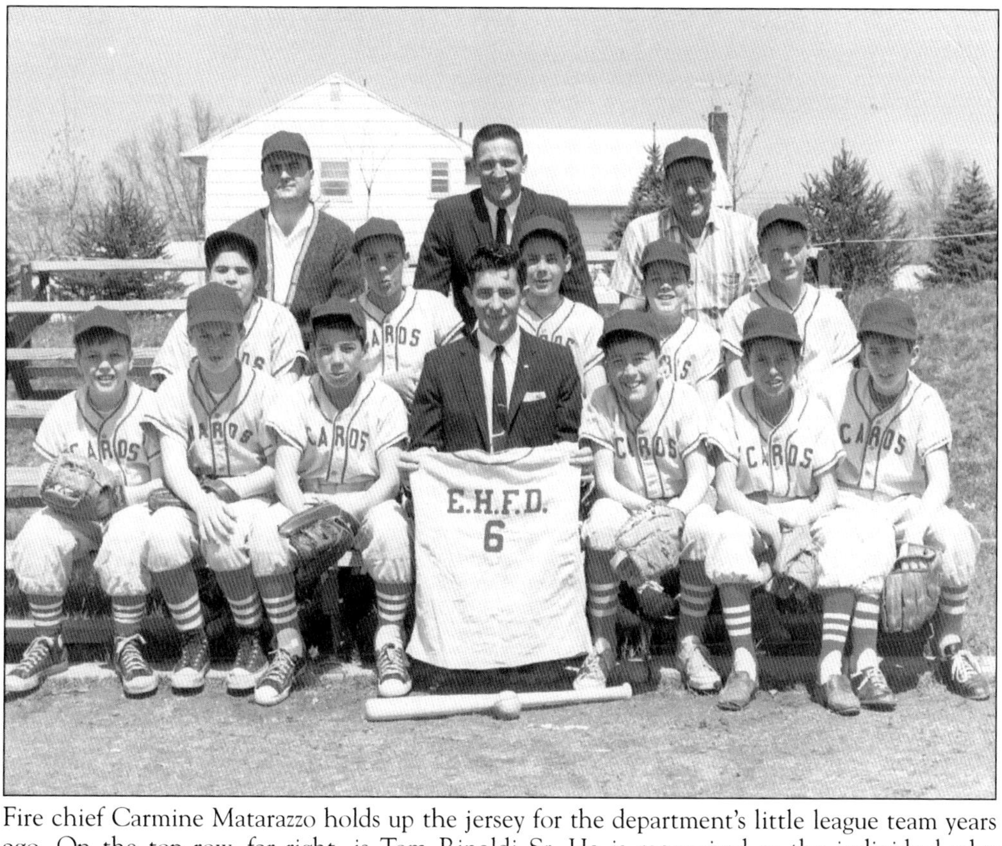

Fire chief Carmine Matarazzo holds up the jersey for the department's little league team years ago. On the top row, far right, is Tom Rinaldi Sr. He is recognized as the individual who developed the town's fledgling recreation program into a top-notch organization. (Courtesy of the East Hanover Fire Department.)

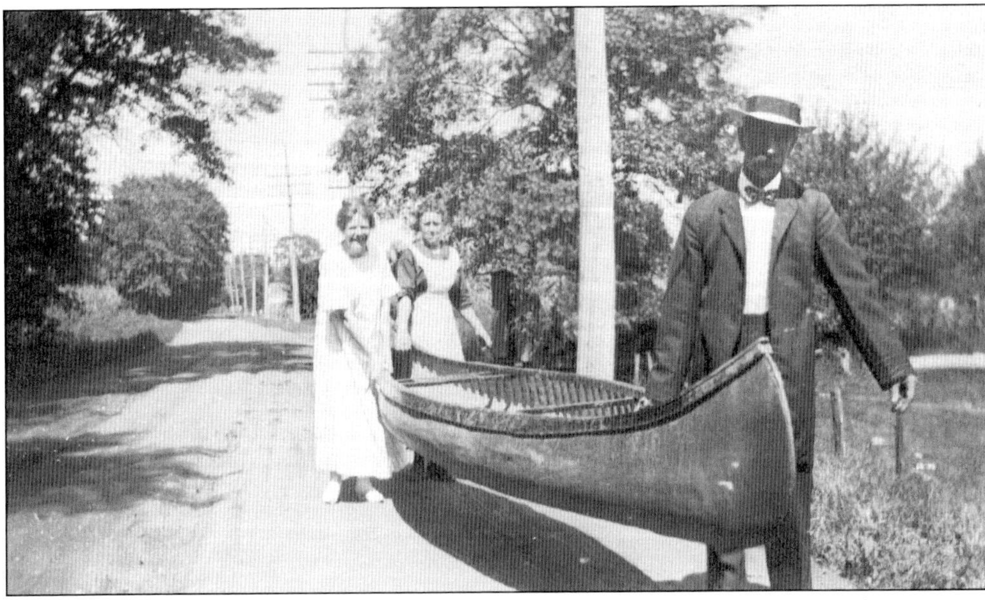

The Passaic River used to be a great source of recreation for boaters, bathers, fishermen, and ice-skaters. These local canoeists are putting in near Mount Pleasant Avenue in a pre-1920 excursion. (Courtesy of Margaret Griffith.)

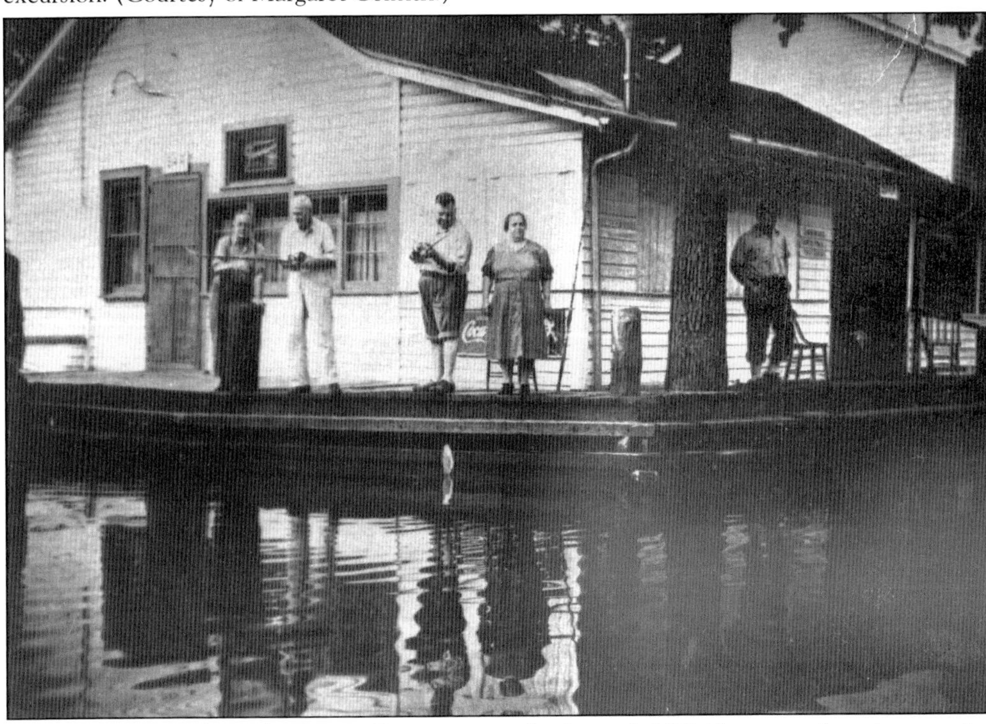

Champi's Tavern, along the Passaic River next to the Swinefield Bridge, was a favorite watering hole from the 1930s into the 1960s. On this day in the mid-1930s, the river rose above its banks, so several regulars decided to try their luck with their rods. They are, from left to right, Al Bannister, Oscar Kent, Patsy Champi, Rose Champi, and Al Champi. (Courtesy of Don Courter.)

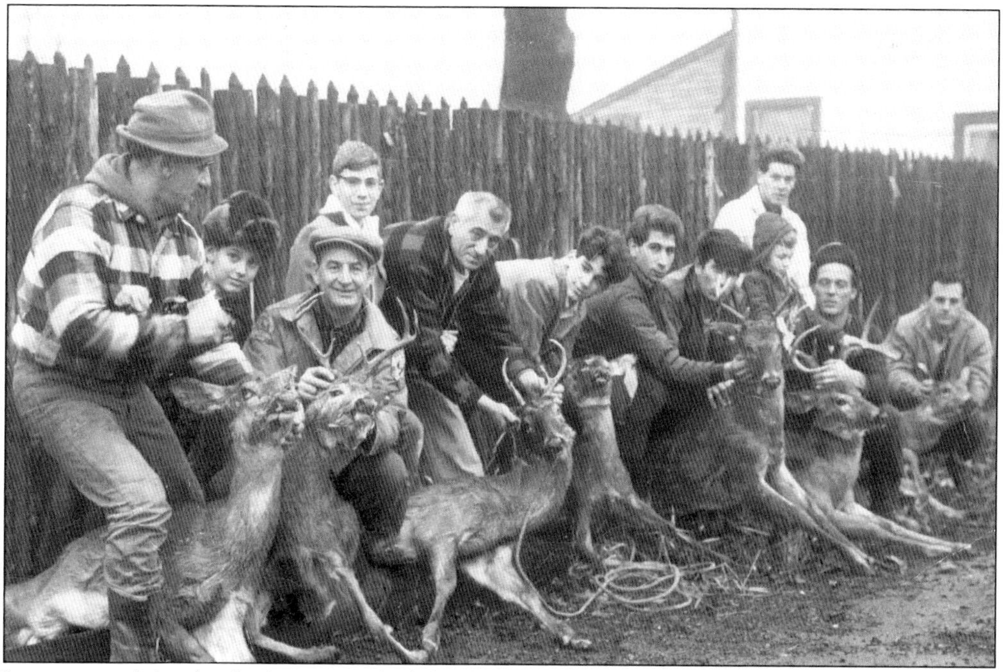

It was a good day for the hunters, a bad day for the deer. Hunting was both a popular sport and a means of putting food on the table throughout the town's history until open lands dwindled. The hunters include, from left to right, Joe Esposito, Richie Esposito, Frank McCauley, Tom Esposito Jr., Tom Esposito Sr., Tom Esposito, Philip Esposito, Jim Esposito, Master Finehauls, Bob Esposito, Rich Finehauls, and Herb Crozier. (Courtesy of John Esposito.)

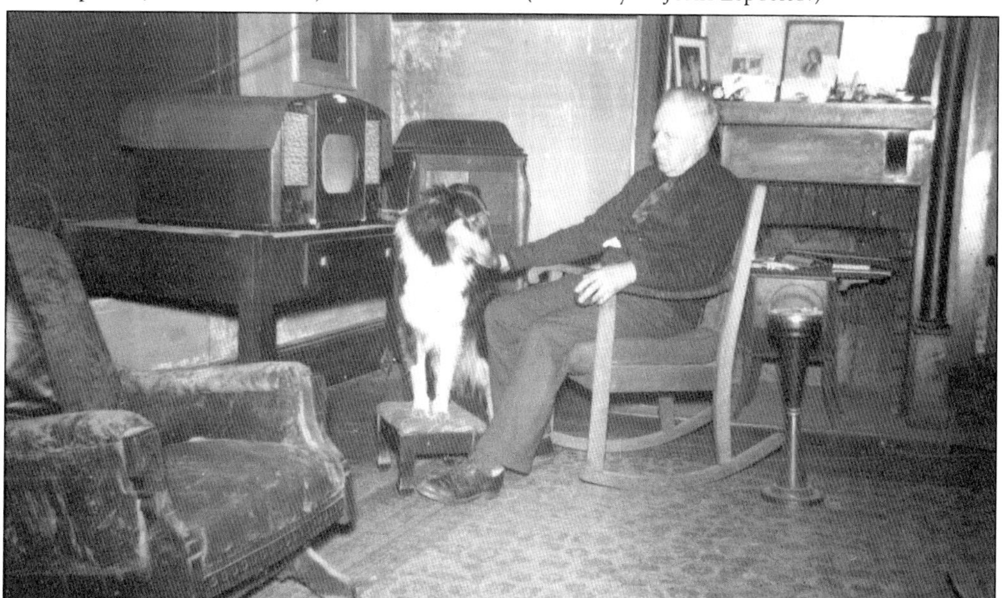

Eugene Johnston and his dog Lassie get ready to watch a show in 1950 on what was one of the first television sets in town. Since TVs were quite expensive then, and most families did not own one, the Johnstons would set up chairs theater style in the TV room so that neighbors who stopped by could enjoy the programs with them. (Courtesy of Herb Johnston.)

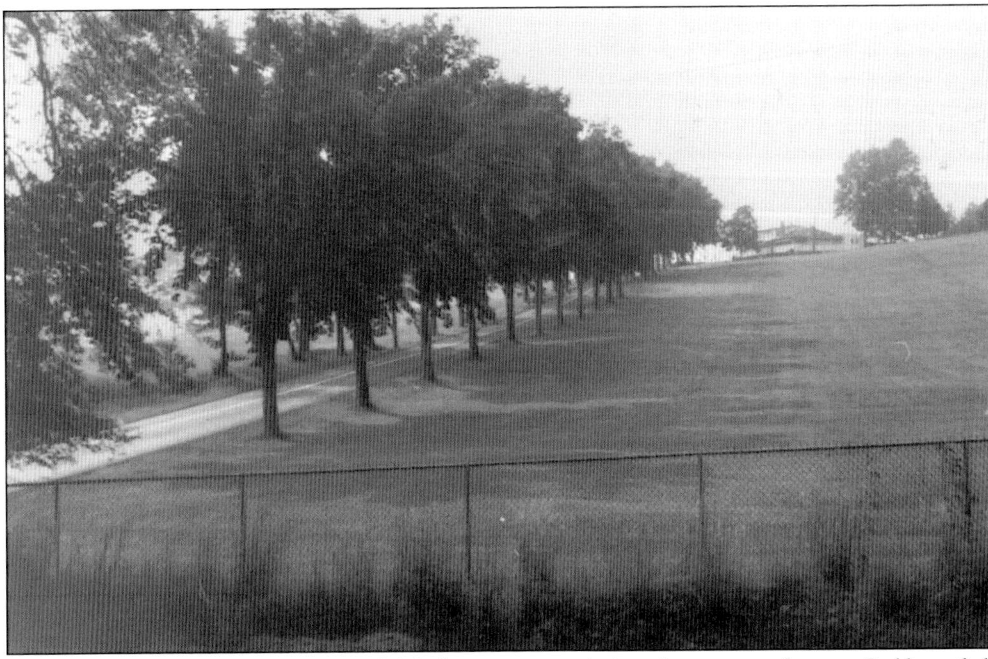

Valley View Golf Club was a beautiful, hilly course nestled in the center of town. Golfers of all ages and skill levels honed their handicaps for many years at Valley View. The hills also offered great sleigh riding in the winter. In the 1970s, caddies were replaced by corporate executives when Nabisco bought the property. (Courtesy of Catherine Froling.)

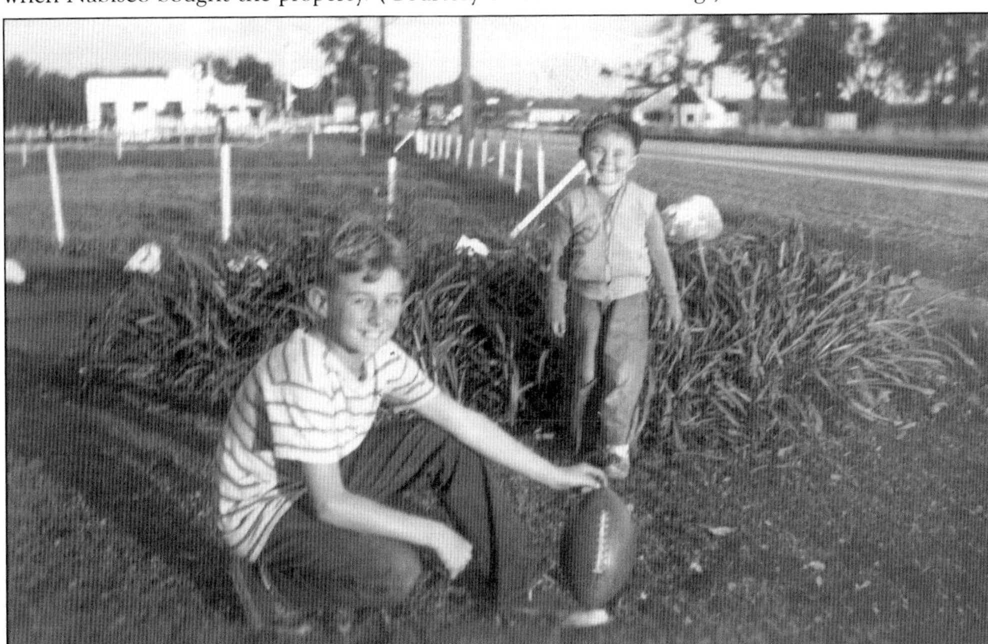

Backyard football has been an important pastime since Rutgers first played Princeton. Anyone who has ever held the ball for a young place kicker knows that it's best not to look at what's coming—you just might let the ball go too soon. Not that Bob Riley would have done that to his younger brother Rich in this 1940s practice. (Courtesy of Bob Riley.)

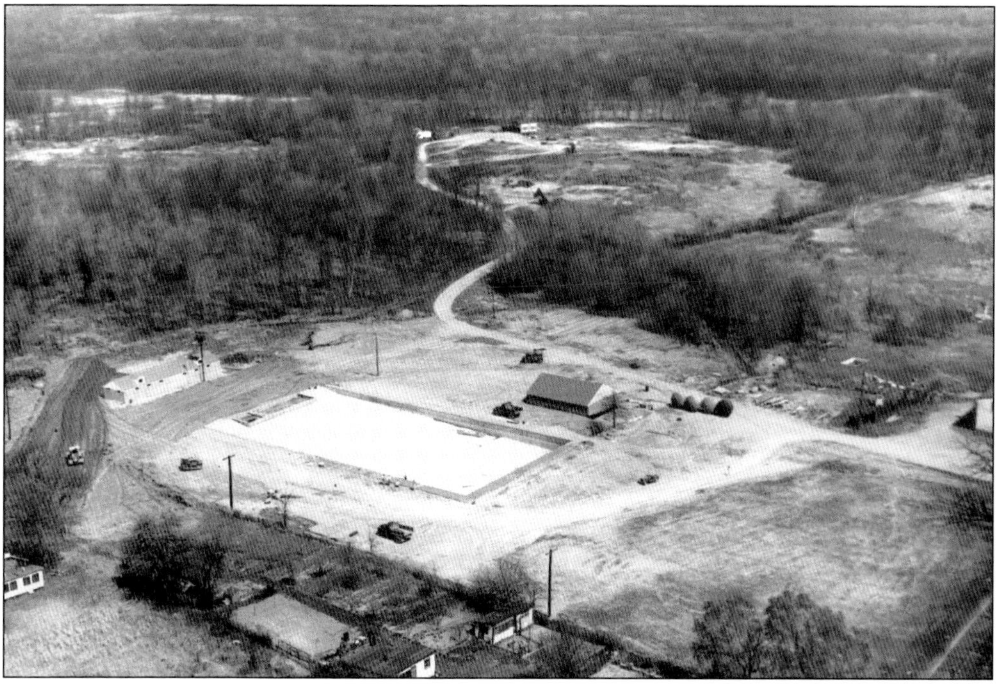

The Rello family built the East Hanover Swim Club in the early 1950s on Eagle Rock Avenue where the executive offices are today. The pool site is under construction in the top photograph. Four huge water filters can be seen outside the filter house. The locker room building is on the left side of the pool. The bottom photograph shows a good summer crowd in 1952 or 1953. Rello's Pool drew members from East Hanover as well as nearby towns. At the end of the swimming season, St. Rose of Lima Church often held its annual picnic at the pool. Rello's closed in 1983. (Above and below courtesy of John Rello.)

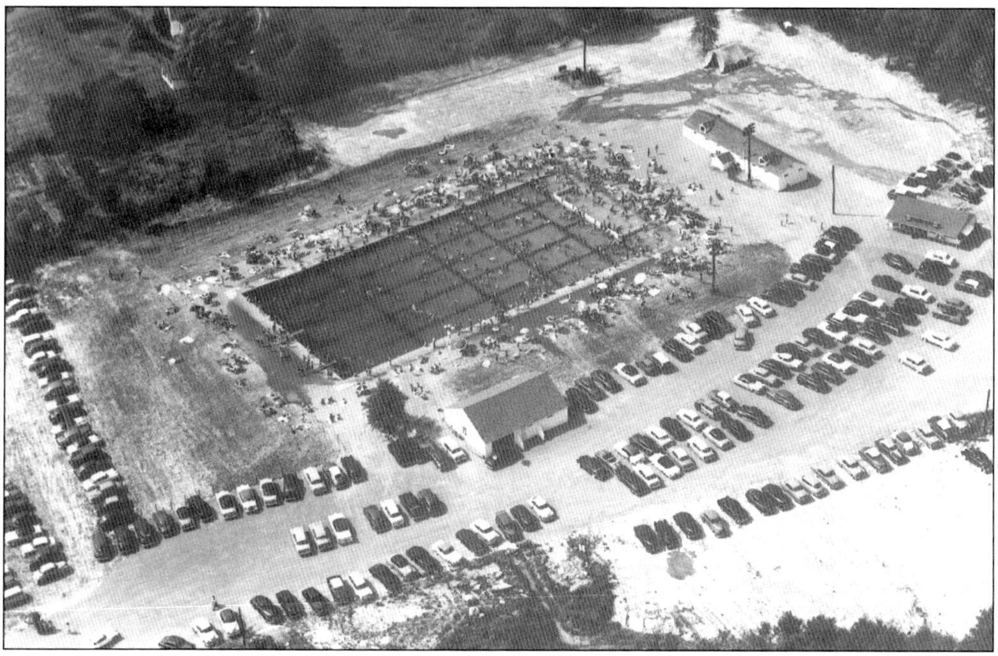

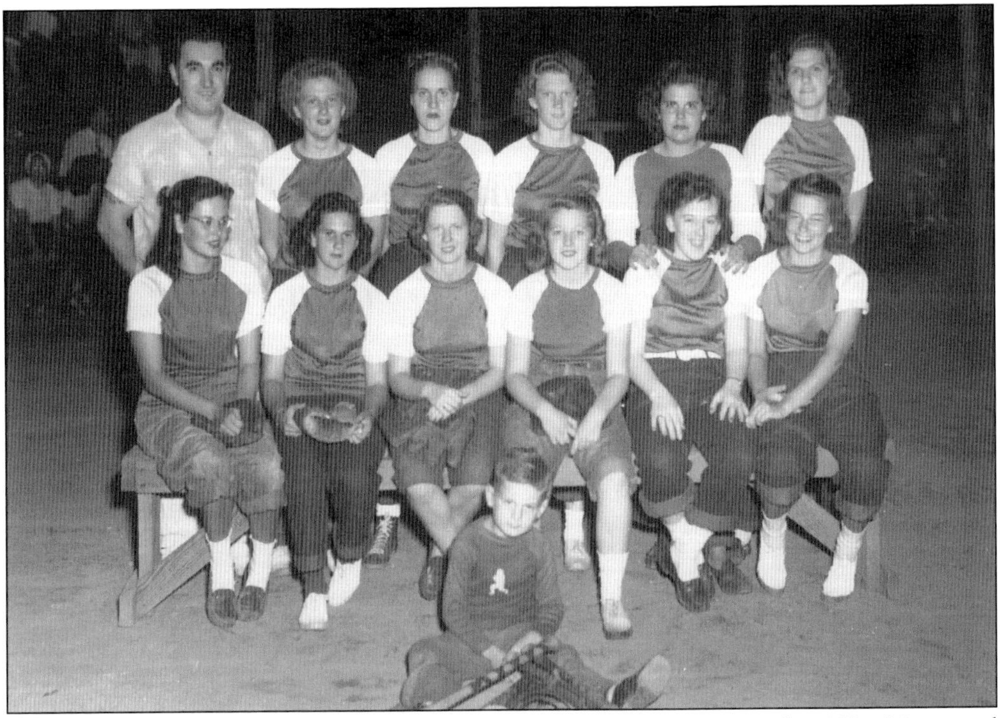

John Bauk sponsored this women's softball team in the late 1940s or early 1950s. He owned the Old Firehouse Tavern, which later became the Red Fox. (Courtesy of Anthony and Anne Pellecchia.)

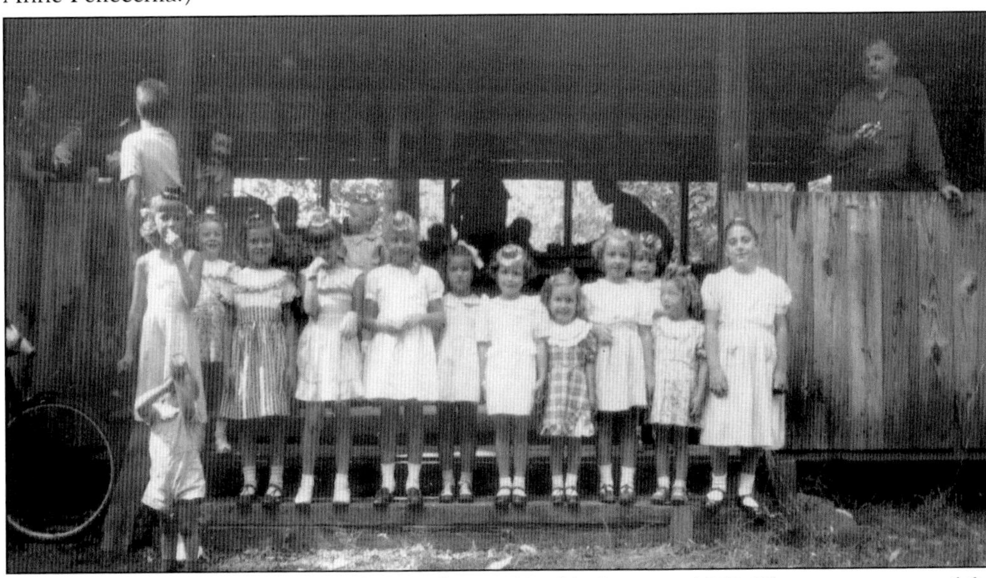

This birthday party took place at the pavilion in Buck's Grove c. 1950. The grove was used for various public and private activities, including picnics, clambakes, and ball games. A typical picnic menu included roast beef and sausage sandwiches, hamburgers, hot dogs, corn-on-the-cob, potato salad, coleslaw, clam chowder, clams on the half shell, and soda. The price per head was $3.50; soda was $2.50 per case. Dorothy Swet prepared the menu in her home. She and her husband, Walter, owned the business on Cedar Street. (Courtesy of Dorothy Swet.)

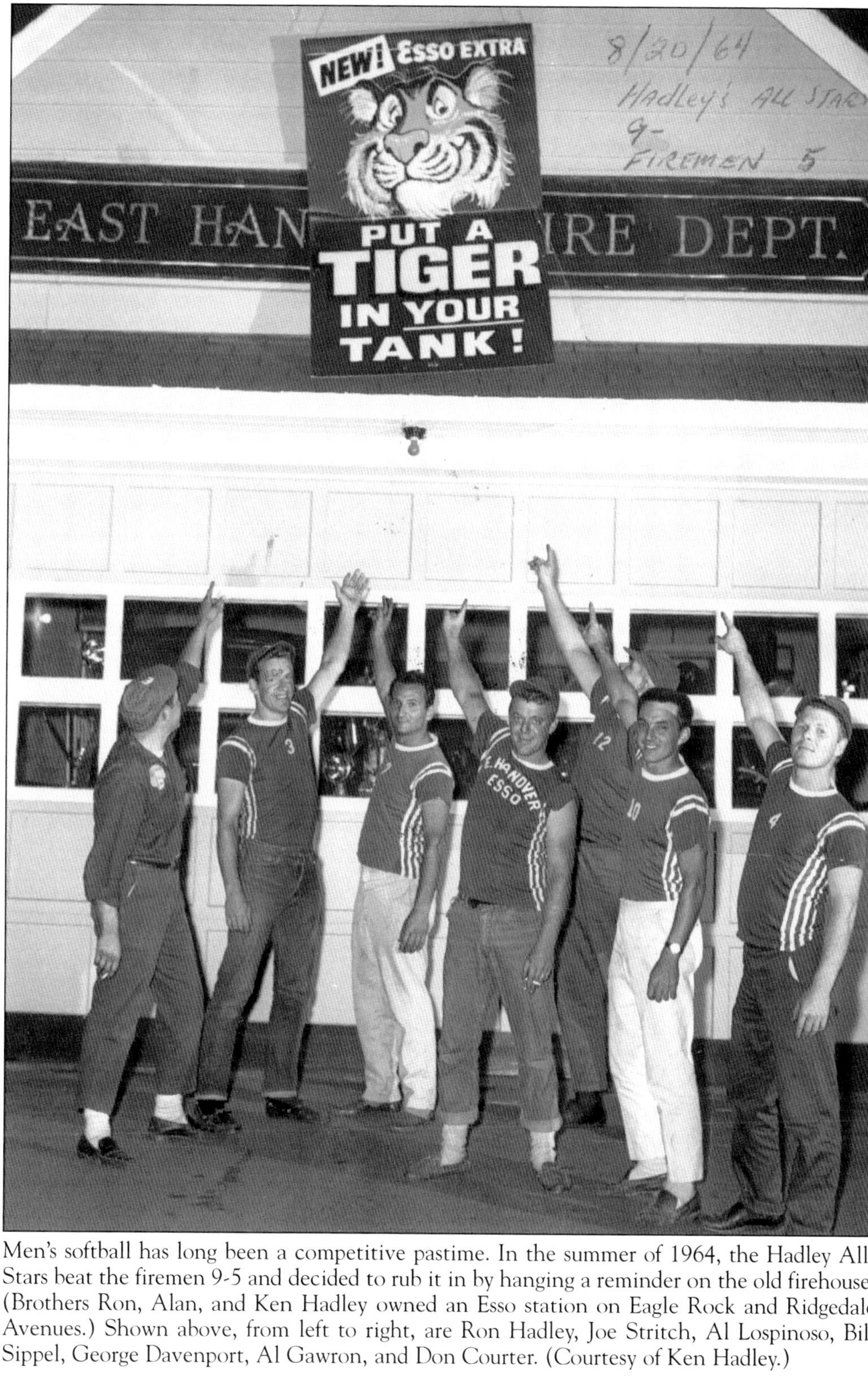

Men's softball has long been a competitive pastime. In the summer of 1964, the Hadley All-Stars beat the firemen 9-5 and decided to rub it in by hanging a reminder on the old firehouse. (Brothers Ron, Alan, and Ken Hadley owned an Esso station on Eagle Rock and Ridgedale Avenues.) Shown above, from left to right, are Ron Hadley, Joe Stritch, Al Lospinoso, Bill Sippel, George Davenport, Al Gawron, and Don Courter. (Courtesy of Ken Hadley.)

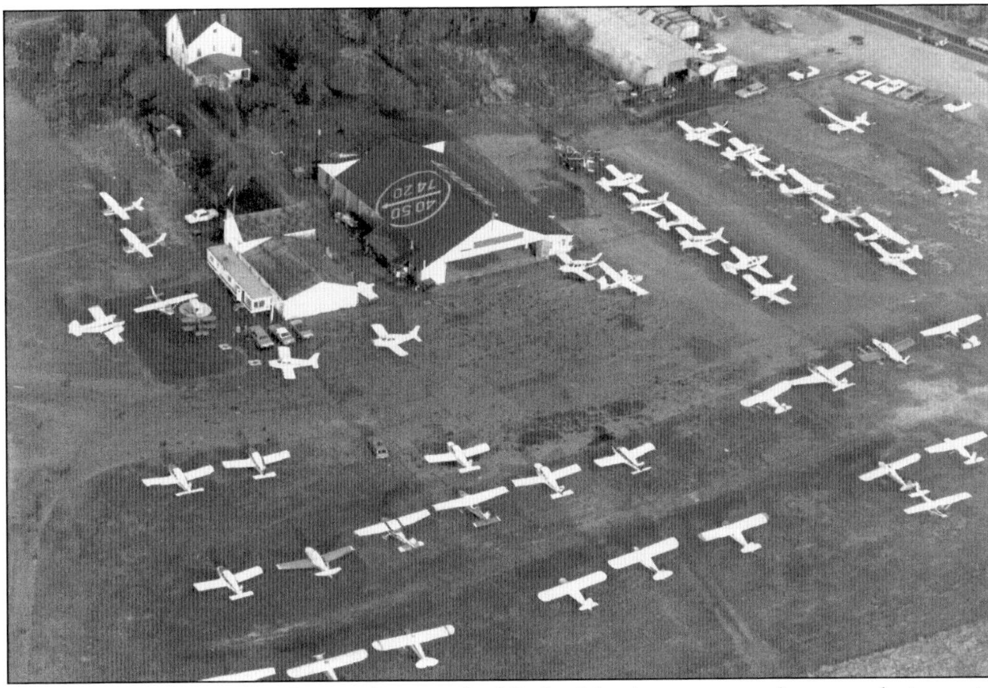

The Hanover Airport, at the northern end of Ridgedale Avenue, was the second airport in town. It was opened in 1939 by Abe, Ethel, and Gertrude Steppel. (The first airfield operated in the 1920s and 1930s along Route 10.) When it was in full swing, there were an average of 100 small planes based at this airport. It was a full-service, small airport, offering tie-down for plane owners, maintenance, flight instruction, rides, banner tours, gliders, biplanes, and helicopters. Fire destroyed the hanger in the 1970s. There were several fatal crashes over the years. The airport ceased operations in 1985. (Above courtesy of Bill Schaeffer; below courtesy of Catherine Froling.)

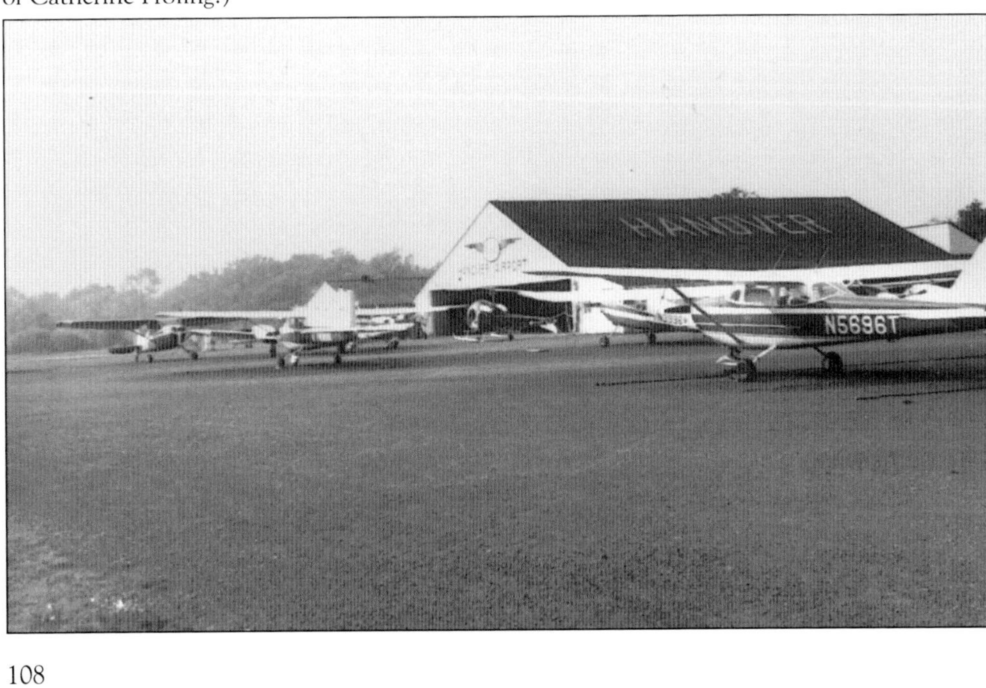

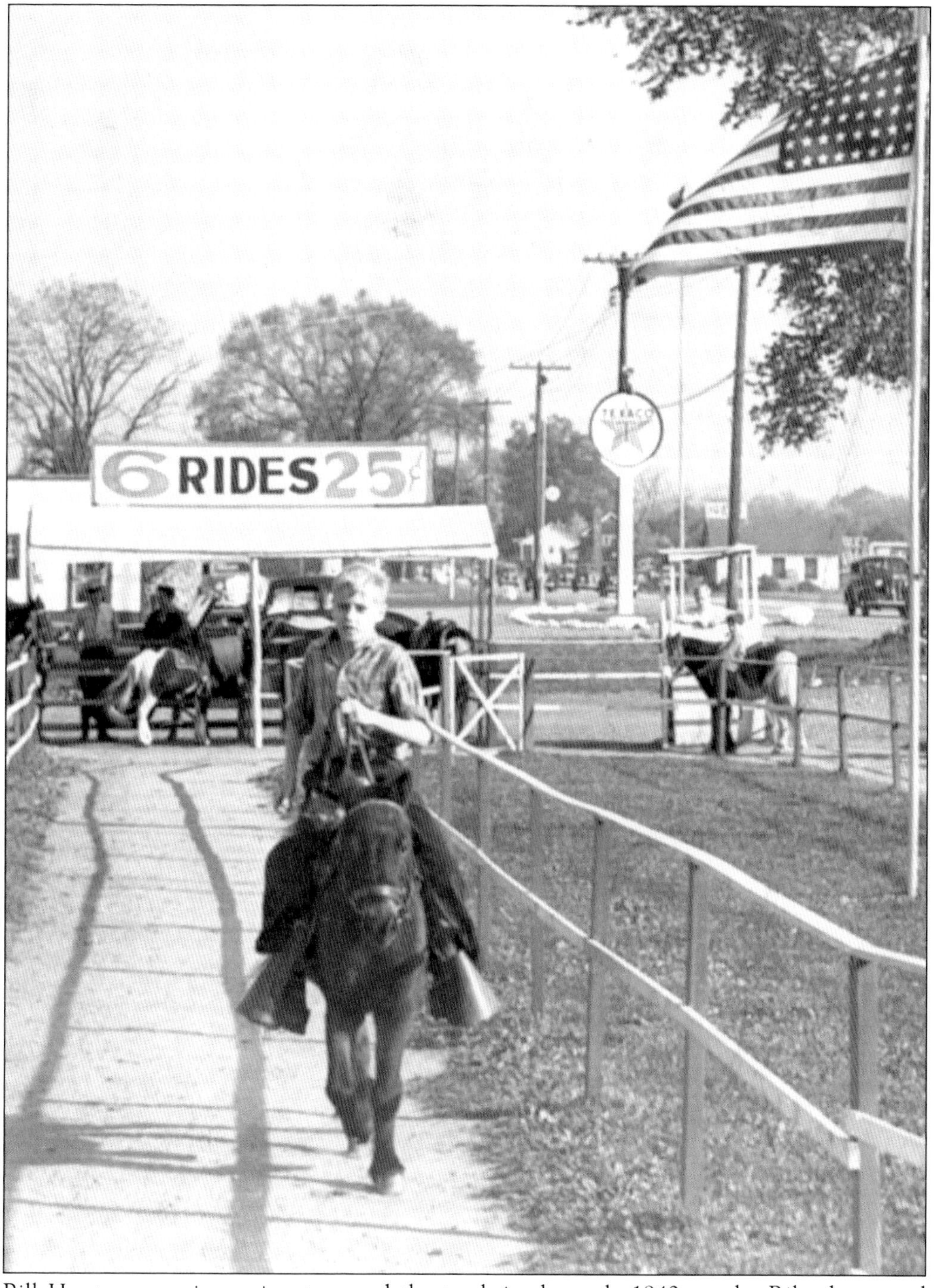

Bill Horstmann enjoys a jaunt around the track in the early 1940s at the Riley horse and pony farm on Route 10 (where Ingersoll Rand is today). Tom Riley started the business, which trained wild horses that were brought in from the West. One of their customers was the Ringling Brothers, Barnum & Bailey Circus. The Rileys also had a small stagecoach that gave free rides to patrons of the Livingston drive-in movie theater down the street. Horstmann went on to raise a family and become a successful businessman in town. (Courtesy of Bob Riley.)

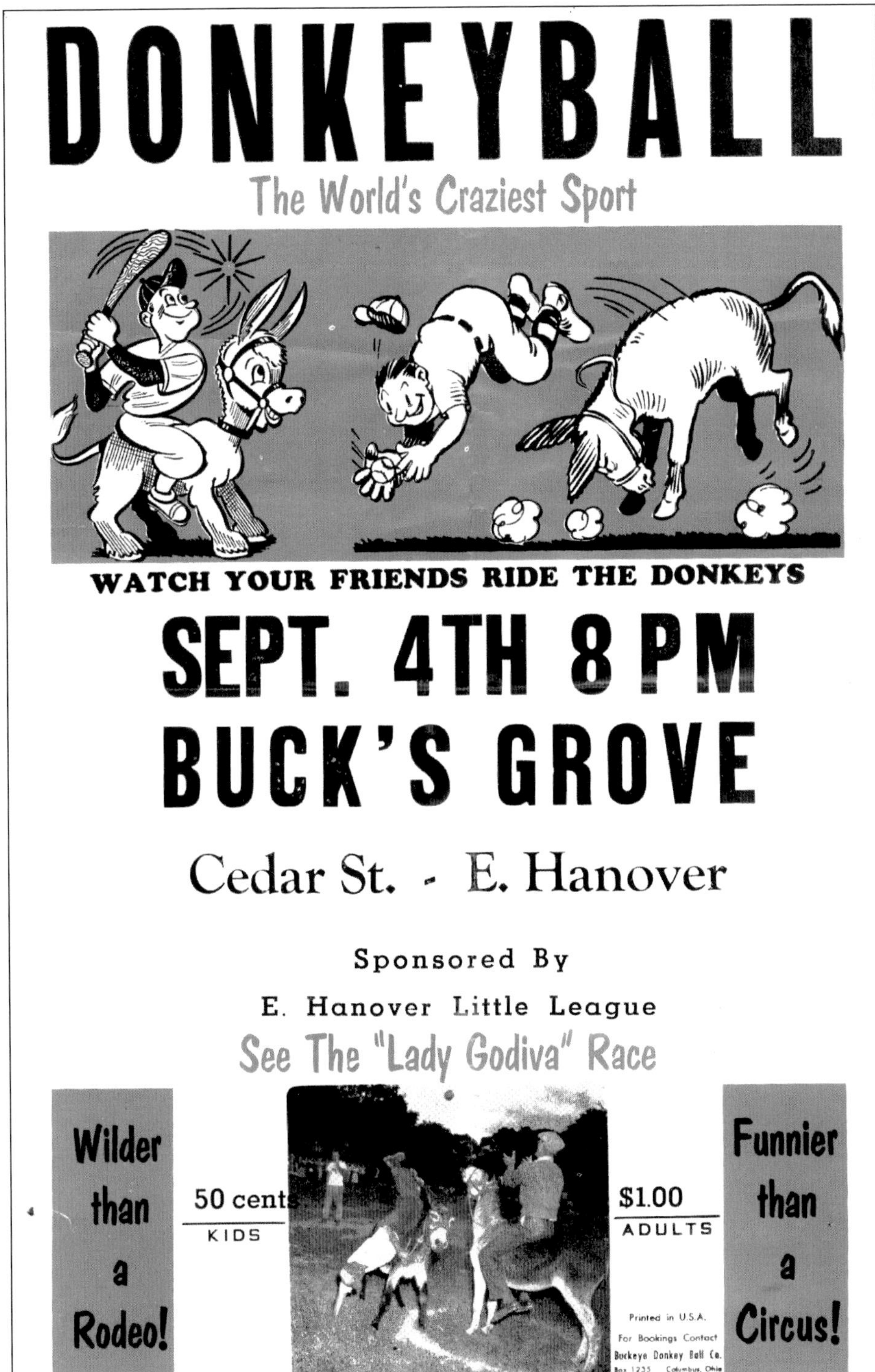

Buck's Grove on Cedar Street hosted all kinds of sports and recreational events from 1933 until 1959. Donkeyball featured local ballplayers aboard jackasses competing against one another. It was always good for laughs. (Courtesy of Dorothy Swet.)

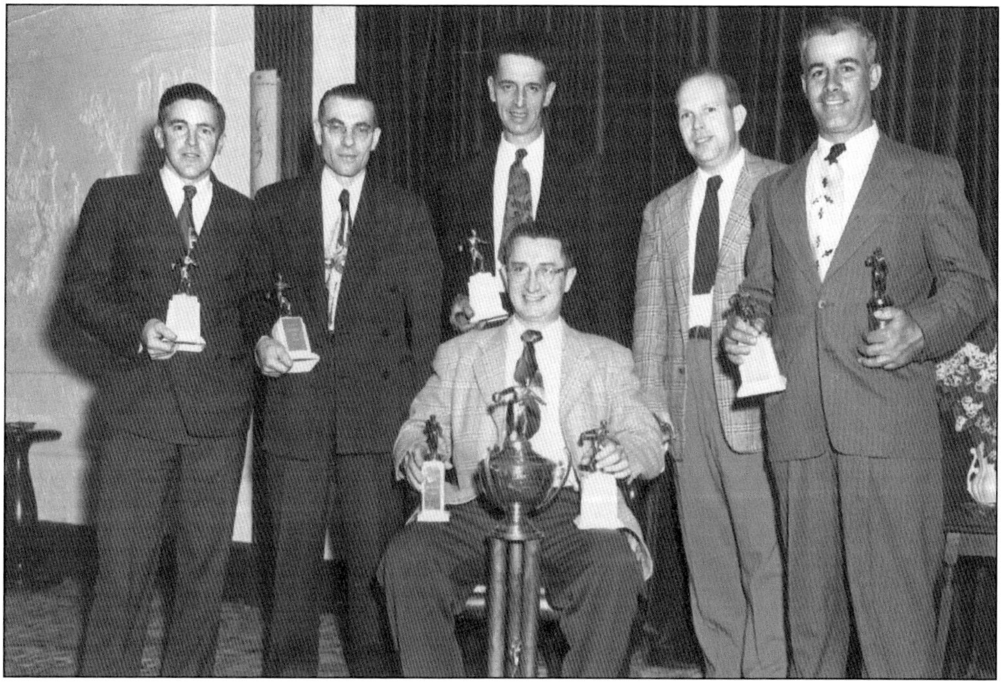

This men's bowling team walked away with the trophies in 1951. The bowlers include, from left to right, the following: (sitting) Gil Ziler; (standing) Milton Petry, John Cutter, Ray Poppendieck, Fred Shrader, and Ernie Vanacore. (Courtesy of the East Hanover Fire Department.)

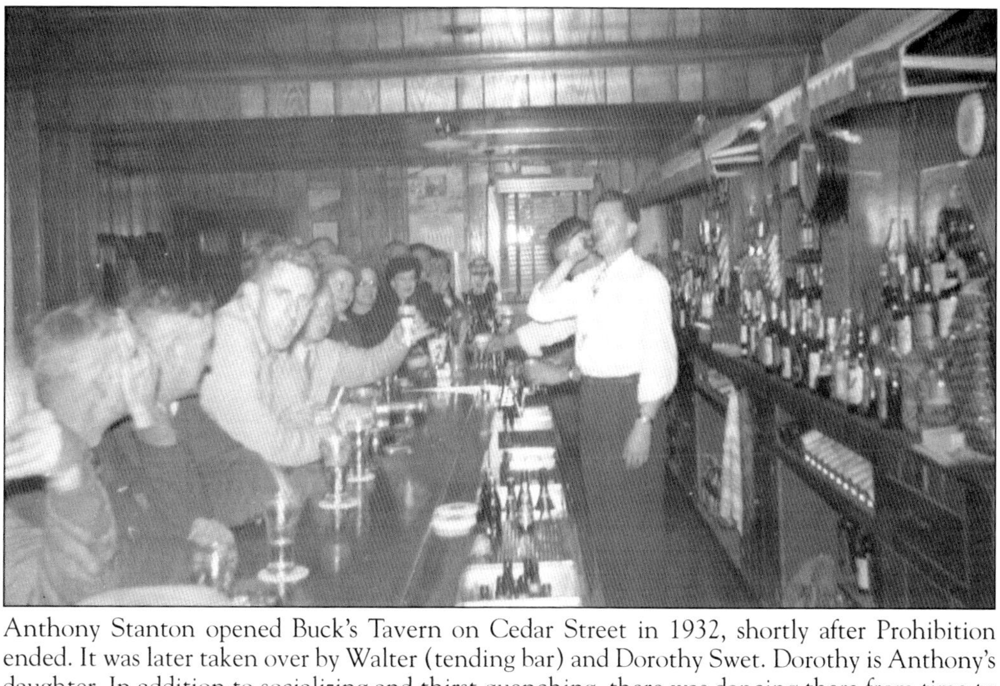

Anthony Stanton opened Buck's Tavern on Cedar Street in 1932, shortly after Prohibition ended. It was later taken over by Walter (tending bar) and Dorothy Swet. Dorothy is Anthony's daughter. In addition to socializing and thirst quenching, there was dancing there from time to time on Saturday nights. (Courtesy of Dorothy Swet.)

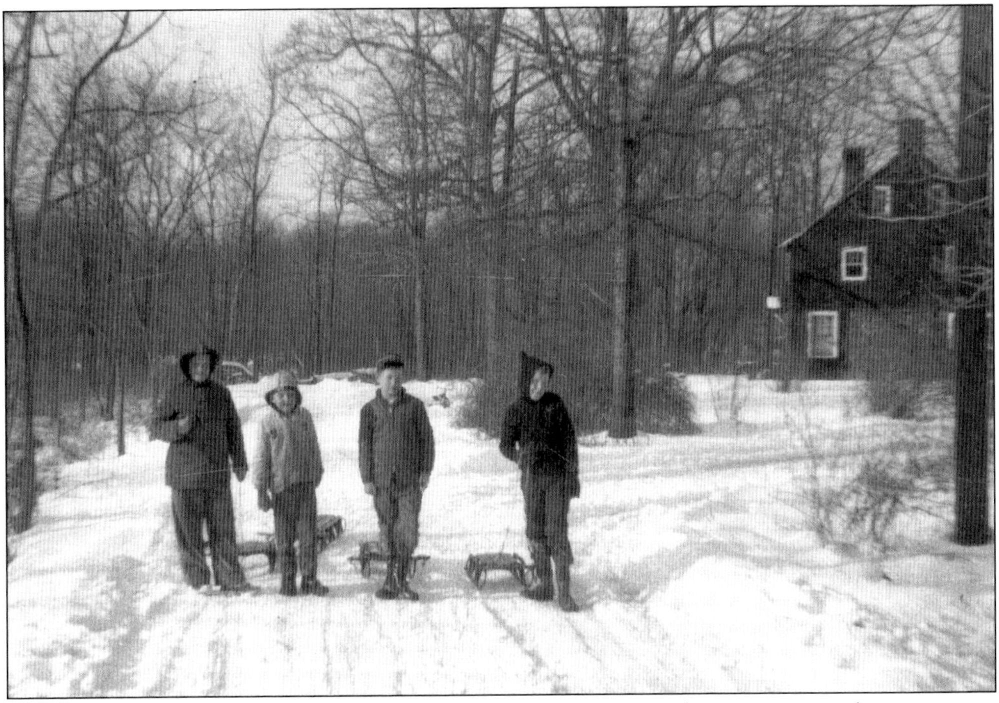

Just about everyone enjoyed sleigh riding years ago. It seems that winters used to get more snowfall back then. In this photograph, four hearty sledders tackle a good hill on Ward Place. The best hills in town for sleigh riding, however, were at Valley View Golf Club. (Courtesy of Shirley Shrader.)

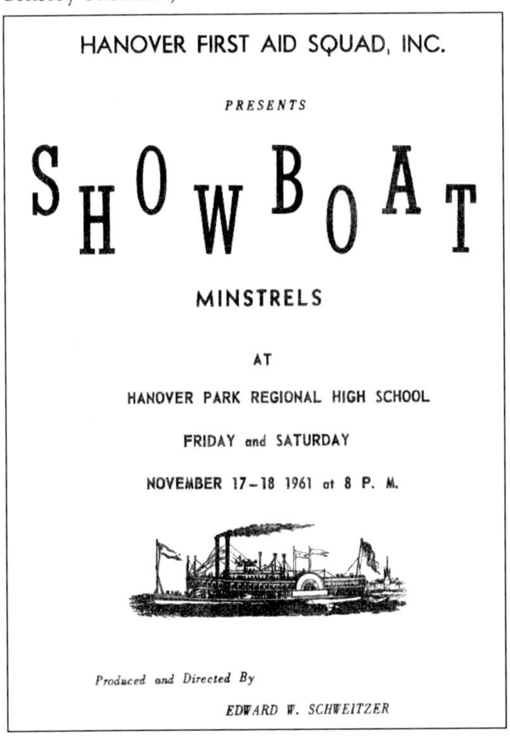

HANOVER FIRST AID SQUAD, INC.

PRESENTS

SHOWBOAT

MINSTRELS

AT

HANOVER PARK REGIONAL HIGH SCHOOL

FRIDAY and SATURDAY

NOVEMBER 17–18 1961 at 8 P. M.

Produced and Directed By

EDWARD W. SCHWEITZER

Members of the first-aid squad got into the act with their production of *Showboat* in 1961. Number 21 in the musical's program listed East Hanover's Finest Dancers. They included Larry Bode, Conrad Rittweger, Bill Scioscia, and Al Schweitzer, assisted by Mary Ann Darlington, True Schmaler, Imogene Stallings, and Ann Tillard. (Courtesy of Weetona Hobby.)

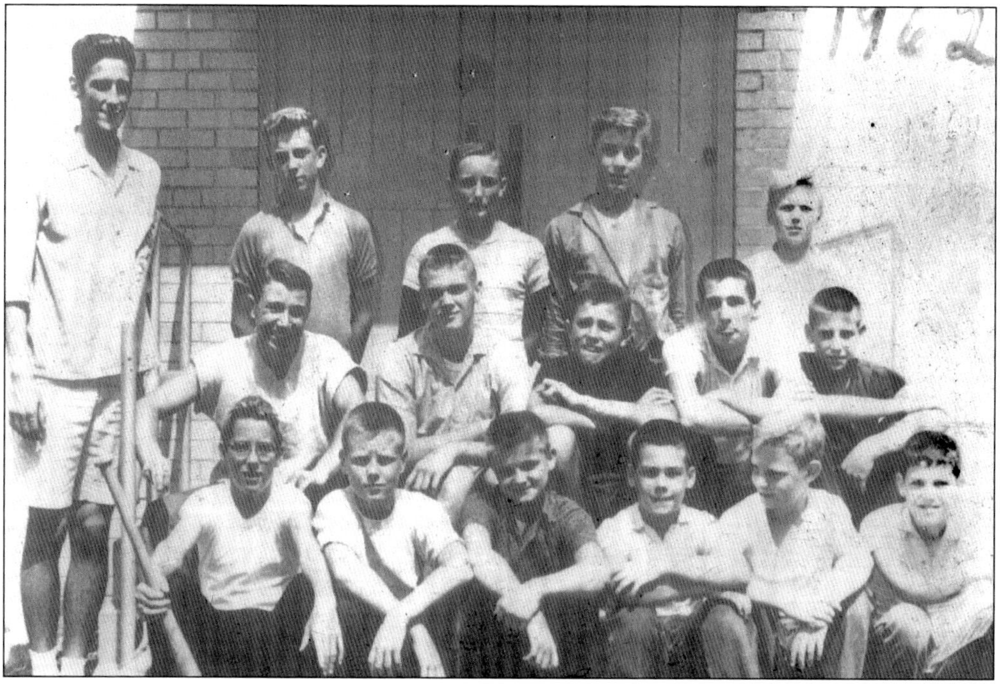

This was a pretty good team four decades ago. The sluggers include, from left to right, the following: (front row) Robbie Field, unidentified, Davie Crane, Timmy Rinaldi, Bobby Phillips, and Ricky Leonard; (middle row) Frankie Valvano, Tad Wood, Tony Kungl, Ricky McGuire, and Billy Tillard; (back row) Danny Delaney, Glen Schmaler, Ronnie Williams, and Johnny Elias. Bill Guerny is standing on the far left. (Courtesy of Freddie's Barbershop.)

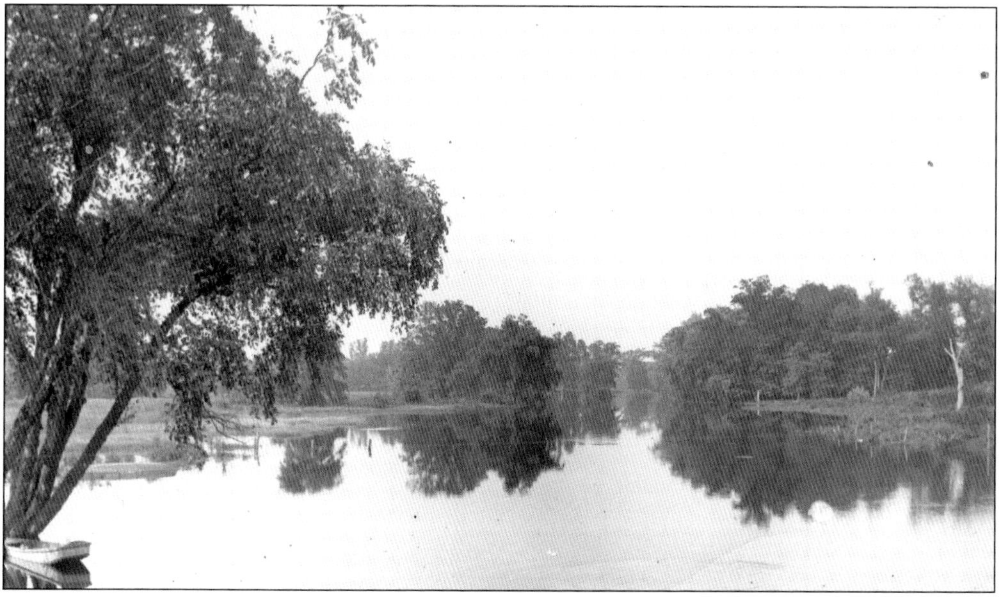

The Passaic River occasionally flooded its banks. Flooding caused problems certain times of the year but created excellent ice-skating opportunities in the winter. Skaters could wander in and out of trees and far into ice-covered terrain. The government eventually dredged the river in an effort to curb the flooding. (Courtesy of Everett Rowley Jr.)

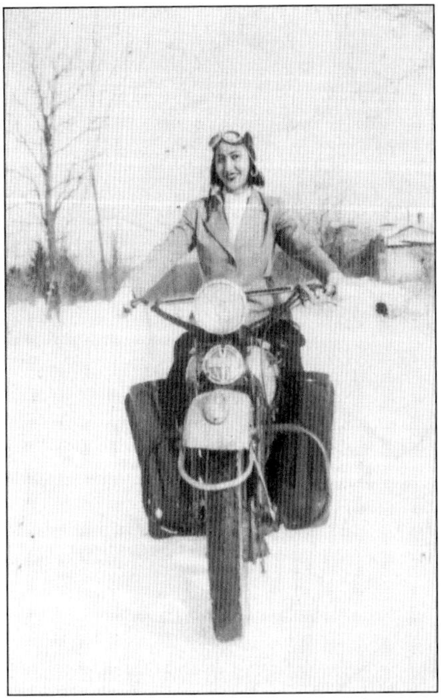

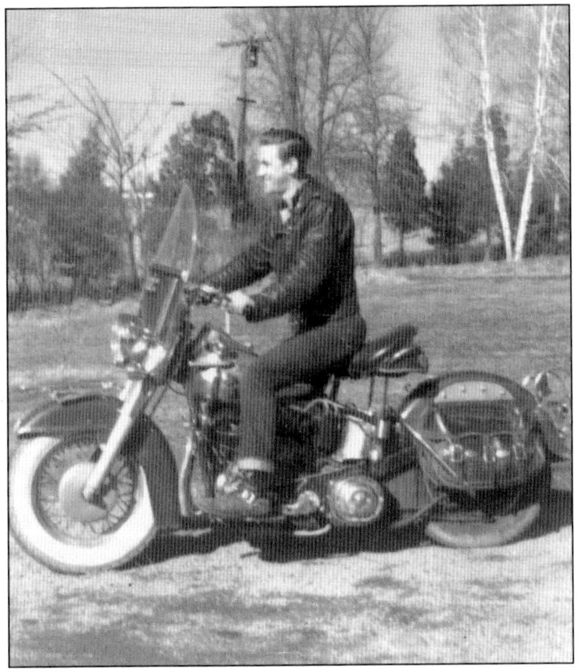

Young men and women alike have enjoyed fast motorcycles since the first Harley came roaring into town. Pictured above are Lucille Iradi and Alan Hadley riding their machines. (Photographs courtesy of Tom Iradi and Ken Hadley.)

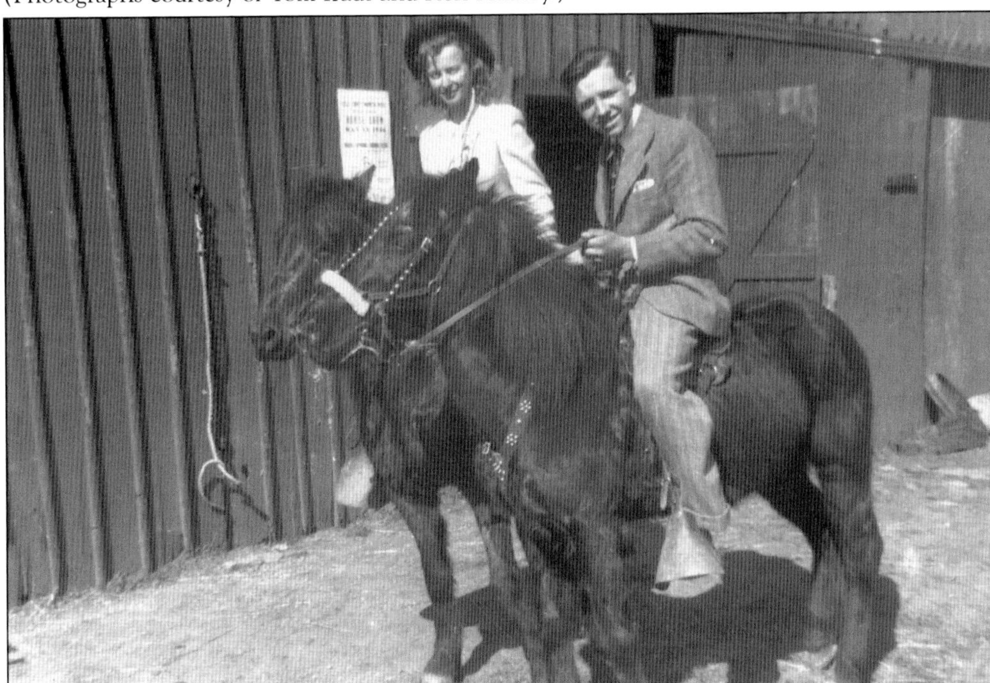

Those who were looking for a more leisurely pace might opt for a horse or pony ride. There were a number of places to ride throughout town. Pictured above are Helen Sippel and Lenny Rykozi going for a ride near Ridgedale Avenue West c. 1946. (Courtesy of Tom Iradi.)

Seven

AROUND TOWN

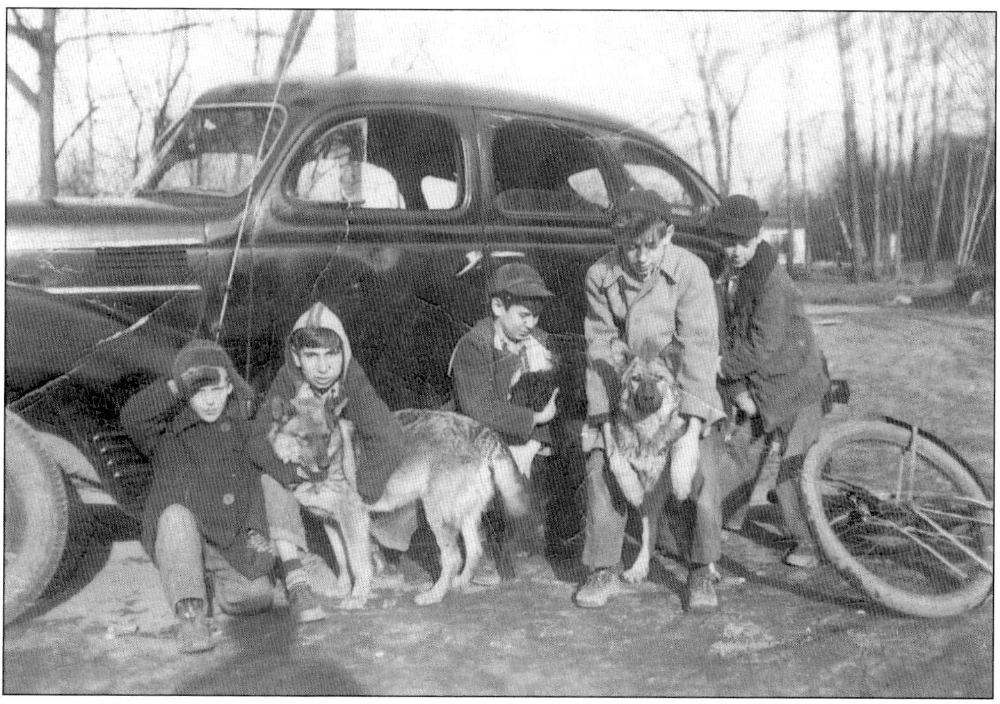

Before there were organized after-school activities, children would come home from school, change their clothes, and go outside and play. It was easy to find things to do. Here, the Esposito boys enjoy a cold afternoon in 1948 on Peach Tree Avenue with their two dogs. Pictured are, from left to right, John, Philip, Jimmy, Joe, and Bobby Esposito. (Courtesy of John Esposito.)

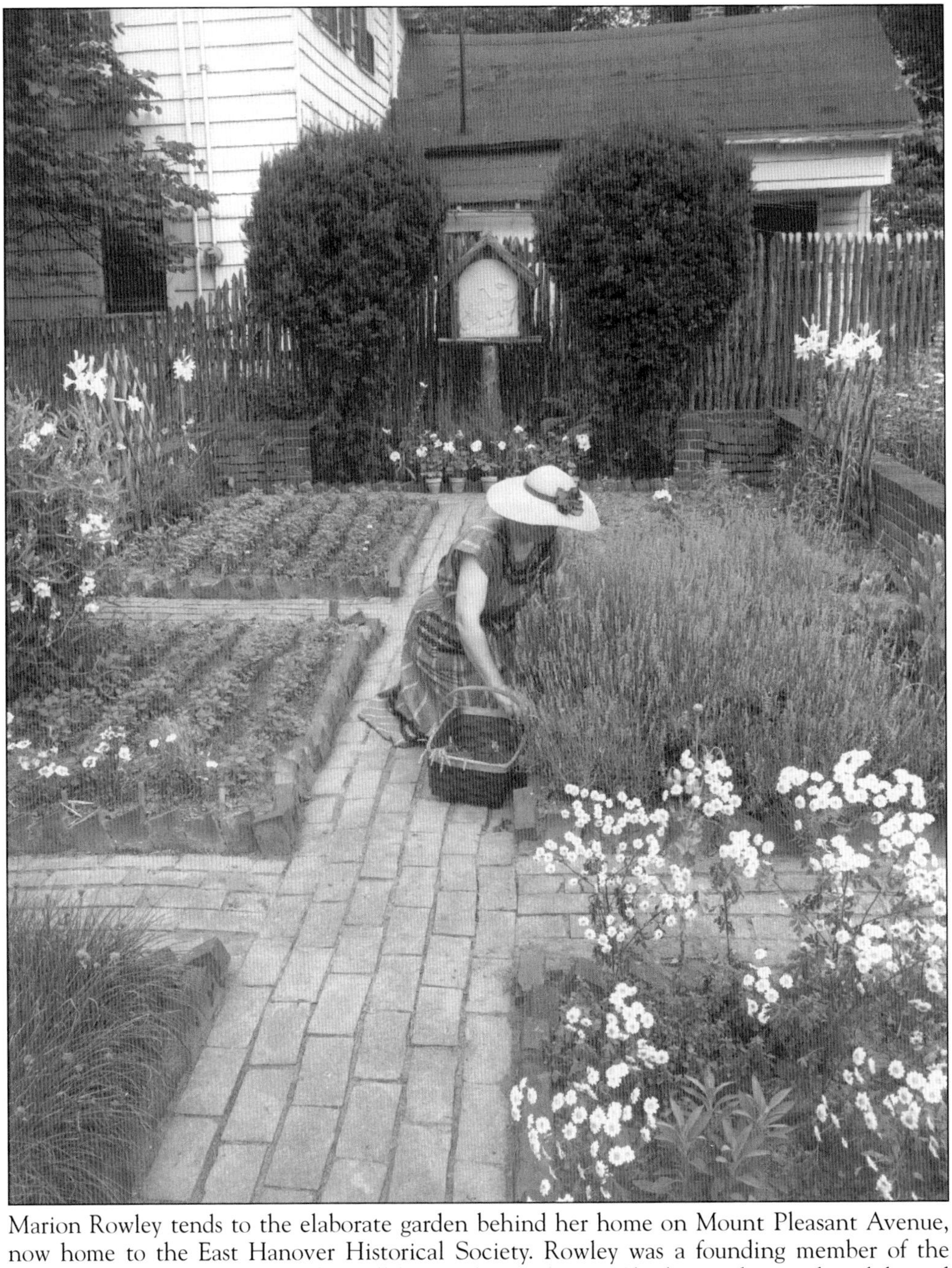

Marion Rowley tends to the elaborate garden behind her home on Mount Pleasant Avenue, now home to the East Hanover Historical Society. Rowley was a founding member of the East Hanover Garden Club and a well-known horticulturist. She lectured at garden clubs and participated in flower shows throughout the metropolitan area. (Courtesy of Roche.)

The llama at Newark Monument on Ridgedale Avenue was practically a town mascot 40 years ago. He had other pals as well, a donkey and several deer. Here, Barbara Glutting (left) and Kathy Jordan stop to say hello. That was about as close as anyone wanted to get to that llama. (Courtesy of Marge Glutting.)

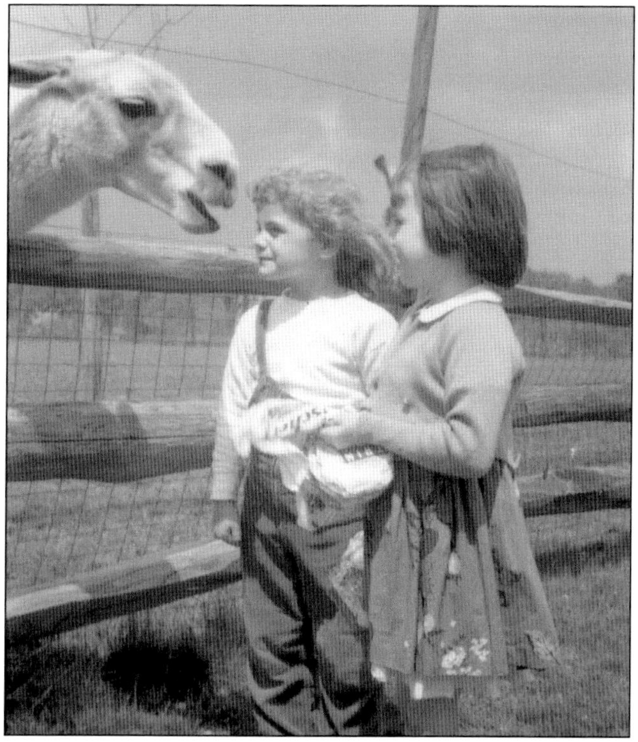

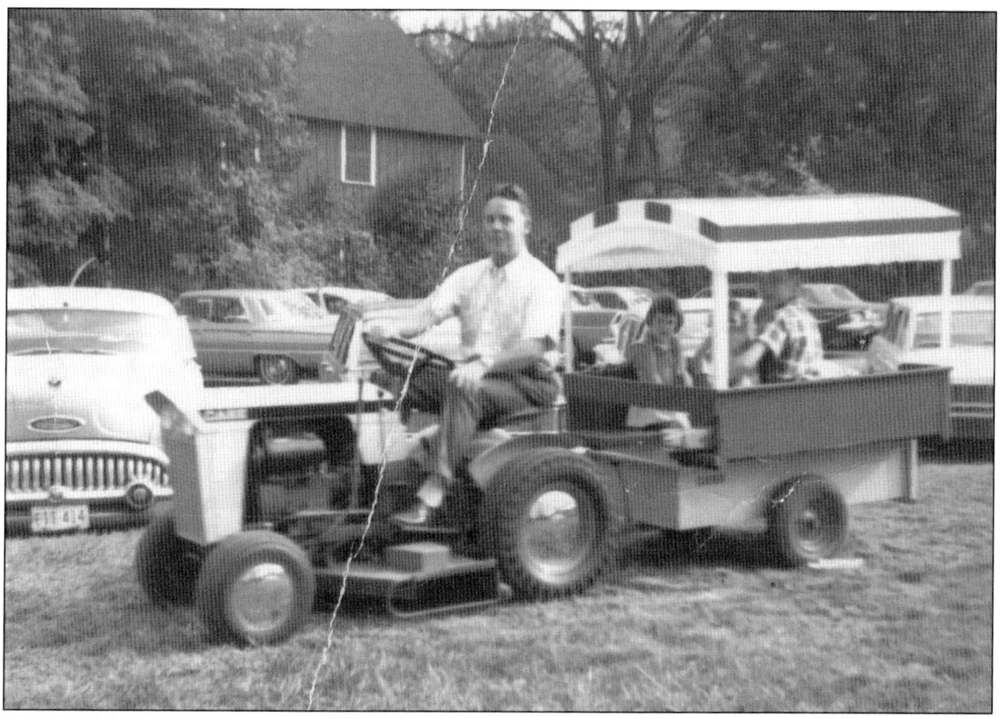

Ken Stoll keeps the children entertained at the church fair and chicken barbecue in 1965. The fair is held every September across the street from the First Presbyterian Church of Hanover. (Courtesy of the First Presbyterian Church of Hanover.)

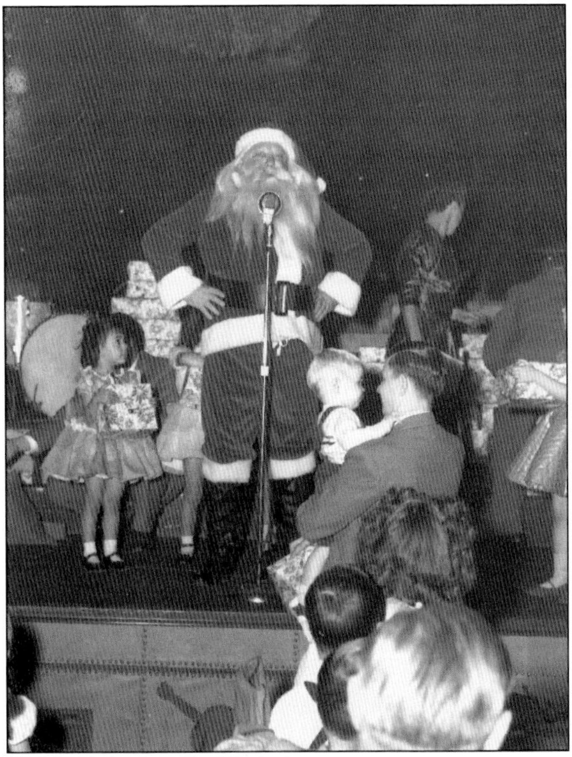

Rose Valera (left) is awed by Santa Claus on a December afternoon in the 1950s. Santa often pays a visit to town shortly before Christmas to double-check who's been naughty or nice throughout the year. (Courtesy of Tom Iradi.)

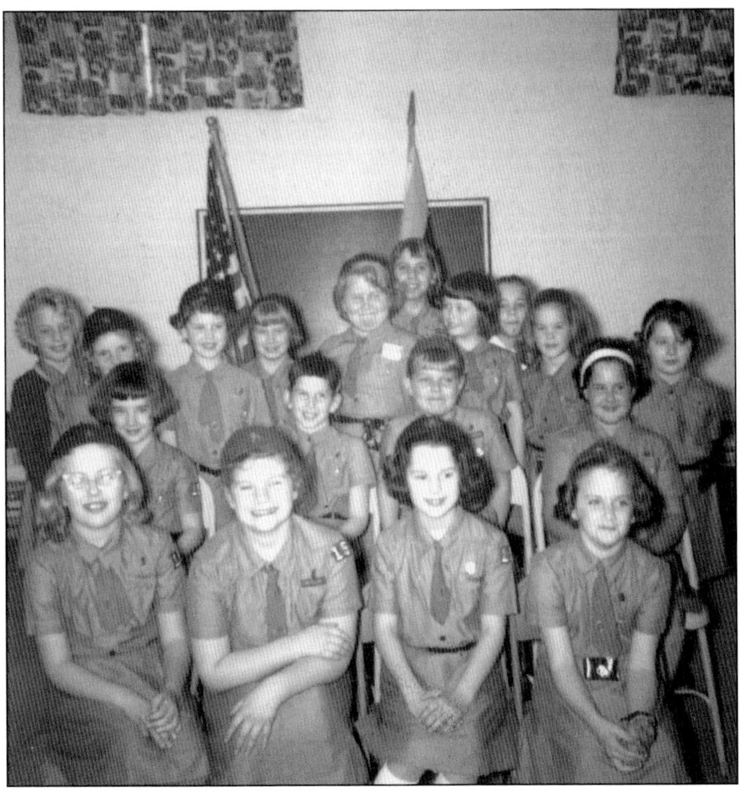

Brownie Troop 152 takes a break during a meeting at Kitchell Church in 1963. Troop leaders were D. Hall and Marge Glutting. The Brownies include Barbara Glutting, Susan Rapa, Gail McDonald, Michaele Maragulio, Kathryn Hoffman, Linda Fergusson, Suzanne Esposito, Karen Hall, Karen Koenen, Karen Richards, Ann Cummings, Marcy Goldblatt, Diane Zern, and Virginia Allen. (Courtesy of Marge Glutting.)

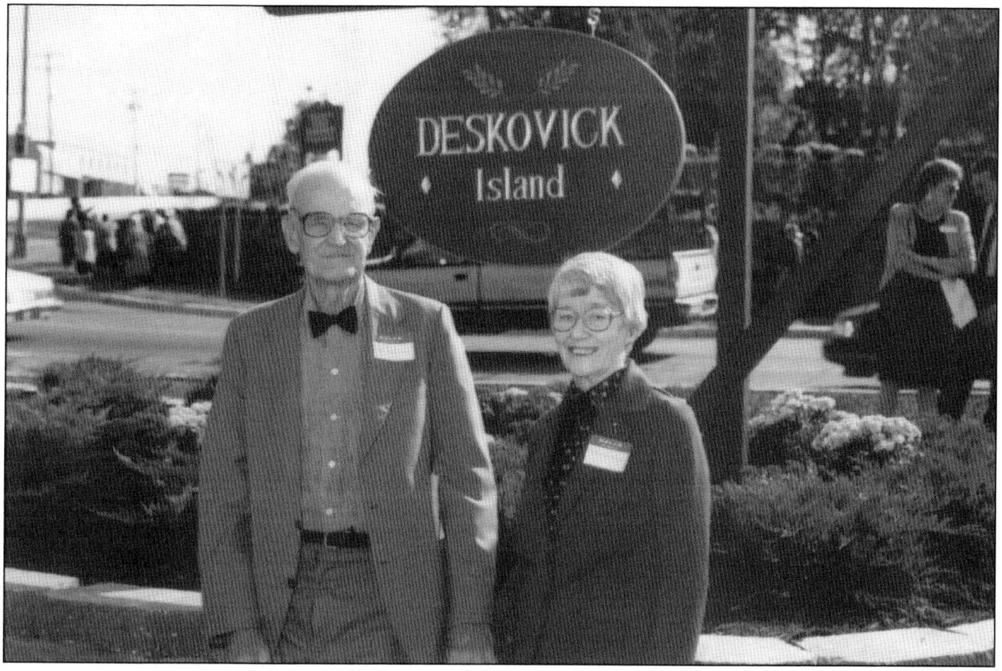

Mike Deskovick and Catherine Froling are shown at the dedication of Deskovick Island at Ridgedale Avenue and Route 10. The tribute to Deskovick was initiated by the East Hanover Garden Club in recognition of the many contributions he had made to the town over the years. (Courtesy of Catherine Froling.)

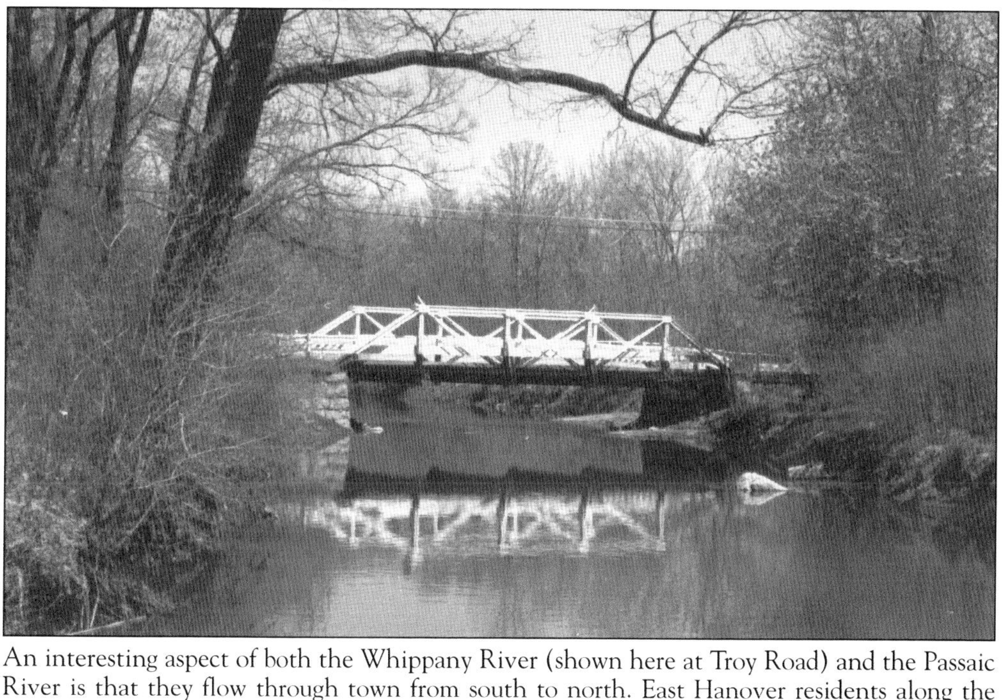
An interesting aspect of both the Whippany River (shown here at Troy Road) and the Passaic River is that they flow through town from south to north. East Hanover residents along the Whippany River would have preferred it ran the other way when the mills in Whippany started dumping who knows what into the waters back in the 1800s. (Courtesy of Gus Auermuller.)

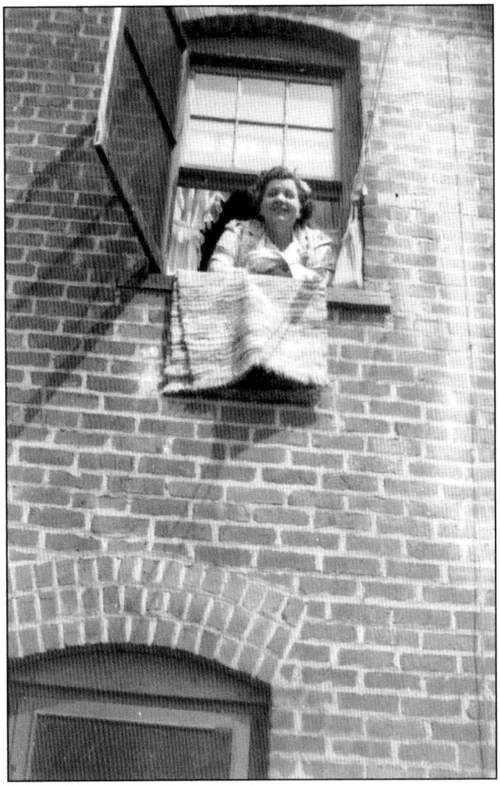

Although this looks like it could be Brooklyn in 1949, it is downtown East Hanover. Willie Freda Ross enjoys the sunshine and fresh air from her apartment window above Ross' grocery store on Ridgedale Avenue. (Courtesy of Evelyn and Jim Ross.)

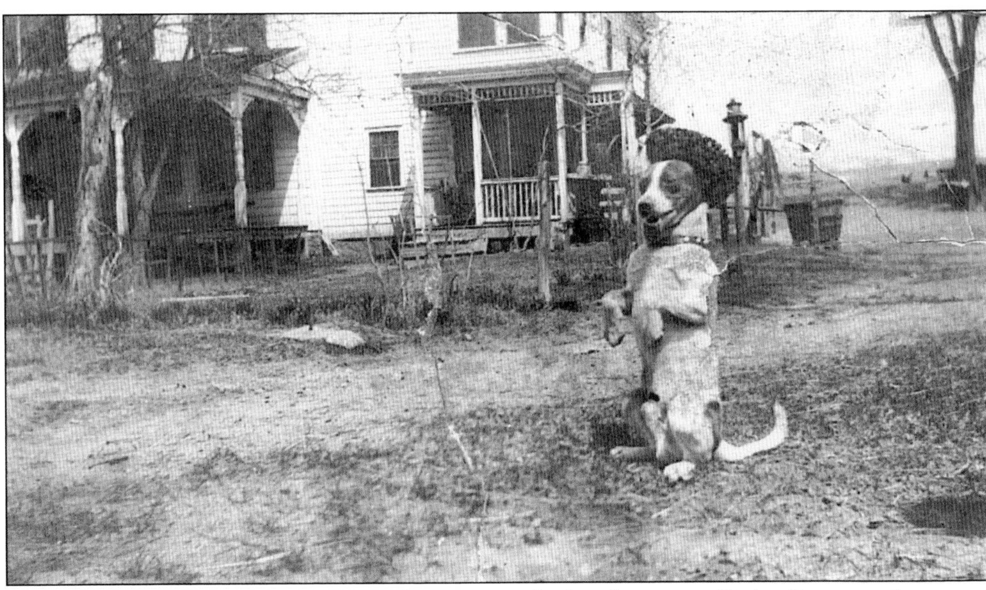

This obedient puppy is sitting patiently in front of a farmhouse on Cedar Street at the corner of Ridgedale Avenue prior to 1907. The original Colonial home was built sometime in the late 1700s or early 1800s. The farm had approximately 11 acres, where the farmers grew potatoes and other crops. In the 1950s and 1960s, horses grazed here in a fenced pasture. (Courtesy of Gregory and Pamela Smith.)

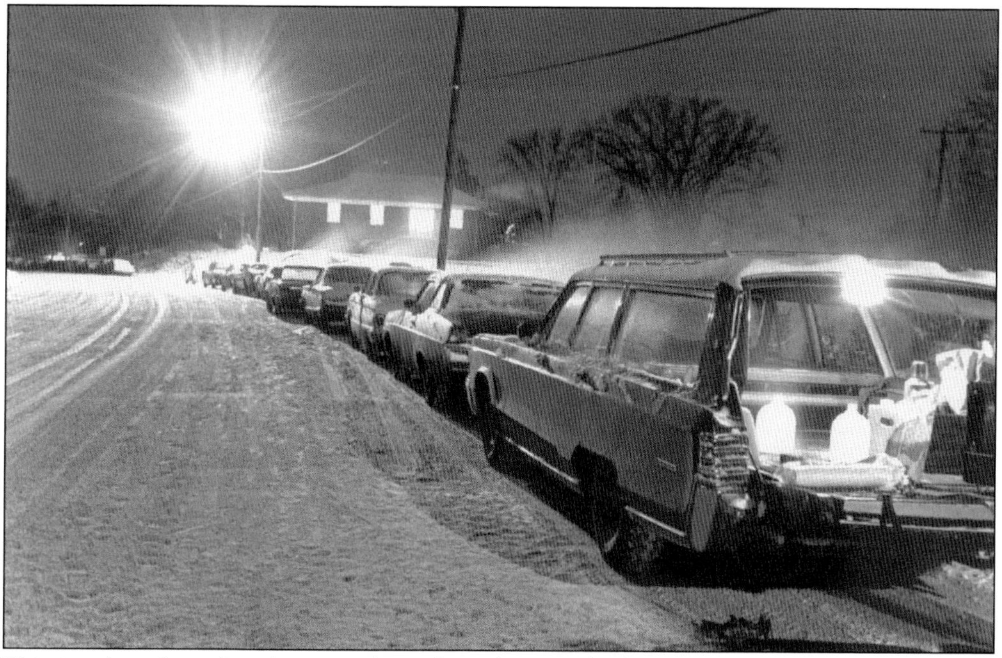

This is what the oil embargo and gasoline shortage looked like on Ridgedale Avenue on February 9, 1974. Drivers would get in line, park their cars overnight, and come back in the morning when the gas station opened. Some stations sold by appointment only, others only to regular customers. Some had limited hours. Others limited the amount of gas to $1 or $2. Occasionally, it got ugly. (Courtesy of Bill Schaeffer.)

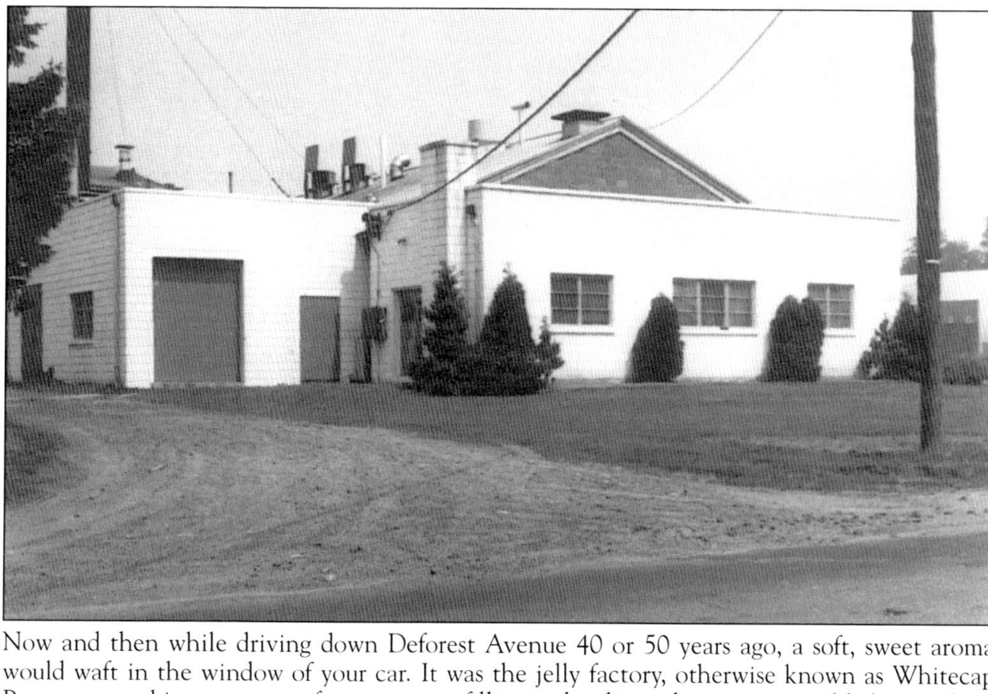

Now and then while driving down Deforest Avenue 40 or 50 years ago, a soft, sweet aroma would waft in the window of your car. It was the jelly factory, otherwise known as Whitecap Preserves, cooking up a vat of sweet pastry filling to be shipped to commercial bakeries along the East Coast. (Courtesy of Catherine Froling.)

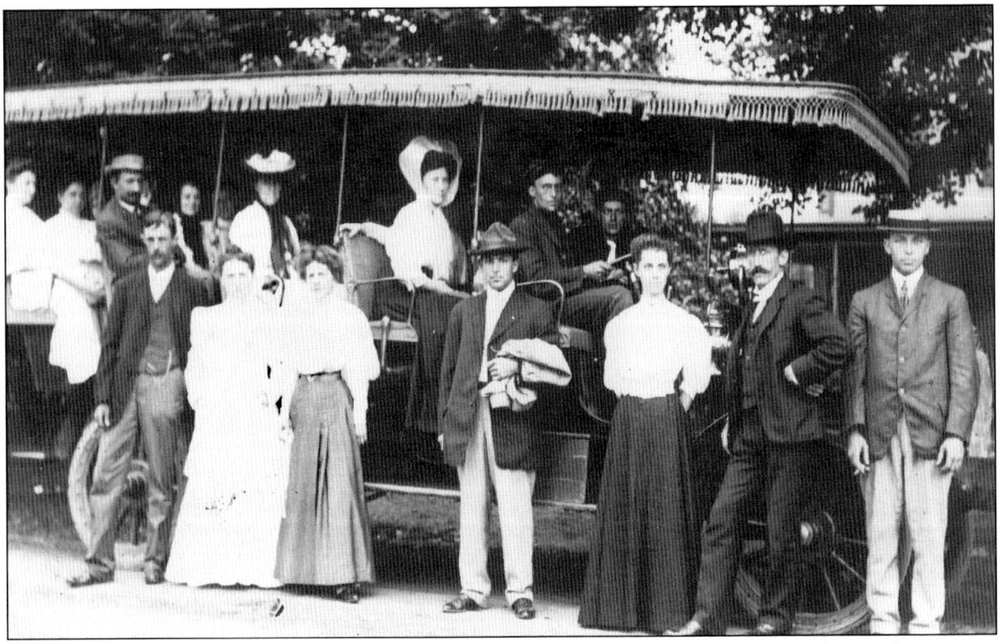

An afternoon outing in a motorized carriage was exciting in the early 1900s. These adventurers include (standing, from left to right) Gilbert Squier, Grace Squier, Jeanne Speer, Edwin Speer, Jennie Ward, Thomas Ward, and George Cook. Estelle Hopping is seated in the center with the scarf. (Courtesy of the East Hanover Historical Society.)

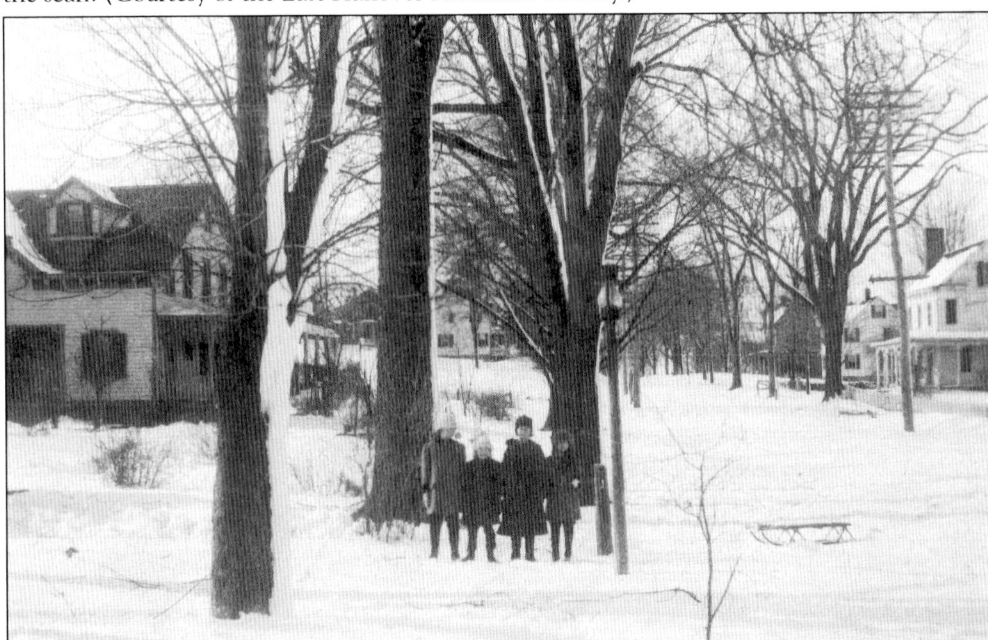

This is a winter scene on Mount Pleasant Avenue before 1920. The photographer is standing next to the steps of the general store and looking west. The children are on Mount Pleasant Avenue across from River Road. The sled is in the middle of the road; good thing no cars were coming. (Courtesy of Margaret Griffith.)

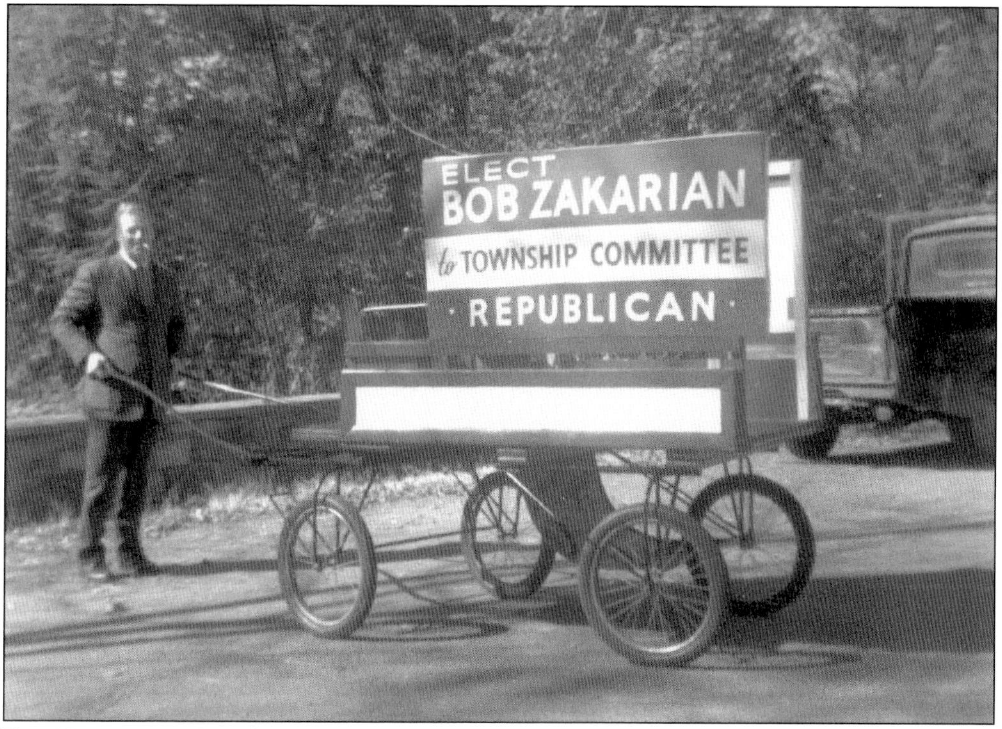

East Hanover's political arena has always been spirited. While the county is predominately Republican, Democrats often win local elections. Here, Republican Bob Zakarian hits the campaign trail. It was a successful effort. He served as township committeeman and mayor in the 1960s. (Courtesy of Vivian Zakarian.)

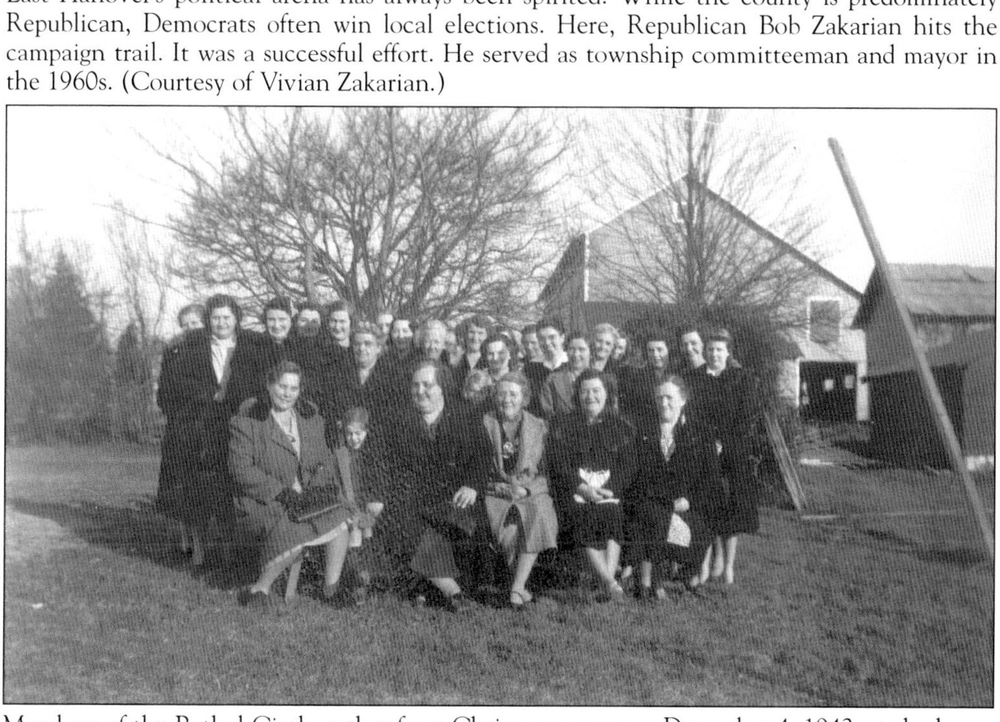

Members of the Bethel Circle gather for a Christmas party on December 4, 1942, at the home of Marie Hicks on Ridgedale Avenue. The Bethel Circle was a church group that donated time and talents to a number of church and civic causes. (Courtesy of George and Sylvia Busold.)

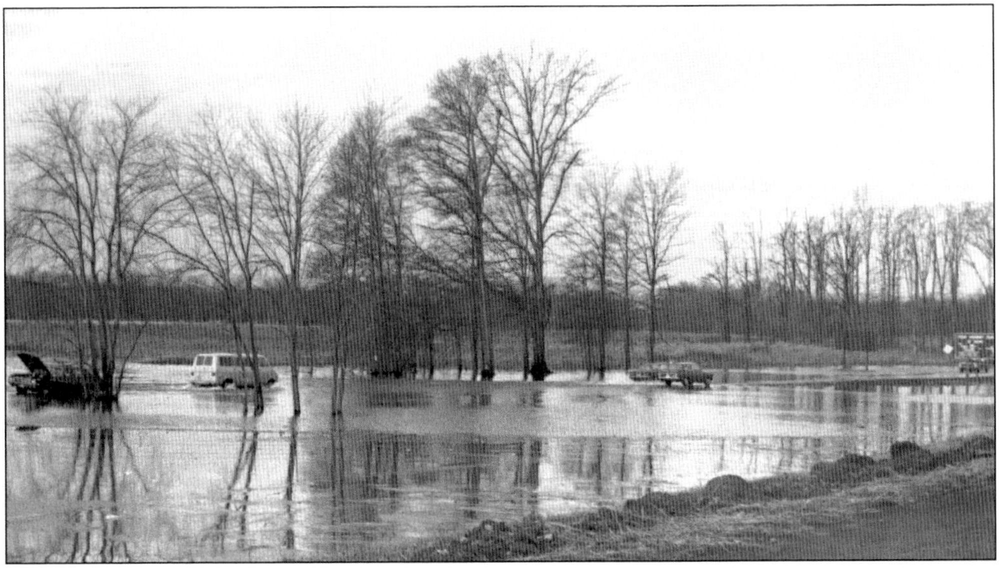

The town's elevation ranges from about 170 to 200 feet above sea level, and parts of it are in the flood plain. Some roads got a little soggy from time to time when it rained too much. This stretch of Ridgedale Avenue near Route 280 has been raised to prevent the flooding that it used to endure. (Courtesy of George and Pamela Schaeffer.)

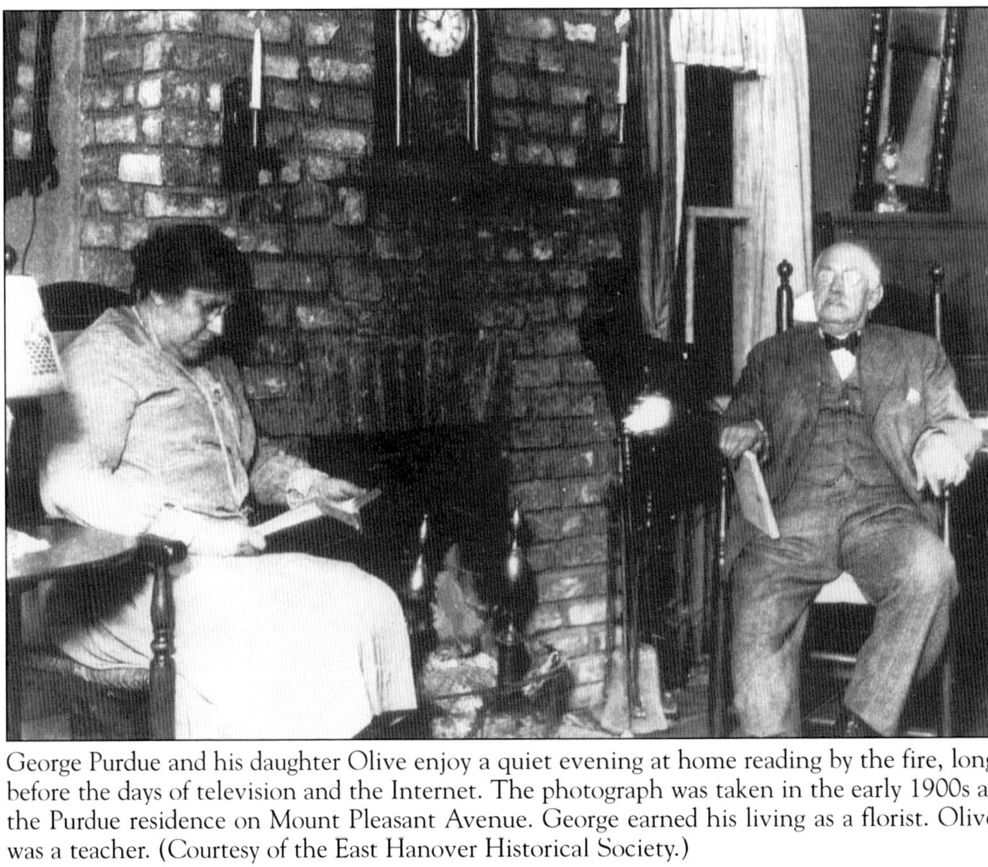

George Purdue and his daughter Olive enjoy a quiet evening at home reading by the fire, long before the days of television and the Internet. The photograph was taken in the early 1900s at the Purdue residence on Mount Pleasant Avenue. George earned his living as a florist. Olive was a teacher. (Courtesy of the East Hanover Historical Society.)

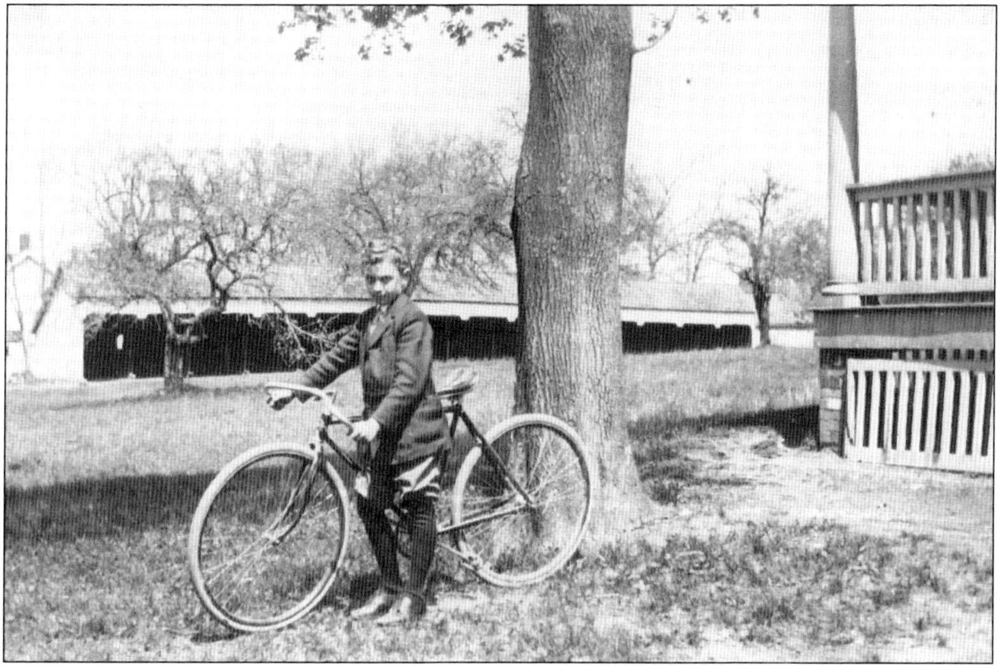

This unidentified biker is across the street from the First Presbyterian Church of Hanover on Mount Pleasant Avenue. In the background of this early-1900s photograph is the shelter where churchgoers would park their horses and carriages during inclement weather. A bike like that was a valuable piece of equipment in those days. (Courtesy of Everett Rowley Jr.)

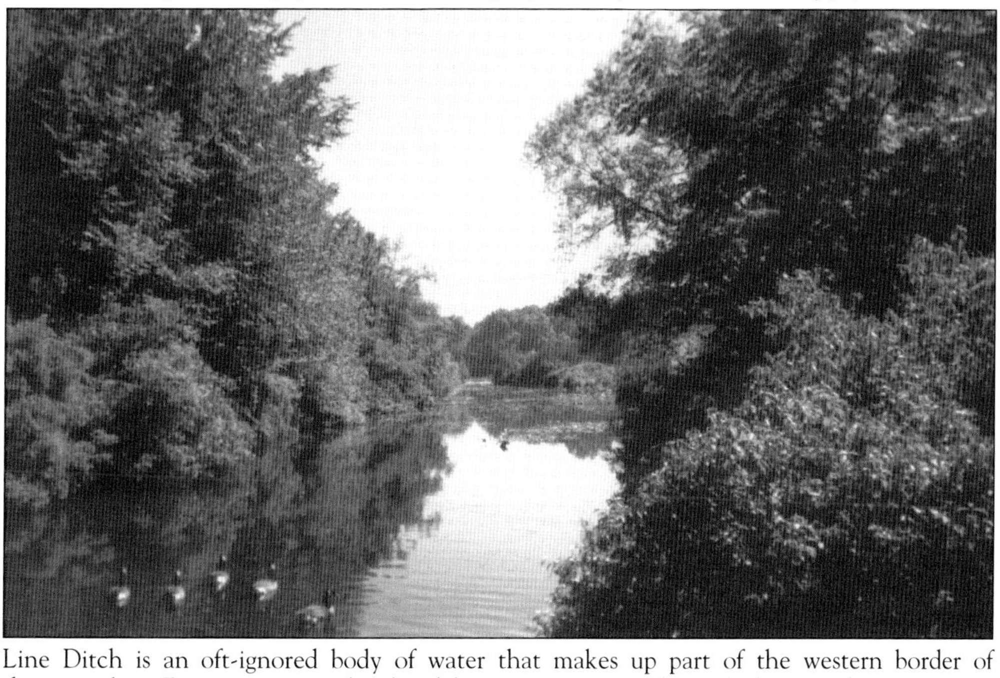

Line Ditch is an oft-ignored body of water that makes up part of the western border of the township. East Hanover is bordered by Hanover Township, Florham Park, Livingston, Roseland, West Caldwell, Fairfield, Montville, and Parsippany-Troy Hills. Children used to swim in the ditch near the Troy Road bridge.

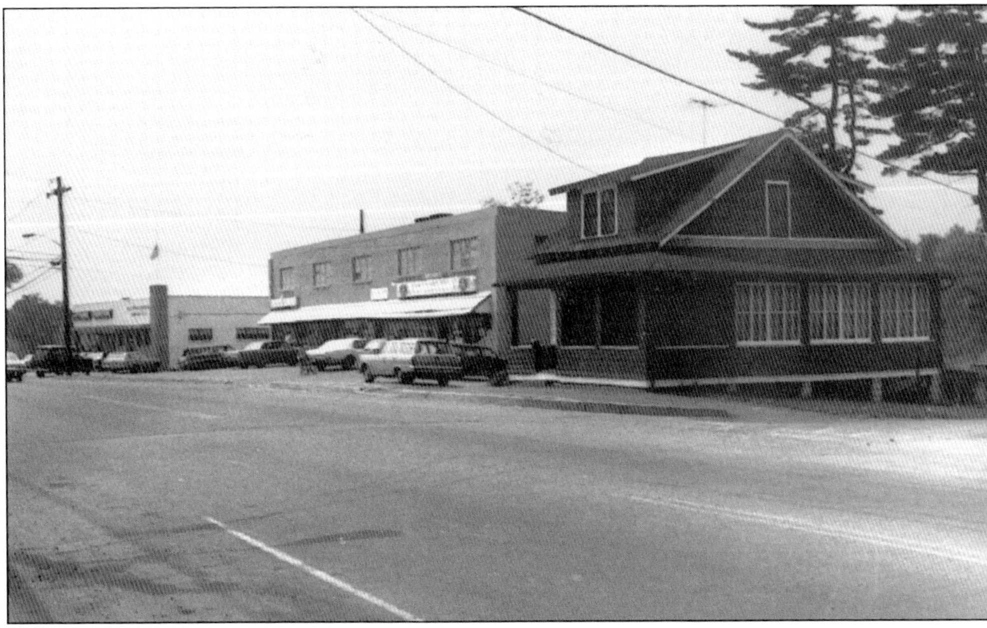

The building in the center of the photograph housed the Hanover Sweet Shop in the 1960s. It was a typical sweetshop of the era, offering a soda fountain, jukebox, candy counter, magazine and comic book racks, newspapers, school supplies, small toys, and other odds and ends. Sweetshops seem to have gone the way of the five-and-dime stores. (Courtesy of Catherine Froling.)

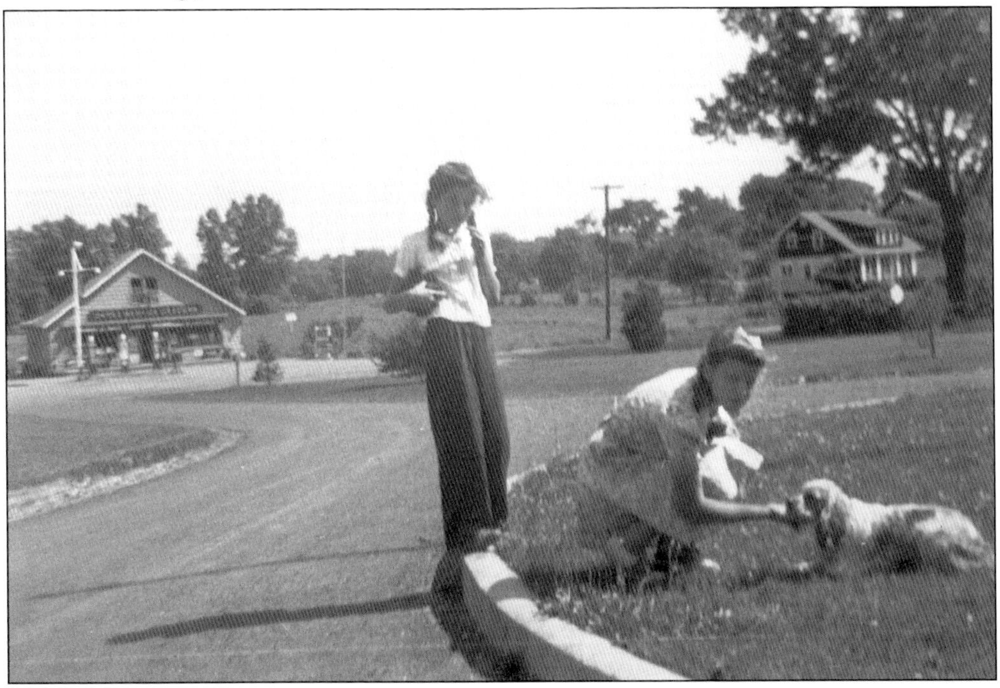

Bahr's general store can be seen in the left background of this photograph, which was taken c. 1940. Located across from Central School, the store offered groceries, general merchandise, hardware items, and gasoline. (Courtesy of Bill Shrader.)

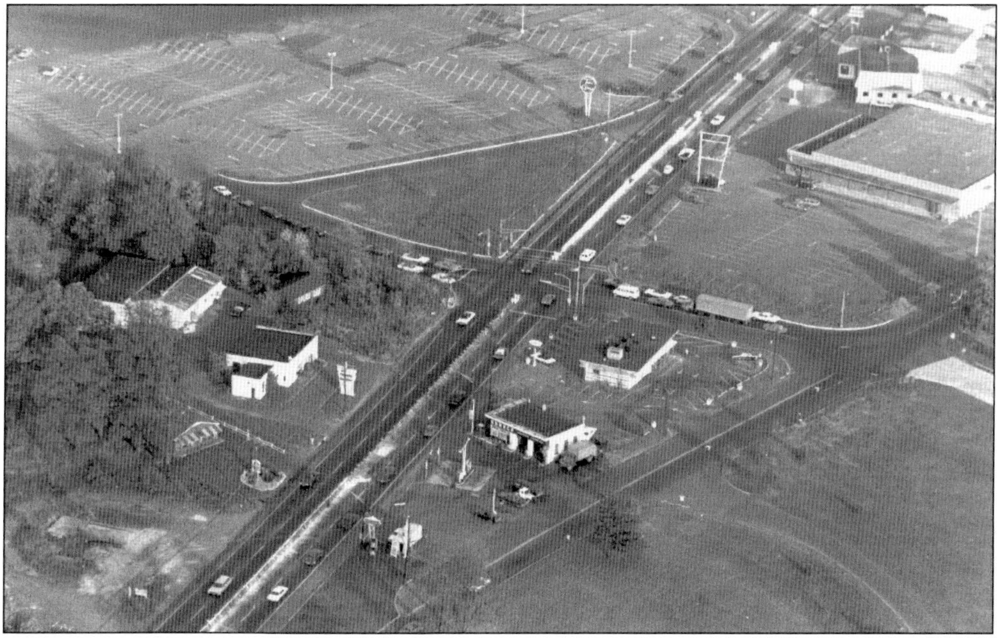

General stores had given way to mass merchants by the 1960s, and Route 10's destiny was emerging. Two Guys From Harrison became the retailer of choice for many local shoppers. The round Two Guys sign can be seen in the top center of the photograph. (Courtesy of Bill Schaeffer.)

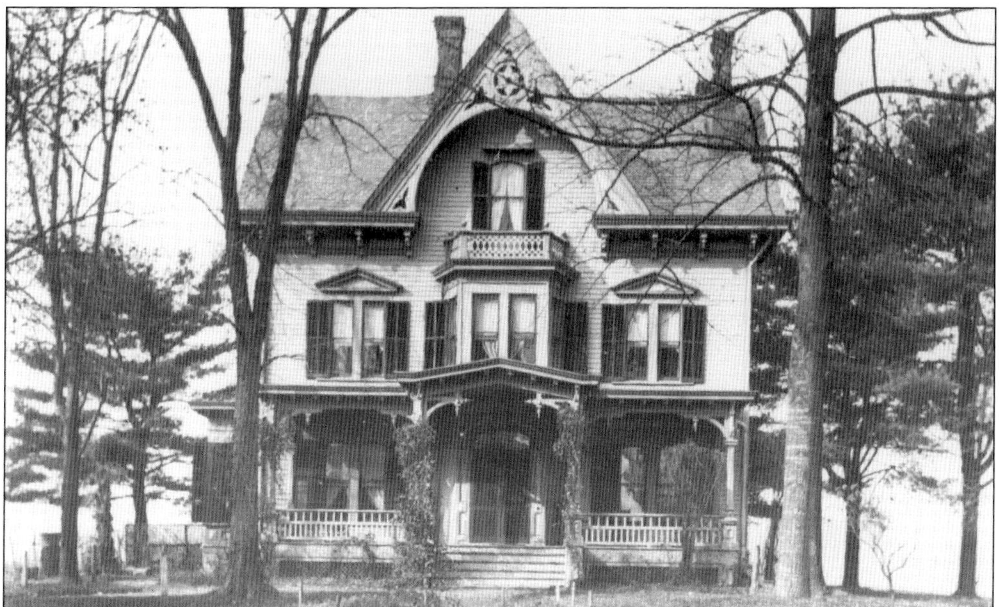

This big, beautiful Victorian house was perched on River Road near where Daffy's is today. The home was built in the 1800s with great attention to detail. Around 1960, a new owner wanted to use the property for a Route 10 retail store. He offered the house for free to anyone who would move it away. There were no takers, so the old farmhouse was razed. (Courtesy of Gus Auermuller.)

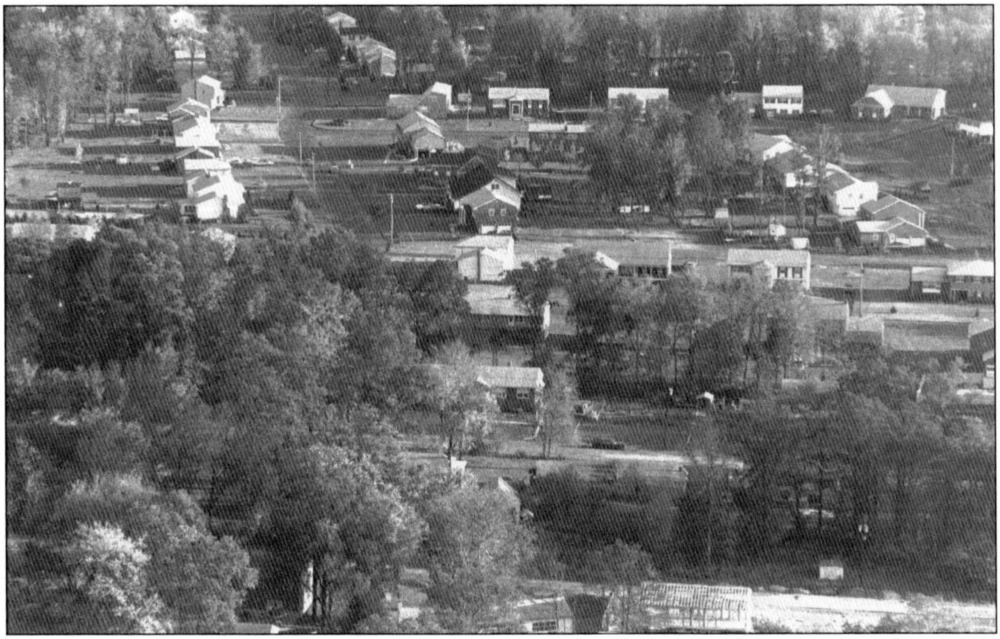

East Hanover's population increased from 946 in 1930 to 2,151 in 1950. It more than doubled again in the 1950s and reached 7,734 by 1970. There were reasons for the growth: soldiers returned from war, started families, and bought houses, as shown in this Ridgedale Avenue scene. Roadways improved and commuting became commonplace. Urban areas were decaying, and people wanted out. Businesses came to town. (Courtesy of Bill Schaeffer.)

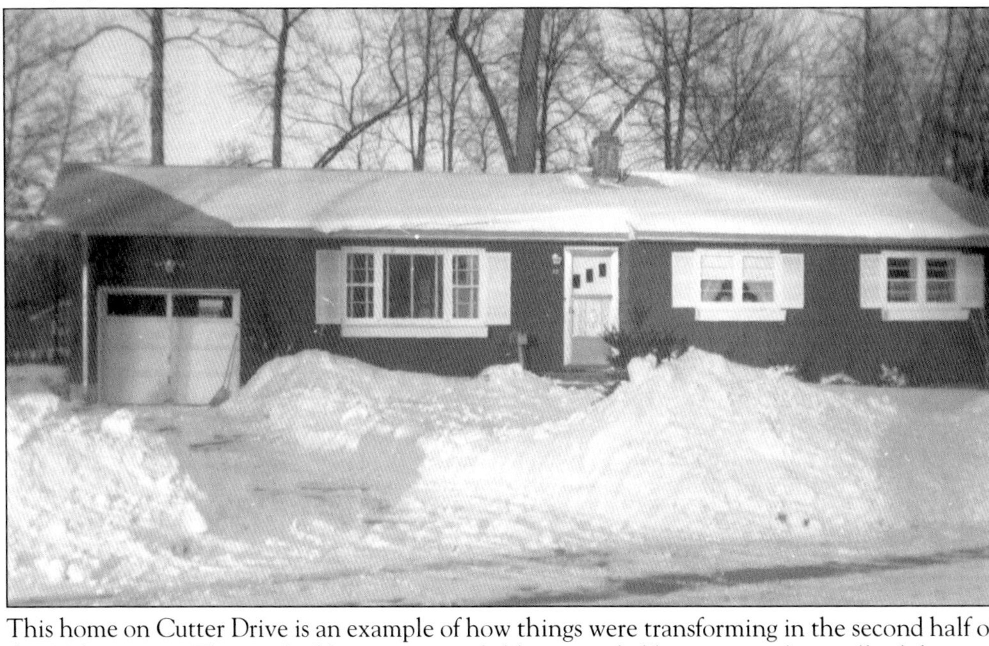

This home on Cutter Drive is an example of how things were transforming in the second half of the 20th century. The site had been an open field surrounded by trees until a small subdivision was developed. Leonard and Adina Swanbeck bought the three-bedroom ranch new in 1961 for $21,000. As time moved ahead, other fields disappeared and the houses got bigger and more expensive.